Child of the Sea

Aventura

Yo ho ho the wind blows free
Oh for the life on the rolling sea.

The Ballad of the Eddystone Light

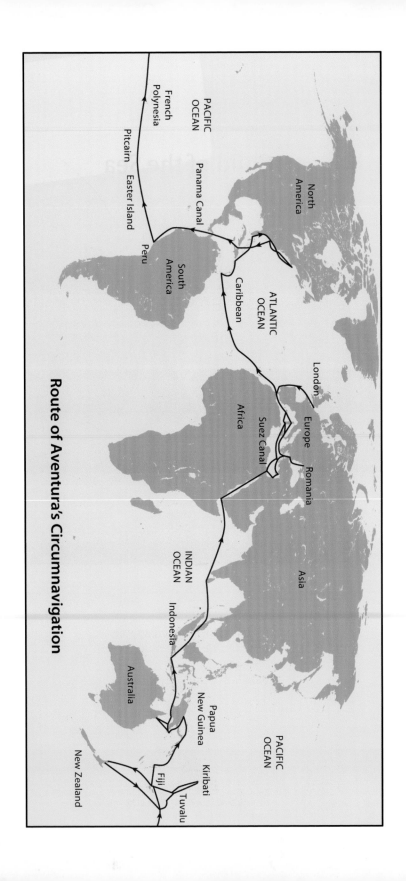

Route of Aventura's Circumnavigation

Child of the Sea

Doina Cornell

Enjoy the journey!

Doina

Dudley 16. 6. 16

ADLARD COLES NAUTICAL • LONDON

To Nera and Dan

Published by Adlard Coles Nautical
an imprint of Bloomsbury Publishing Plc
50 Bedford Square, London WC1B 3DP
www.adlardcoles.com

Copyright © Doina Cornell 2012
Photographs copyright © Doina and Jimmy Cornell
Illustrations by Doina Cornell
Aventura layout and route of circumnavigation by Mark Silver

First edition published 2012

ISBN 978-1-4081-7859-1

A CIP catalogue record for this book is available from the British Library.

This book is produced using paper that is made from wood grown in managed, sustainable forests. It is natural, renewable and recyclable. The logging and manufacturing processes conform to the environmental regulations of the country of origin.

Printed and bound in Germany by Druckerei Girzig+Gottschalk GmbH

Note: while all reasonable care has been taken in the publication of this book, the publisher takes no responsibility for the use of the methods or products described in the book.

www.childofthesea.org

Contents

Aventura Layout

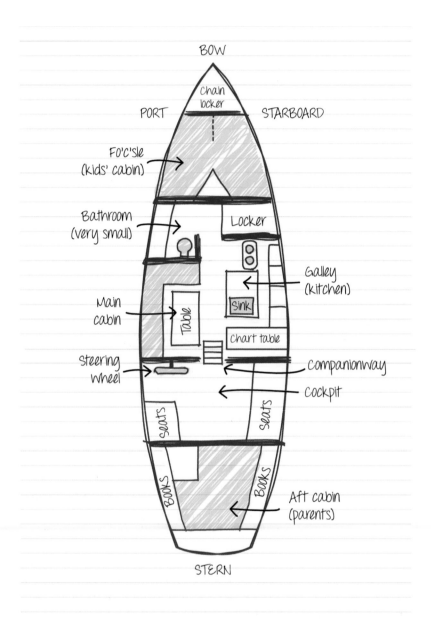

Aventura was a 36 foot (11 metre) long ketch called a Trintella III by her Dutch designer. She was a ketch because she had two masts. The fiberglass hull was built in 1974 by a boatyard but my father fitted out the hull himself, building the furniture, installing the Perkins engine and all the other equipment.

England 1981

I WASN'T WORRIED about my first day at school. After all, I'd been looking forward to this moment for a very long time. I hadn't been to school for seven years, not properly anyway. I was fourteen now and I was ready.

'Excited?' Mum asked and squeezed my hand. I didn't need to answer.

The school was a modern building block with hundreds of windows. We walked past the playground where a crowd was milling about, kicking balls, chatting and laughing. A bell rang like an alarm and there was a great rush as everyone moved towards the school entrance.

Mum left my brother and I at the headmaster's office.

'Bye,' she said, giving me a little wave. 'Good luck.'

A girl was told to show me to my form for register. She pulled a tissue from her sleeve and noisily blew her nose.

'Hi.' I grinned.

'This way,' she said without looking at me.

'What's your name?' I asked as we climbed the stairs but there were crowds going up with us and I guess she didn't hear. On the top floor she pointed to a door.

'Thanks,' I said, but she had already gone.

The classroom was filling up as people came in and sat down. My new form teacher waved me to a seat.

'This is Doina, she's starting today,' he said cheerily.

I smiled at him, and then looked around the class, still smiling. Rows of faces, pale above their red uniforms, stared at me. No one smiled back.

I couldn't help but remember the bright smiles of children who lived on islands on the other side of the world. Welcoming me to their school, even if it was just a visit for a day. And now, here, a few miles from where I was born, I'd assumed it would be the same. In fact, I'd assumed it would be far, far better.

A blonde girl sitting at a desk in front of me leaned towards her friend and whispered, loud enough so I could hear, 'What does *she* look like?'

I said nothing and smoothed down the red jumper my grandmother had knitted for me. Only yesterday I'd stood proudly in the sunshine outside Granny's house for a photo. Yesterday seemed so far away now. Even the car ride this morning, when my heart beat fast and sweet with excitement, seemed very far away.

A thin smile hooked up the side of the blonde girl's mouth. 'Maybe she's a Paki.'

My cheeks smarted like I'd been slapped, and my smile felt stiff and painted. Despite the red uniforms, the outside world seemed to be switching to black and white. Inside me was a riot of colour. Seven years of great memories. Could I hang on to those, to get me through? Because even now, I was sure it would get better. I knew it would.

For two years the blonde girl and her friends called me Paki. Jana of the Jungle. 'Go back to Bongo Bongo Land,' they said. 'Where you came from.'

Well, if I went back anywhere, it wouldn't be to the land. I'd go back to the sea.

The Beginning 1974–75

The Boat Comes to Life

I REMEMBERED SO vividly the first time I saw the boat. I remembered the smells and the feel of that day.

'Children, we have something to show you,' my parents had said.

'What is it?' we wanted to know, but they wouldn't say. We drove from our house through southeast London and across the river Thames.

'Where are we going?'

'To the Royal Albert Dock.'

All around us stretched wastelands and abandoned buildings. Nothing very Royal at all. Dad stopped the car between a huge metal shed and an old dock that led to the Thames. There was rubbish piled everywhere, spilling out of disused warehouses with broken windows. The brown river water sloshed against the quay and smelled of rot and mud.

'There she is,' Dad said, pointing towards a large white shape inside the shed. 'Our new boat.'

I saw now that the shape was a smooth hull. It looked a bit like my brother's toy boat. Only this boat didn't have any masts or sails.

Or any cabins. Or even any floors. Inside was an open space that was difficult to walk on as it was pointed at the bottom, following the shape of the keel. There was a strong smell like glue that made me want to sneeze. Everything was made of a yellowy-green material out of which stuck tiny fibres. When I touched them my hands began to itch.

'Fibreglass,' Dad explained. 'That's what it's made of. Very strong.'

'Couldn't we have got a proper boat?' I asked.

'We could only afford the hull,' said Mum, trying to stand upright.

'I'll do all the rest,' he added. 'It's my dream. We're going sailing.'

* * *

So Ivan and I spent our weekends at the Docks while Dad worked on the boat. Once, this place had been alive with ships loading and unloading cargo from all over the world. Now there were only ruined warehouses, and a few people like Dad, building their boats and following their dreams. We clambered over the hills of rubbish and dragged out bits of broken furniture to make into dens. Once we found a dead cat, all swollen with its legs sticking out. Ivan poked it with a stick and then we ran away laughing.

Soon the boat had a floor, and wooden bulkheads dividing it into cabins. So many things were needed: masts and sails, ropes and winches. Ivan was always asking, what's this? what's that? All that interested me was when the boat would be ready. But months passed and there was still a lot to be done.

We were sent to stay with Granny in Cornwall for a month. Mum had to finish her teacher training course.

'I'm going to be teaching you,' she explained, 'when we go sailing.'

'So we won't go to our school anymore?'

'Yes, that's right.'

I wasn't sure I wanted to leave my friends behind. And I liked school. But I didn't mind going to Granny's. She made cakes for tea and we walked along the beach with her dog. I went to the village school and Ivan went to the playgroup and we made a few friends.

When we returned to London Mum said, 'I've a job for you.'

I frowned. I didn't really want a job.

'Don't look like that,' she added sharply. 'It's a nice job! The boat is going to be launched soon, and you can say a little speech.'

'Why do I have to say a speech?'

'Because boats are like people and have to be christened. Marianne will be coming over for the summer holidays and she can help you.'

Marianne was my 12 year old cousin. She seemed so grown up and elegant with her dark curly hair and neat clothes. My clothes started off clean but always ended up scruffy and food-stained, and I never remembered to brush my hair.

'This is what you will say.' Marianne handed me a slip of paper. 'You'll say it in English and I will say it in Romanian. Shall we practise?'

On the launch day she and I dressed in matching white Romanian blouses, embroidered with red and black and gold thread.

'You both look lovely,' said Mum.

A crowd gathered on the dockside. The boat hung in straps from a crane, dangling over the water. It looked rather helpless. I clutched my scrap of paper

and said: 'We name this boat *Aventura* and God bless all who sail in her.'

Marianne repeated it in Romanian, then she took hold of a champagne bottle that was hanging off the front part of the boat. She held my hand, I put my other hand on the champagne, and then together we swung it hard onto the bow, where the glass smashed into pieces. The champagne fizzed and bubbled, and everyone cheered and clapped.

The boat was slowly lowered down into the water, and as the muddy Thames touched the hull for the first time and it floated, it didn't look helpless any more. In fact, it seemed to come to life. Not an 'it' now, but a she, and she had a name. *Aventura*. It meant 'adventure.'

The Maiden Voyage

'ARE WE GOING straight away?' I asked.

'Soon,' said Mum. 'We still have a lot to do.'

Though the boat was not completely finished, plans were made for *Aventura*'s first voyage. Marianne and her brother Klausi were coming with us across the Channel, and their father Klaus would collect them on the other side.

We left the docks behind and motored down the Thames. The summer sun shone and I talked excitedly to my cousins. Like me, they'd never been on a sailing boat before.

Out of the protected waters of the Thames estuary, the skies suddenly turned grey and the wind started to blow strongly. The waves grabbed the boat and made her roll from side to side. My stomach heaved and a terrible feeling of sickness swept through me. I struggled to the side of the boat, grabbed the lifelines, and threw up. Lumps of my breakfast stuck to the hull before the waves washed them away.

'Get away from there,' shouted Dad, shoving a pink beach bucket into my hands. 'You haven't got a safety harness.'

I stepped back down into the cockpit. The boat moved and I fell on my knees. The cockpit floor was covered with a wooden grill and it hurt.

'First sailors' rule,' Dad yelled. 'One hand for yourself, the other for the boat.'

I looked at him without understanding. 'What?' I said weakly.

'*Always hold on!*'

I bent over the bucket and retched again. Out came a watery green liquid that burnt my throat. It felt like my whole stomach was trying to get out. Strings of spit dangled from my mouth. I spat and spat and then sat still for a moment, my eyes closed.

'You'd better get below with the others,' Dad said.

The waves were bigger now and spray was hurling itself onto the decks. At least the cockpit was protected by the wheelhouse. I glanced up at Mum sitting at the steering wheel. She gave me a weak smile. She looked pale and ill too.

I staggered from handhold to handhold to the companionway, where the steps led down to the main cabin. My hands trembled but I tried to hold on firmly as I put my foot on the first step.

'Doina, turn around!' I was being yelled at again. 'Have you forgotten how to go down the steps?'

'Mmm,' I said, trying to move my mouth as little as possible. Turn around and go down backwards. Hold on. How could I remember all these rules, when I was feeling so sick?

Down below the boat's movement was even worse.

'There's nowhere to lie down,' I moaned. If only this banging up and down would stop. Ivan sat on the floor, clutching the washing-up bowl. Marianne and Klausi lay on the hard wooden seats, their faces grey.

'Lie on the floor.' Dad came down the companionway. He didn't feel even the slightest tinge of seasickness. 'The movement isn't so bad there.' He spread out some cushions and swapped Ivan's full bowl for a clean bucket.

All four of us squeezed together like sardines on the floor.

'Doina,' Ivan whispered.

'What?' I said crossly.

'Will it get better? I feel horrible.'

'I don't know. I feel horrible too.'

Marianne and Klausi said nothing, just groaned.

'This is a real gale,' I heard Dad saying to Mum. 'We'll have to head for shelter.'

We spent the night in Ramsgate tied up to a rusty old fishing boat. In the still waters of the harbour I felt alright, and the sickness seemed like a bad dream.

'You'll get your sea legs soon,' Dad said.

'What are sea legs?'

'Getting used to the movement – after a few days at sea, you'll find that you don't get sick anymore.'

When we left port the next day, and *Aventura* began to move, I looked at my legs and hoped they had turned into sea legs. But no. I grabbed the nearest bucket and curled up on the floor.

As we drew nearer to Boulogne on the French coast, the sea calmed a little bit. I felt slightly better and climbed up into the cockpit. There were ships and ferries everywhere.

'Is it always this crowded?' I asked.

'I hope not,' Dad said. 'It's been pretty scary trying to steer our way through.'

He dropped the sails and tied them down as we motored into the marina.

'I'll get the mooring lines and fenders ready,' he said to Mum. 'Aim for that pontoon, look, where the man is waving for us to go.'

She turned the wheel and headed towards the pontoon.

'Now stop!' Dad told her as he went onto the foredeck.

Mum pulled at the gear levers. The boat kept on going forwards without slowing down at all. The man waved his arms wildly.

'It's Papa,' cried Marianne, peering above the wheelhouse. She started waving back.

'Stop!' Dad yelled.

'She just won't stop!' Mum shouted back.

The boat crunched into the pontoon at full speed as Klaus put up his arms and tried to fend her off.

After Dad had tied the ropes, Mum said, 'Why didn't the boat stop? I put the gears into neutral.'

'It's not a car! You have to put it into reverse. Astern, I mean.'

'Well, why didn't you say so!'

Klaus stood on the pontoon looking shaken.

'Welcome to France,' he said.

My Father's Dream

OUR SUMMER SAILING was over and we spent the winter in London. We hardly saw Dad. If he wasn't on a day or night shift, he was down at the docks working like mad on the boat. He was determined to have everything finished so we could spend next summer in the Mediterranean.

When Dad was a very little boy he was taken from the mountains where he lived to the coast for a holiday. As soon as he saw the sea for the first time he knew his dream was to sail on it to far away lands. However, he was growing up in Romania, just after the Second World War, when the country was falling into the grip of a cruel dictatorship, and no one was allowed to travel abroad.

Fortunately, many years later, a beautiful piece of luck brought him to a street corner in a dusty border town. Here he met Mum. She was on holiday driving around Europe with friends. Within a year she'd left her job in England and come to live with him in Romania. But foreigners were looked on with much suspicion. The police followed them everywhere. The government refused to give them permission to get married.

When she was eight months pregnant Mum drove two thousand miles back to England so I could be born there. Then she drove right back again with me strapped into my car seat. I was her spitting image, with the dark brown hair and green eyes of her Welsh father. My Dad was also dark. He came from Transylvania, where different nationalities had lived together for hundreds of years, Romanian, Hungarian and German. His father was Romanian and he married a Hungarian, my grandmother Omi, who looked after me when my parents were working. Dad's sister married a German, and their children were Marianne and Klausi. Only my aunt died when I was little, and the cousins left and moved to Germany.

Until I was two I lived in Romania. Then finally my parents were allowed to marry, and Dad could leave the country. We came to London, and Dad was offered a job with the Romanian language section of the BBC World Service, which broadcast radio news and other programmes back to Romania. They bought a house, and Ivan was born.

But Dad's boyhood dream was still there, stronger than ever. Every spare penny was saved towards buying a boat.

'People tell me I'm crazy,' he said on one of those rare occasions when we were all at home together. 'Wanting to give up such a good job to go off sailing. But I will have to resign from the BBC.'

'What are we going to live on?' wondered Mum. 'The boat has taken all our savings. If we rent the house to tenants, that'll be a bit of income.'

'I've been thinking. I could make programmes about our travels in Romanian. What do you think?' Dad never did anything without discussing it with Mum first.

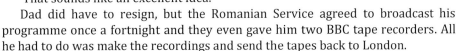

'That sounds like an excellent idea.'

Dad did have to resign, but the Romanian Service agreed to broadcast his programme once a fortnight and they even gave him two BBC tape recorders. All he had to do was make the recordings and send the tapes back to London.

'These are *Uhers*,' he said, as he unbuckled the black leather case of one of the recorders. 'All the best journalists use them.'

I laid my fingers lightly on the big silver buttons.

'I've plenty of tapes too.' He showed us the square boxes, each one containing a spool of brown magnetic tape. The tape gave off a faintly chemical smell that I rather liked.

'I've got a great name for my programme,' he said.

'What, Daddy?'

'*Aventura*, of course!'

* * *

'Where are we going to put all our stuff?' Mum asked. 'Our clothes and books, and all the food we'll need.'

'No problem,' Dad replied. He built lockers under all the bunks and behind the seats, and shelves and cubby holes in any corners left over.

Mum sewed cushions, sheets and duvet covers. She collected empty coffee jars to use as storage for flour and rice. In the main cabin was a space for the kitchen, or *galley* as I had to call it now, with shelves that had shock cord stretched across to stop things falling out at sea, and a little gas cooker that swung backwards and forwards on gimbals, so that the saucepans would stay level when the boat was moving. There were handles everywhere for holding onto, and the main seat had a lee cloth so you could lie there without falling out.

At the back of the boat was the aft cabin with a double sized bunk, for my parents. Next to the main cabin there was a little space for a bathroom sink and a toilet but there was no bath, not even a shower.

Right at the front of the boat was the very best bit of all – the triangle-shaped cabin that I was to share with Ivan.

'This is the fo'c'sle,' Dad explained. 'The forecastle. In the old sailing ships the

crew always slept in this part of the boat. Before the mast, that's what they used to say.'

There was a bunk on each side, with bright orange cushions as mattresses, and there were cubbyholes for clothes and shelves for books as well as a triangular shelf at the foot of the bunks that was crammed with our collection of toy animals. Light came in through small portholes on the side, and a large hatch in the ceiling. It was very cheerful, as all the wood was painted yellow and orange. Ivan and I had chosen the colours ourselves.

'This is my side,' I said, sitting on the left bunk. 'The port side. And Ivan is sleeping there, on the starboard. And look at this!' I stood on my bunk and opened the hatch. 'You can climb out this way.'

I heaved myself up and scrambled out onto the deck.

With a struggle, Emma followed.

'*That*,' I said, 'is a much better way to get out than just walking through the door.'

Emma fished a scrumpled piece of paper out of her pocket and handed it to me.

'You have it,' she said.

It was the secret list we'd written of all the things we were going to take when we ran away from home.

'We never got to run away,' she said. 'Not together anyway.'

Across the Bay of Biscay

BY SPRING THE boat was ready and we sailed down to Cornwall. Granny lived in a little village near the river Fowey, and *Aventura* was moored to a buoy at the river entrance.

'Daddy,' said Ivan, as the adults chatted in the cockpit.

'Ssh. Don't interrupt.'

'But Daddy...' Ivan persisted, and tugged at Dad's sleeve.

'Yes?' he said impatiently.

'Why are those boats moving?'

'Because that's what boats do. Now don't worry about it.'

'But why?'

Dad looked, finally, at the other boats.

'It's not the other boats moving, it's us!'

Aventura was happily drifting down the river with the tide and out to sea.

'You're very observant,' Mum said to Ivan, once the boat was safely tied up again.

'The hero of the hour!' agreed Dad.

Ivan looked pleased. I decided I would look out for things too. I'm just as observant as he is, I said to myself. What does he know? He's only five.

* * *

'Gale warnings on the radio,' said Dad. 'But only for Plymouth. Biscay is clear. Ready to make a run for it?'

Mum nodded.

'Where are we going?' we asked.

'We're not going. We're *bound for* Lisbon. That's what you should say. It's an old sailors' superstition.'

'Why?'

'Because you can never be sure you'll get there, until you do. Don't tempt fate.'

Aventura slipped out of the river, heading for the Bay of Biscay. The wind blew strong from the northwest and the boat was soon sailing fast and away from the shelter of land.

Dad brought our duvets and a few toys and books into the main cabin and we lay one at each end of the main seat, with the lee cloth up so we wouldn't fall out. We felt too sick to move.

Towards evening Dad managed to get us into the cockpit. The fresh air helped a bit, but not much.

'We're going to have good routines on board,' he insisted, dishing up a stew Mum had made before leaving, 'and that means an evening meal which we all eat together. I read about it in a book. It's supposed to keep the crew happy.'

'Aren't we going to stop for the night?' I asked, clutching my plate in my lap.

'No!' he laughed. 'Boats don't do that. Anyway, there's nowhere to stop.'

All around were big waves, and a rough, grey sea that didn't look very friendly. There was no land in sight.

'We'll take it in turns to keep watch,' he assured me.

'Kids, off to bed,' said Mum. 'We don't want to be worrying about you too.'

Ivan and I retreated to our base in the main cabin. We stayed there for five days.

On the sixth day Mum finally persuaded us to get out of our pyjamas and get dressed.

'Come up on deck,' she said. 'It's lovely.'

Dad dug out our safety harnesses and we sat together on the aft deck. The grey

was gone – the sun was out and the sea sparkled blue. We were very close to the coast of Portugal.

'I'm really pleased with the boat,' Dad said. 'She sails beautifully. Better than we hoped for.'

'Look, fishing boats,' I was trying to be observant.

'And I can see a tanker, and another one,' Ivan pointed. 'And that grey one must be a warship.'

'Not long to Lisbon now,' said Mum. 'I will really enjoy a full night's sleep!'

'The wind's dropped a bit. Do you children want to help put up the mizzen?'

Aventura was a ketch, so she had two masts. The mainsail needed a lot of strength and winch power to raise it, but Dad thought we could have a go at the smaller mizzen sail.

'Heave!' he cried and we pulled on the halyard with all our might as the sail slowly made its way up the mast.

'Can I go on deck now?' I asked when the mizzen was right up.

'Okay. But keep your safety harness clipped on to the lifelines.'

Ivan stayed in the cockpit, asking more questions about the ropes. I was glad – I wanted to go on my own. Hand over hand, off I set. I was aiming for the pulpit, a curved metal rail at the front of the boat. I'd sat there when we were in port. As I went forward I realised – I didn't feel sick anymore. Not one little bit, even though the swell was making the boat rise up and down.

I sat down on the pulpit. Above me the sails pulled, full and round with the wind and gleaming white in the sunshine. Below, the sharp bow cut into the water, turning the blue waves white with lacy foam. Now and then a bigger wave came and slapped the hull hard, sending cool spray over my feet. The sea never stopped moving, and each wave was different.

I felt so happy then, sitting on the bow, watching and listening to the sea and the wind and the boat.

Mediterranean 1975–76

Getting Used to Our New Life

'SHALL WE GO and take a look at the apes?' suggested Mum.

We climbed the Rock of Gibraltar that stood at the mouth of the Mediterranean, a tiny bit of British land attached to Spain. The Straits of Gibraltar were busy with shipping and we could see all the way across to Africa, only some thirty miles away.

A few Barbary Apes, which lived on the Rock, sidled towards us. One reached its paw into Mum's bag and grabbed a tourist brochure. It ran off and sat on the wall.

'Is he going to read it?' Mum laughed.

'Look, Mummy. He's *eating* it!'

Another suddenly jumped onto Dad's arm and from there to his shoulder.

'He likes you,' we yelled with glee.

'Let me get a picture,' Mum took out the camera.

Ivan gasped. A large damp patch was spreading across Dad's back.

'He's weeing!'

The ape leapt for the wall and sat next to his friend who had finished chewing the brochure. They stared at us while Dad examined his jacket. It was his only one, saved for special outings.

'He must have realised that I'm not British.'

* * *

We didn't stay long in Gibraltar. Even though Dad was a UK resident they only gave him a 2 day visa. He'd had to give up his citizenship when he left Romania so he was now a stateless person and had to get visas for every country we visited, which were stuck into his stateless passport, which wasn't really a passport at all,but a big folded up piece of paper.

Also, it didn't stop raining, and the Rock had clouds permanently wrapped around its peak.

The sun came out as soon as we sailed away.

'Let's play,' I said to Ivan. We grabbed an armful of toy animals each and took them into the main cabin.

Mum looked through the companionway.

'Good, I see you've got your sea legs. You can start on some schoolwork.'

'No!' we protested, but we had to do it. There were plenty of English and Maths books, given to us by our London school before we left. Mum sat with Ivan, listening to him read. I started copying out a list of spellings.

'This is stupid,' I complained. 'The sea makes my writing all wobbly.'

'Children, come quickly!' Dad shouted.

We dumped our books and raced into the cockpit. Dolphins were breaking the surface of the sea next to the boat, their blue-grey skins shiny from the water. 'Quick, go up to the bow.'

'What about harnesses?' Mum asked.

'Never mind that!'

I peered over the pulpit and there they were, a group of them, speeding fast through the water. Grey and silver bodies, smooth as torpedoes, slid beneath the surface, keeping up with the boat effortlessly. They wove from side to side right in front of the bow, and now and then broke the surface of the water in little playful jumps.

'Do you realise, kids, they're riding the boat's bow wave,' said Mum.

'Why?'

'They like the feel of it on their skins, I guess.'

'Maybe it tickles.'

All of a sudden one big dolphin jumped very high out of the water. It was a wonderful, exciting sight. I thought my eyes would pop out of my head.

* * *

We sailed along the Spanish coast and stopped in Almeria.

'Can we explore?' I asked after a quick breakfast.

'No, school work first,' said Mum firmly.

We settled down in the main cabin with our books.

'You'll do three hours a day and get a routine going,' she told us.

'Even if there's a big storm?'

'Well, obviously not then.'

After lunch we were at last free and Dad said we could have a go at rowing the inflatable dinghy.

'Lifejackets,' said Mum.

'Oh, do we have to?' I could already swim quite well.

'Ivan's not so good, you know.' That shut me up. He wasn't very confident in the water and I hadn't helped this by pushing him into our local swimming pool when he was about two.

Rowing wasn't as easy as I thought it would be and we splashed more than we went forwards. After a while I began to get the hang of it, though, and managed to dig the oars deep enough into the water so that we moved. *Aventura* was moored on the quay right in the middle of the town and a crowd gathered to watch us.

'We're going forward,' said Ivan. 'Look at those boats. What flags are they flying?'

'I don't know.' I was concentrating on my rowing.

'Did you like it?' Dad asked when we managed to get back alongside *Aventura*.

'Oh yes,' I said. 'It was really fun.'

'I haven't heard any complaints about no TV,' I overheard Mum saying to Dad.

TV! I'd completely forgotten about it. There wasn't time to think about TV.

We Nearly Miss Italy

'I CAN'T UNDERSTAND IT,' said Dad, after we'd been at sea for two nights and two days. 'We should be able to see Sardinia. My navigation can't be that bad.'

He was sitting at the small desk in the main cabin that he used as his navigation station and looking at a paper chart of the Mediterranean.

He went into the cockpit and peered again at the compass.

'You're on course,' he said to Mum. 'Something is wrong, it just doesn't make sense.'

Suddenly he leapt down the steps and rummaged in a locker.

'Look,' he said, waving a radio at us. 'This was in the locker just beneath the compass!'

We looked at him without understanding.

'It's got a magnet inside the loudspeaker. It's put the compass out by 5°. We've been sailing right off course. We're too far south to get to Sardinia now.'

'What shall we do then?'

'Go on to Sicily.'

'Remember, don't put anything metal or magnetic near the compass. We could have ended up in Africa!'

He found some shock cord and fixed the radio to the bulkhead. After dinner he tuned to the shortwave frequencies to pick up the BBC World Service for the news in English. Then he managed to get his own *Aventura* programme on the Romanian Service. I couldn't understand anything, because it was all in Romanian, but I liked hearing his voice coming out of the radio.

That night I lay in my bunk but I could not sleep. The water was rushing past on the other side of the hull, and I knew it was only a few inches away.

'Ivan...' I whispered but there was no reply.

I lay there for a while, then climbed out of my bunk and felt my way to the cockpit. It was very dark out there, and Dad was a dim shape sitting at the wheel.

'What is it?'

'I can't sleep.'

'Are you scared?'

'No.'

He let me come up for a moment. All around us were the coloured navigation lights from other vessels. *Aventura's* own lights burned red for port and green for starboard, with a white one on the aft rail.

A huge passenger ferry was passing on its way to Italy, lit up like a Christmas tree. It looked ten times bigger than little *Aventura*.

'We're changing watches now,' he said, going to wake Mum. She came up bleary-eyed.

'I'll go and lie down,' he said, after he had made her a coffee, 'but call me if you're worried about anything.'

'Doina, back to bed.'

I lay in my bunk and tried to stay awake as long as I could, listening to the sounds of the sea, the creak of the masts, the flap of sails, and many other little noises that I couldn't identify, as the boat moved about and things slid backwards and forwards in the lockers and shelves. It was never silent. I found all those sounds comforting. I liked being at sea at night.

* * *

'Mum, I feel a bit funny.'

I was reading in my bunk. In fact, I was reading upside down, which might have had something to do with it. And I had just eaten a big piece of bread that Mum had made yesterday, the first bread she'd baked on board. Ivan was leaping around the main cabin, playing with his favourite toy, Yellow Teddy.

Mum glanced below and laughed.

'You feel a *bit funny*?! Don't you two realise that it's blowing a *Force Eight gale* out here!'

We scrambled into the cockpit. The sky was blue and it didn't look much like gale weather to us, but Mum was right, the wind was really blowing, and there were foamy white horses on the tops of the waves. Dad was on deck reefing the main and putting up a smaller foresail.

'We're hungry,' we said.

'Don't you two ever stop eating?'

* * *

Later that day we arrived in Palermo in Sicily.

'We've already done 2,000 miles.' Dad looked at his captain's log book where he wrote down everything to do with the voyage, like wind speed and direction, and how far *Aventura* had sailed every day. 'We're really putting in the miles to Greece.'

'It feels like we're almost there,' Mum said.

We sailed slowly round Sicily and then began the last leg of our journey to Greece through the Ionian Sea. The wind vanished. The sails flapped about and all the ropes on the mast clanked this way and that. The sea was so calm it looked like someone had spread oil all over it.

'We're doing about one knot,' Dad calculated.

'We'll never get there!' I moaned.

'You could try whistling,' Dad suggested. 'Whistle for a wind.'

I sat on the aft deck and tried whistling. I wasn't very good.

That night Ivan and I went to sleep to the sounds of the engine pushing *Aventura* on through the calms.

Greece at Last

WE WOKE TO the sunlight streaming through the hatch above us and a strange quiet. The boat wasn't moving at all. We rushed up on deck in our pyjamas. It was always exciting to get to a new port, and we were now moored in Patras harbour.

'You do realise you slept through a horrendous wind,' said Dad, who was on deck tidying the sails and ropes. 'Mummy was scared out of her wits!'

'We did have all the sails up in a Force Seven blowing us onto the shore,' Mum added. 'I couldn't even steer so Daddy had to take over.'

I had a sinking feeling in my stomach.

'Sorry,' I said. 'Maybe it was my fault.'

'What do you mean?'

'I was whistling for a wind yesterday.'

'I think it was the mountains,' Dad laughed. 'Not you! They do funny things to the wind.'

There were certainly plenty of mountains. We sailed into the Gulf of Corinth with the Peloponnese on one side and the Greek mainland on the other. A rugged green coastline rose up out of a sea that was so blue I could stare at it for hours, and the bright sun made it sparkle with silver.

* * *

In the port of Corinth I had my eighth birthday. My favourite present was a book – *Greek Myths and Legends*. That evening someone let off fireworks on the sea front, which weren't for me, I knew, but made me feel very happy nevertheless.

The following day we headed for the Corinth Canal. It was a useful shortcut to save us having to sail right round the Peloponnese, but the fee for *Aventura* to go through turned out to be ten times more than it had said in the guide book.

'Our budget is down to the minimum now,' said Mum as we motored through the narrow canal.

'At least fruit and veg are cheap and good.'

'And the sea is free,' I added.

* * *

Aventura anchored off the little island of Delos in the Aegean Sea. I read in my

Greek Myths and Legends that Delos was said to be the birthplace of the beautiful brother and sister gods Apollo and Artemis, children of Zeus. Even now it was a holy place and no one was allowed to sleep on the island overnight.

As we rowed ashore in the dinghy I looked back at the white hull of *Aventura*, gently rocking at anchor. The sea and the sky were very blue and the heat made the air shimmer. Broken remains of marble walls and statues lay here and there.

It felt to me like I was entering the place of a fairy tale. I could almost imagine a goddess stepping lightly onto the dry white stone, feeling the dry grass under her feet and the sun beating down on her head.

We toured the ruins then sat on a rock to rest. I closed my eyes and listened to the chirping of the noisy cicadas.

'Mummy, I'm thirsty,' said Ivan.

He had insisted on taking Yellow Teddy, and now the two of them were drooping in the heat.

A soft breeze touched my face. I opened my eyes. Just next to my hand, a lizard lay quite still in the sun, basking on the warm stone. I stared and tried not to breathe. Its tiny toes were spread out, gripping the rock, and its tail curled around like a question mark.

'Mummy, look,' I whispered, but the lizard heard me and whisked off into the nearest clump of dry grass.

'Where's Ivan gone?' said Mum, when it was time to row back.

'He was just here...' Dad's voice trailed away. I looked about but no one moved on the island.

'I'll run back to the kiosk where they were selling drinks, see if anyone saw him there,' and he ran off, shouting for Ivan as he went.

Mum and I followed more slowly. Ivan could not be seen anywhere. Then we heard a yell from Dad. He was standing behind the kiosk, a small skinny figure next to him. With an empty bottle of beer clutched in its hand.

'What d'you suppose he was up to!' cried Dad. 'Draining the empty beer bottles to see if there was any left.' He gestured towards the pile of crates.

'Ivan!' Mum was shocked.

Ivan just stood there and gave us a silly grin. A very silly grin.

Toilets, Treats and an Escaping Octopus

'WELL, I HOPE you won't mind using a bucket,' said Dad. He had just spent the morning taking the toilet to bits. 'The valve is broken and I'll have to order one from England when we get to the next town.'

There were no other boats anchored in the bay so Ivan and I didn't bother with the bucket.

'You're a boy so it's easier for you,' I said.

'Just remember the rule: never wee to windward,' Dad told Ivan. 'You know the *meltemi* wind blows quite strongly sometimes.'

I didn't see why being a girl should be a disadvantage and I got quite good at sticking my bottom over the back of the boat. Even when the toilet was fixed, I still preferred it, because it was much less work than having to pump the toilet bowl dry. Because it was a special boat toilet, there was no flush, and it could only be emptied by pumping a handle up and down about ten times. It was boring, hard work, so if there was no one about, I always went over the side.

* * *

On the island of Tinos we waited for the new valve for our toilet to come in the post. There was a holy icon in a church on top of the hill, which people believed could heal them. Crowds of pilgrims arrived each day by ferry in the port and crawled on their hands and knees up the hill to the church.

'We could pray for the toilet,' joked Dad. He had just come back from the post office. The part had still not come, but there were lots of letters from home.

'Granny wants to know what you two would like as birthday presents,' said Mum.

'Lego,' we both agreed.

There was a shout from the quay. A man was standing there.

'It's George,' said Dad. 'I made friends with him, he works at the post office.'

Dad could speak some Greek. He was fluent in so many languages – Romanian, Hungarian, German, French and English – that he found it really easy to pick up new ones. Even Ivan and I were learning to decipher the Greek alphabet and understood when local children cried after us, *pos se lene*, what's your name?

'*Yia sas*,' said George. He had brought us a box of *baklava* and *kataifi* pastries dripping with honey. The adults talked and Ivan and I focussed on eating the pastries. We very rarely got such a treat.

* * *

We spent a week anchored in Despotiko Bay on the island of Antiparos. According to Mum it had been a favourite haunt of pirates in days gone by. There was no one there and Dad needed a quiet place to record his programme. Ivan and I were sent to the beach with a picnic.

'Off you go,' said Mum. 'School later.'

Of course we didn't mind that at all.

'Can I try rowing this time?' Ivan asked, but his skinny arms didn't take us very far.

'Oh, let me,' I said impatiently.

At the beach I put on my mask and snorkel and dipped my head under the water. A lot of little fishes looked right back at me. The water was very clear, and I tried to peer off into the blue distance.

Ivan swam and splashed about on the surface. He refused to take his arm bands off, however much Mum tried to persuade him.

'Time I tried getting some fish,' Dad announced that afternoon. He took his mask, fins and snorkel, and strapped the sheath of his diving knife to his shin. With his spear gun in one hand he plunged into the water and snorkelled off.

An hour later he was back.

'Well, it beats diving in England. The water's so warm and clear. But there's nothing much to catch. Overfished, that's the problem. I'll try tonight and take a torch. That might attract the fish.'

Once it was dark he took his underwater torch and jumped into the inky black water. I couldn't imagine myself swimming through that darkness, not knowing what creatures were swimming by me, unseen.

Ivan yawned. So did I.

'Time for bed,' said Mum.

'But –'

'Look at you two. It's really late.'

As we were brushing our teeth we heard a shout from Dad. He was in the water next to the boat. We peered into the dark. All we could see was an enormous octopus waving around in the air.

'Take the gun!' he shouted to Mum. 'I can't get it off the spear.'

Mum took the gun gingerly. The octopus, speared right through its pulpy body, wriggled all its tentacles, trying to grab hold of whatever it could. Mum held it at arm's length and put it on the aft deck. Dad climbed back on board.

'Where's the octopus? It was just here...'

'Look!' we yelled.

The octopus was walking off the back of the boat, dragging the harpoon and the spear gun behind it. Dad grabbed for the gun just in time. He pulled the creature into the cockpit and stabbed it with his knife.

'Is it dead now?' I asked doubtfully.

'Yes, now it is.'

In the morning Mum prodded the dead octopus.

'It looks like a lump of rubber. How do they cook it so nicely in restaurants?'

'I'll have to take it ashore and beat it on the rocks,' Dad said. 'I've seen fishermen doing that.'

He rowed ashore and beat the octopus on the rocks until it was tender. And when Mum fried it in the pan it tasted delicious.

Dad became pretty good at spear-fishing, and we got to eat octopus, fish and eel for lunch and dinner every day we stayed in Despotiko Bay. I would help Mum look in her book *Mediterranean Seafood* to identify fish we didn't know, and Dad showed me how to gut and clean the fish to get them ready for eating.

'Write some notes in your science book about what you've found,' said Mum.

'I like science when you can eat what you've been studying!' I said.

'Me too,' agreed Ivan.

'And best of all,' she added. 'It doesn't cost us a thing.'

* * *

When Ivan and I next set off to row to the beach the wind started to blow more strongly.

'Ooh,' said Ivan, clutching at the sides of the dinghy. 'It's that *meltemi* thing.'

Gusts of wind darkened the water. With its flat bottom the inflatable dinghy slid over the waves, and although I rowed with all my might, we were being blown away from *Aventura* and out to sea.

'Help!' we yelled. 'Help!' But our words blew away on the wind.

We kept yelling, and at last we saw Dad's head appear in the cockpit. He looked casually round for us, but when he saw how far we had drifted, he dove into the water.

Mum stood on the deck and clasped her hands.

Even with his most powerful strokes, it was a few minutes before he got to us. He hauled himself in and took over the rowing, mumbling something we couldn't understand. Why wouldn't he open his mouth?

When we got back to the boat he spat something into his hand and grinned. There was a big gap in his front teeth, and with his tanned skin and his long black hair plastered wetly over his face, he looked just like a wild Despotiko pirate.

'My tooth,' he lisped. 'I knocked it out when I dove in.'

It was his false front tooth, from an accident of his rugby-playing days many years before.

'What I do for you children!' He was still lisping. 'How can I do any recording when I sound like this?'

Mum found some chewing gum for him to stick the tooth back in so he could finish recording. And eventually, he found a dentist.

I decided I didn't want to be rescued again. I would practise and practise until my rowing was perfect.

Lost in the Labyrinth

THE GREEK ISLAND of Thira had a massive hole in the middle of it where a volcanic eruption blew the island apart thousands of years ago. *Aventura* was tied to a huge mooring buoy; we couldn't anchor because we were inside the submerged crater which was hundreds of feet deep.

The nearest beach had no sand, just lots of tiny pieces of pumice stones that Ivan and I threw into the water in handfuls and watched float back to the shore. Mum said we could take a few as souvenirs. We went slightly mad with our collecting, and when we emptied our pockets back on the boat we had about eighty stones.

That night I was woken suddenly by the boat rocking wildly from side to side. I heard Dad's footsteps on deck. I stayed in my bunk. The grownups would deal with it.

'What on earth happened last night?' said Dad over breakfast. 'I was really worried our spreaders were going to smash into the boat next door.'

'It was frightening,' agreed Mum. 'The wave just came from nowhere. Maybe it was a giant bubble coming out of the volcano.'

'Whatever it is,' said Dad. 'But I think I've had enough of it. Giant bubbles, or whatever.'

Our course was set for the harbour of Iraklion on the island of Crete. I really wanted to see Knossos, the ancient Cretan capital. I had read so many times the legend of Theseus, who entered the labyrinth and killed the Minotaur. Knossos was where the labyrinth was supposed to have been.

The ruins of Knossos were huge and stretched in all directions. There were rooms, corridors, narrow alleyways, halls and storerooms. Ivan and I crept along behind Mum and Dad, wondering if the Minotaur might spring out at any moment.

Dad made us pose next to some *pithoi*, massive terracotta pots that once stored grain, wine, or oil. All three of us could have fitted into any one of them with plenty of room to spare.

'Come on, Doina,' said Mum, 'we've lots to see.'

I'd spotted a little purple flower growing by the pot. I picked it and said, 'Coming,' but when I looked up, they had gone.

I ran in the direction that I thought they must have taken, but I could not see  them at all. The alleyways twisted and turned and I knew I was lost. My heart began to beat faster and my mouth was dry. I stopped running and walked along, trailing my fingers over the cool stone. What might be around the next corner...

Soon I heard Mum calling. She ran to me. 'Are you okay?'

'I got lost!' I was almost breathless with excitement. 'Really lost, in the real labyrinth!'

'Good thing you got out.' Mum smiled. 'We don't have a ball of string like Ariadne to help you. Anyway, off to the museum now.'

She had made some worksheets for us to fill out. We sat on the floor and copied some of the frescoes. I liked the brightly painted dolphins best, and Ivan liked the acrobats somersaulting over the bull. Mum read to us from the guidebook about how the Cretan civilisation had flourished thousands of years ago, long before the Ancient Greeks came along.

'How it all ended is a bit of a mystery,' she told us. 'But it could have been the eruption that blew Thira apart. It was one of the biggest eruptions in the history of the world.' She was about to say more when a lady attendant came bustling over to us.

'Closing time!' she said.

Ivan started to cry. I didn't want to go either. I hadn't finished my drawing. A tear welled up in my eye and fell down my cheek.

'What is the matter?' The attendant looked puzzled.

'They don't want to go,' said Mum.

The woman disappeared and in a moment came back with a man in a suit.

'I'm the manager of the museum,' he said, gazing at Ivan and I in amazement. 'I've had children crying in the museum before, but that was because they didn't want to come here. Never because they didn't want to *leave*.'

Italians and Dolphins Help Us Out

'TIME TO HEAD west now,' said Dad. 'The summer is nearly over. We'll have to find somewhere to leave the boat for the winter.'

We headed for Sicily, nearly 500 miles away. The engine was playing up, and we arrived in the port of Gela very late. We had meant to get there early, to go out for Ivan's birthday.

'Sorry, Ivan,' I said. The port looked dark and quiet. 'I guess we won't be able to go out now.'

'But it's my birthday. It's not fair.'

'We'll tie up here, next to that motorboat,' said Dad.

A large man immediately appeared on the deck of the boat. I thought he would tell us to go away.

'Come here!' he cried, waving to us to tie up.

'It's such a pity we got here so late,' Dad said to the man when all the mooring was done. 'Because it's my son's sixth birthday today.'

'But why didn't you say! You shall have dinner with me and my family. We must celebrate.'

We drove in his car from place to place, knocking on doors, getting people to open up their shut-up shops. Here he bought a huge cake, here some pizzas, and here a part Dad needed for the engine. We ended up at his house, where we met his large family – his five children, who were all older than us, and lots of other relatives. We ate the pizzas and the adults toasted Ivan's health.

'Too thin,' said the grandmothers, pinching Ivan's cheeks. That was true, I thought, he is skinny.

'Thank you so much,' said Dad, when the man took us back to the boat.

'It was nothing, nothing,' he said, waving his hands. Then he was gone, and we all sat in the cockpit. Ivan leaned against Mum's shoulder, half asleep. He looked much happier.

Mum glanced at Dad, her eyebrows raised.

'He asked what I did and when I said, journalist, he did this' – Dad laid his finger along the side of his nose.

'Who was he, getting all those shops to open?'

'I learnt a lesson when I was very young, which was, never ask questions you don't want to know the answer to. This is Sicily, home of the Mafia, after all.'

The following day the man was back and invited us to spend the day at the yacht club. Ivan and I spent the whole day in the club swimming pool, and then Mum took us to have our first showers for months.

'I think we definitely look one shade lighter now. But then you two are so brown from the sun it's hard to tell.'

Someone brought a box of melons as a present. That made Ivan even more happy because they were his favourite.

'I bet you can't eat a whole one,' Dad challenged him.

Ivan said nothing, just tucked in. Dad lost the bet, and after that we often called Ivan '*meloni.*'

* * *

This time we made it to Sardinia and sailed up the coast, which was very scenic, with mountains dropping down to the sea, but no one enjoyed it very much because the engine broke down again. Dad decided to go to Porto Cervo, which was supposed to be one of the best marinas in the Med, but it turned out to be very expensive and worst of all, didn't even have anyone who could fix marine engines.

'A guy suggested we sail over to Bonifacio, in Corsica,' Dad said eventually, after having spent all day head down in the engine compartment, which was under the cockpit. 'Apparently there's a good yard there.'

'Sail there?' Mum looked worried. 'With no engine? How are we going to do that?'

'We are a sailing boat, aren't we? And Admiral Nelson tacked his whole fleet between Sardinia and Corsica. So why not us?'

A passing motoryacht gave us a tow out of the marina and let us go when we were a mile offshore.

'Force One,' said Dad. 'This is going to take a long time.'

Aventura slowly crept along, with all her sails up. Between us and the clear sea lay a narrow strait of water, dangerous with rocks and swift currents. I perched on my favourite place on the pulpit, watching our progress against the rocky Sardinian coast.

'There's the channel,' said Dad, pointing ahead.

At that very moment, a pod of dolphins broke the water just below me. They looked just like the dolphins I'd seen painted on ancient vases in museums, and in

the Cretan frescos. Perhaps they had helped Odysseus as he wandered the Mediterranean on his way back from Troy, searching for his lost home.

By now the wind had drawn ahead and we had to tack back and forth up the narrow channel. I had to move off the pulpit because I was in the way of the sails. Ivan and I lay on the foredeck on our stomachs and peered over the wooden toerail. The dolphins were still there and we could hear their squeaking through the hull. Each time we changed direction they did too.

Dad came up to the bow. 'Children, look, I'm going to try something.'

When it was time to tack again, he told Mum to keep going, and steer for the rocks beyond the channel. The dolphins immediately started to behave very strangely. They jumped out of the water and swam this way and that.

The rocks came closer. The dolphins grew more agitated.

'Change course!' he shouted. 'Going about!'

'Going about!' replied Mum, turning the wheel.

Aventura switched onto the tack going the other way and came back into safer water. The dolphins calmed down and took up their regular positions at the bow. Again they just looked as if they were playing.

'Let's try it just once more,' suggested Dad, as we came to the other side of the channel. The dolphins acted in the same strange way as we drew near the rocks.

When we came to the end of the channel and out into clear, safe, water, suddenly the dolphins dove, tunnelling down into the sea, blurring to pale blue against the dark depths and out of sight. They had gone.

The sea seemed so empty then.

'There are recorded cases of dolphins guiding sailors,' said Dad. 'But this is still incredible.'

* * *

To get to Bonifacio we had to sail half a mile up a narrow inlet about 100 yards wide. The wind was dead ahead but not very strong. The moon was rising and we could see lights at the other end. We tacked again and again, and each time we came within feet of the rocks. Mum whispered that her heart was 'thumping like mad'. I was sure my heart was thumping louder than hers. On each side huge cliffs plunged sheer to the water. They looked like the clashing rocks Jason had to steer his ship the *Argo* through to safety. At least the *Argo* had oars and heroes to power them. We only had sails, and a dying wind.

When Dad thought we couldn't get any further he dropped the sails and anchored. In the morning he arranged a tow into the marina.

'Good news,' he said when he came back from the marina office, 'they've got a really decent workshop. A mechanic will come and take a look later.'

That was the good news. The bad news was that the mechanic had no idea why the engine wouldn't work. It was a complete mystery.

Ivan and I weren't so bothered. The marina was surrounded by hills on one side and the old town on the other. We climbed up and made ourselves a camp under the trees.

'That's it,' said Dad on the third day. 'The whole engine has been damaged by a seawater leak. It has to be completely overhauled. We'll have to leave the boat here and go back to England for the winter.'

'It's a bit of a sorry end to our summer,' Mum sighed. 'But Bonifacio isn't so bad.'

Winter Interlude

IVAN AND I went back to school in London which at first seemed odd but we soon got used to it again because all our friends were there.

Dad's naturalisation papers came through at last and he became a British citizen. He had to swear allegiance to the Queen, and Mum bought a Union Jack to hang in the living room.

There were tenants living upstairs in our house so we camped out on the ground floor. Piles of things to take back to the boat appeared in the front room, and when spring came and it was time to set off, everything was packed into an old Hillman car bought for the journey.

'Where are the children going to go?' asked Mum, as Dad wedged the box holding a new self-steering wind vane and rudder on the back seat.

'On top!' he said cheerfully as he covered the box with a blanket. 'Now, where can I put my new cameras?'

Ivan and I had to travel all the way to Corsica wedged right up against the roof, so many things were piled underneath us. We took the cheapest tickets on the Channel ferry in the dead of night, and at Calais the French customs unpacked the car and examined every item.

'They're going to fine us *600 francs*.' Dad was furious. 'They said we should have declared the new cameras and the engine parts.'

'Can't you complain?'

'Huh! The chief guy said, if you complain, I'll double it!'

The customs kept us there all day.

'So much for the Common Market,' said Mum bitterly.

* * *

In Bonifacio Mum and Dad had lots of jobs to do, getting the boat ready for another summer sailing. They scrubbed the keel and painted it with special anti-fouling paint, Dad fitted the new self-steering and Mum spent all day sanding and varnishing the woodwork. The good thing for us was that we didn't have to spend much time on school.

'Let's make a house,' I suggested to Ivan. We dragged some sheets and blankets and all our soft toys to the car. We played in there for hours. Other days we found hidey holes in the marina, and used bits of broken wood and scraps of canvas to make our dens.

'I have to patch your jeans every night,' Mum complained, because we tore holes in them as soon as they were mended. We were always hungry, and Mum reckoned we ate almost as much as she did. I loved the fresh loaves of French bread, crusty on the outside and soft and white on the inside.

Friends visited from France – Susie and her daughters Lili and Mayah who were the same age as Ivan and I. Susie was an American and married to a Frenchman. She knew Mum and Dad from a trip she made to Romania long ago, before we children were born. She'd come to London over the winter and Lili had spent a day with me at school. Now I rowed the two girls round the harbour. They wore the lifejackets and I didn't have to. I felt like a real sailor.

Susie wanted to know our plans. 'In the summer we're going to Israel to visit my sister. Why don't you come too?'

This was enough of an invitation for my parents.

'Okay,' they said. 'We'll see you there.'

My Favourite Toy

BY EASTER WE were in Rome, and visited St Peter's Church on Easter Day. I saw the Pope, carried in a special chair on the shoulders of strong men, making his way through the crowds.

Further south, in Naples, *Aventura* was moored in the central harbour, surrounded by little motor boats. As soon as darkness fell they started up their engines, which sounded like the buzzing of angry bees, and set off into the night. Later they came back without any navigation lights and their crews offloaded crates silently onto the dock.

'Smugglers,' Dad said the next morning, after the boats had kept us awake, coming and going all night. 'I expect there was whiskey and American cigarettes in those crates.'

'Good thing we've just given up smoking then,' said Mum.

Near to Naples was Pompeii, the city that was destroyed by the eruption of

Vesuvius. I stared at the white plaster casts of bodies of people who had died, their arms bent, trying to protect themselves from the burning ash.

We climbed up the volcano and looked into the dark gaping crater. Far below steam curled up out of cracks in the ground, as white as the bodies I'd seen before. I didn't completely believe Mum when she said that Vesuvius was sleeping now.

I clutched my favourite toy very tightly. I had had Blulaki since I was a baby. A horrible vision was in my head, that I would let go and Blulaki would drop down into the steaming crater. I knew there was no chance of me letting go, but I was still afraid.

Blulaki didn't look like any animal I knew. He was a dull blue colour, with a head bigger than his lumpy body. He was the oldest of the soft toys we had, but for some reason, Ivan's Yellow Teddy was always considered to be the chief. He did look very impressive, being so bright yellow, and larger than all the others.

There was also Horsy, Floppy the Anteater and Johnny the Elephant who belonged to Ivan. Little Monkey, Long Legs the rabbit, Musical Teddy and Suki the doll were mine. Then there was Betty, a blue rabbit with one eye.

'She is mine!' I said, grabbing her off the shelf. We were in our cabin trying to decide what game to play.

'No, mine!' said Ivan.

'Well, I think she's mine, because I'm the oldest, and I'm sure she was given to me anyway.'

Ivan didn't say anything, but started to cry. That drew Dad to the cabin. I held onto Betty but I wasn't sure I was going to win this time.

'I have the solution,' he said, when he had heard the story. 'You'll share her. Doina, do you want odd or even?'

I thought furiously. What would be to my advantage? I wanted to win this argument. I wanted Betty. The problem was, I had no idea what he was talking about.

'Odd,' I said.

'Fine. So Ivan will get her on even days and you on odd. And since today is the 16th, Ivan gets her today.'

I hurled Betty onto Ivan's bunk and buried my face in the pillow. I didn't need to see his face to know it was covered in a six year old's smirk. My mood didn't last long. By afternoon we were playing together on the dockside. There was a large pile of gravel, where workmen had been repairing the pavement. We dug out caves with our fingers and made homes for our animals. Blulaki looked snug in his mountain lair. Then there was a landslide and Blulaki disappeared under an avalanche of stones. I dug away but I couldn't find him. Now it was my turn to cry.

Evening came as Dad and I searched the pile.

'We'll have to give up,' he said. 'Blulaki is gone. I'm so sorry.'

It was thanks to him the toy had such a silly name. Blulaki was one of his slangy city words from when he was young and hanging out with his mates in the capital of Romania, Bucharest.

I cried myself to sleep.

Come morning, when I opened my eyes, I looked up to the hatch above that was open in the hot air. A familiar blue shape was waving at me from up there.

'Blulaki!'

That evening Dad had moved the entire pile of gravel, stone by stone, until the mountain explorer was found. Italians passing on their evening stroll stared in amazement.

* * *

'You're older now, time you had a few jobs,' announced Mum. 'You can start with washing up the dishes.'

'I know,' said Dad. 'Since Doina has Betty on odd days, that's the day she can wash up, and Ivan can do the even days.'

I didn't like the sound of this at all.

I wasn't very keen on the other job either. If we were to stay in port for a few days, the sail covers had to be put onto the sails in order to protect the canvas from the sun. The covers were made of a blue plastic that had to be laced and hooked around the mast and boom. The plastic was stiff and hard to stretch, and the hooks were fiddly. I was impatient to get it done and I disliked this job almost as much as washing up.

* * *

'The new self-steering is just great,' said Mum. We were sitting in the cockpit, eating our lunch. The wind vane at the back of the boat moved a little this way and that, and ropes attached from it to the tiller on the aft deck made the tiller move a little this way and which moved the rudder and kept *Aventura* on course. I didn't really understand how it worked, but I knew it was clever.

'It doesn't need any power,' said Dad.

'Where does its energy come from then?' piped up Ivan. Dad looked surprised for a minute then laughed. Ivan didn't always say much, but then he would come out with a comment so we all knew he was looking and thinking about things.

'Good question. The energy comes from the boat moving through the water, and the wind. That's it.'

'Wow!' Ivan's eyes were wide.

'Well, I think it's fantastic,' said Mum. 'I don't have to spend all my time at the wheel.'

'It won't work in a flat calm though. And it doesn't go in a very straight line. You're a better helmsman, Gwenda.'

'Helmslady,' I said.

'Thank you,' said Mum.

To Turkey and Romania

NO CORINTH CANAL this time, we sailed round the Peloponnese. On the west coast we anchored in Pylos bay that was protected to seaward by a long island.

We rowed ashore and had our first swim of the year off the beach. The water was cold. Afterwards we climbed up the slopes of the island. A few broken stone walls crossed our path, but there was nothing much else to see. Ivan raced ahead. I went more slowly, looking at the wild flowers that covered the hill in colour.

At the top we sat and had sips of water. Mum took out a book.

'This is your school today,' she said, 'and this hill is your classroom. A famous battle took place in the bay down there, more than two thousand years ago, between the Athenians and the Spartans. I'll read to you what the ancient historian Thucydides wrote about it.'

So we sat there among the flowers, and listened to the story. The bay below us was very quiet, and the only vessel there now was *Aventura*, a white dot, turning slowly with the wind. But I tried to imagine the clashing triremes and the shouts of the men. On the island where we were sitting, Sphacteria, the Spartans made their last stand, until the Athenians forced them to surrender.

School was good on days like these.

* * *

We slowly made our way through the Greek islands, heading north towards Turkey and after that through the Bosphorus into the Black Sea to Romania. This would be Dad's first visit since leaving seven years before. Now he had a British passport, he could visit again.

'We'll be in Turkey soon,' Mum said. 'I'll have a go at sewing the flag.'

Each country we visited required us to fly a courtesy flag. The Turkish flag was quite tricky, with its crescent moon and star, but when it was finished Mum said, 'I'm quite proud of that.'

When we left Greek waters, Ivan asked if he could haul down the Greek courtesy flag from where it was flying on a little halyard, below the starboard spreader on the main mast. He had a copy of *The Observer Book of Flags* which he studied so often he knew most of them by heart. Any ship that passed by he would tell us where it was from long before we'd even seen the name of its home port painted on the stern.

'You know what,' said Dad. 'If I am captain and Mummy is first mate, Doina can be second mate.'

'I don't want to be third mate,' said Ivan.

'Well exactly. You'll be the Flag Officer.'

Ivan looked very pleased. When we arrived in Turkey he immediately said, 'Can I raise the flags, Daddy?' He hoisted the yellow quarantine flag, which was code for 'We are waiting for clearance,' and then the Turkish flag underneath.

The first official who came aboard to complete our entry formalities looked up at the flag and snorted.

'That flag is shameful to my country, you cannot fly it!'

'Isn't it correct?' Dad asked.

'It is not good enough. Take it down!'

Before our eyes he took out his car keys and started to rip the flag up, picking off Mum's careful stitches. It took him quite a long time, and we could only stare.

He said a few words to another man who had come with him, and they produced a brand-new flag twice as big as our old one.

'Fly this, please,' he said.

So Ivan took down the yellow flag, because we were now cleared into Turkey, and hoisted the brand new Turkish flag.

The next day the official returned, smiled and pointed at the flag. He'd brought two embroidered bags as a present for Mum and me.

As we sailed towards the Straits of Bosphorus Mum started to sing:

Istanbul was Constantinople
Now it's Istanbul, not Constantinople

'Mum!' We always got embarrassed when she started singing.

'That's an old song, I remember from when I was a girl,' she said, ignoring our protests.

The tune was very catchy. Ivan and I found ourselves singing *Istanbul, Constantinople* over and over, as the Turkish city crowded the land on either side of us. To our left was Europe, and Asia was on the other, and the city of Istanbul united them.

'We won't do any sightseeing now,' said Mum, 'we'll spend time here when we come back with Omi.'

Dad phoned my grandmother Omi as soon as we moored.

'She's very excited,' he said when he came back. 'She's got her passport and visas all arranged. She'll be able to sail with us all summer.'

The Sea of Marmara was busy with ships, which steamed through very fast, leaving a terrible wash that tossed *Aventura* about.

'They're Russian,' observed Ivan, looking at the flags the ships flew at their sterns.

'That water is horrid,' I said, peering over the side. The sea was a horrible grey-green colour. A film of dirty oil covered the surface, and underneath floated lots of jellyfish.

Aventura fought against the current until we got into the Black Sea, and then the sailing was better. Mum even had time to give Dad a hair cut and to sew the Romanian flag.

Omi arrived about half an hour after we arrived in the port of Constanța. I was happy to see her again. Her hugs were warm and she smelt of perfume. Her hair was grey but she had dyed it with some mysterious dye that made it go faintly purple. I couldn't quite work out why you would want to do that.

My grandfather had died many years before. In fact, both my grandfathers had died long before I was born. So I only had Granny and Omi.

Romania was hectic. Lots of relatives and friends came to the boat, and they gave Ivan and I boxes of chocolates and pinched our cheeks until it hurt. How lovely they said. *Ce frumos!*

'Thank you, *mulțumesc*,' we said politely, and smiled and started to eat the chocolates. Getting chocolates was a real treat. I chewed on one slowly. It tasted horrid.

I glanced at Ivan. I didn't know if I could swallow it but Mum was staring at us to be polite. It was hard though, as more chocolate arrived.

When at last everyone except Omi had gone, Ivan and I looked at all the chocolate boxes and then at each other.

'It doesn't taste like chocolate at all.'

'I know. Horrid,' and Ivan threw the box into the corner of his bunk.

Then I chased after him saying *Ce frumos!* and trying to pinch his cheek, because I knew it annoyed him so much.

We went for a walk in the town. There were police everywhere, stopping cars to check papers. As we crossed the street, Dad stepped over a bollard. Suddenly a policeman appeared and started shouting at him. A great deal of talking went on, which I didn't understand, and we ended up at the police station.

'He called me a sheep,' he explained later. 'And he said, take your *gypsy rabble* with you. Well, it was ruder what he said, in Romanian.'

'Are we the rabble?' I asked, though I knew the answer.

Dad wasn't really listening to me. 'The sooner I leave this country the better,' he said to Mum. 'I just feel wrong here.'

We travelled inland to Bucharest and Braşov, the city Dad came from.

'I don't remember anything much,' I said to Mum. 'I was so little when we came here last time.'

'Yes,' she said. 'That was when we came for the funeral. When Dad's sister died, Aunt Doina. Dad couldn't come, because he still had his stateless passport.'

My aunt's name wasn't mentioned much, but when it was, it always gave me a jolt, because it was the same as mine. I wondered if Ivan felt the same. He shared his name with his grandfather, and he was dead as well.

In Bucharest while Mum and Dad did tours of the embassies sorting out visas, Omi took us for a walk in the park. I put Blulaki in my Turkish embroidered bag and swung him around my head. He seemed to like it.

When we got to the end of the park we stopped for ice creams, but when we took our first lick, they didn't taste very nice. Omi looked at her ice cream too. She made a face, and gestured to us that we should throw them in the bin.

I put my hand in my bag. Blulaki was gone.

We walked back through the park slowly but we never found Blulaki. Omi was very kind but nothing she could say made it any better. She took me to a toy shop and bought me new toys, a little brown bear, and a white duck.

'Thank you, *mulţumesc*,' I said, through my tears, and held the toys. They didn't have half the character of Blulaki.

A Boatful of Relatives

'WE'LL STOP AT that island,' said Dad, looking at the chart. 'Just for the night.'

We were sailing through the Sea of Marmara, heading back to the Mediterranean. We'd left Istanbul behind, and had made good progress but night was falling, and the sea was busy with ships and ferries.

Ivan and I were already in our bunks by the time Dad got the anchor ready. I heard the chain go rattling out and the quiet when Mum turned off the engine. At that moment there came the noise of another, rougher engine. It sounded like a boat had zoomed up beside us and I could hear men's voices shouting. Omi looked into our cabin and saw we were awake.

'Sleep,' she said, patting my hand, and she sang softly:

Noapte buna somn usor
Şapte purici pe-un picior

Good night sweet dreams
Seven fleas on one leg

'Sing it again, Omi,' Ivan and I whispered. The voices outside had stopped, Dad was pulling up the anchor chain and we were underway again. We fell asleep, and in the morning were in a different place altogether.

'There was a prison there,' Mum explained. 'So they came and chased us away. But it didn't say anything about a prison in any of the pilot books or on the charts. How were we to know?'

* * *

The Tale of Troy by Roger Lancelyn Green was my latest favourite book, and now we were going to visit actual Troy. But there was nothing there except mounds of

earth. I was disappointed though Mum said the views over the plains to the sea were impressive.

'The Greek ships would have been pulled up over there,' she said. 'For ten years they made their camp on the beach.'

I tried to imagine it, but without much success. The only good bit was a life size replica of the Trojan horse that the Greek warriors hid

inside and the Trojans foolishly pulled into their city and thereby ensured their downfall. The replica was definitely big enough to hold a few warriors.

On the Greek island of Chios my cousin Klaus joined us. He had just finished school, or *gymnasium* as they called it in Germany. He slept on deck, the nights were so hot. Omi occupied the main cabin. The boat was full.

'It's nearly your birthday,' said Mum to me.

'We'll find a nice place to stop,' Dad promised.

'And I make you a cake,' said Omi. This was exciting, because Mum, as she admitted herself, was terrible at making any sort of cake or pudding.

'Somewhere quiet,' added Dad. 'I need to do some recording.'

We anchored off a peaceful uninhabited island, near to Kos.

'Nice and relaxing,' said Mum. She sat down to write all our news in a letter to Granny.

Dad disappeared into the aft cabin and we could hear the typewriter bashing away as he wrote his script. Klaus sat on the foredeck and strummed his guitar. Ivan sat at his feet. He followed Klaus around everywhere.

Omi was busy in the galley. I watched as she mixed cake batters and baked thin layers of sponge in the tiny oven of the gimballed stove.

There was no sign of life on the island and Ivan and I were keen to go to the beach.

'Can we sleep ashore in the tent?' we asked. 'Klaus said he'd go with us.'

Mum agreed. We quickly packed the tent and a few other things and climbed into the dinghy.

'What's that?' Ivan said. A large goat had appeared out of nowhere and was walking down the beach.

'Oh.' I looked at Ivan. We weren't so keen now.

'What!' laughed Klaus when we asked if we could unpack the dinghy.

The grownups thought it was very funny. Dad kept teasing us about the goat.

It didn't matter. Next day was my ninth birthday. Omi had assembled all the parts of the cake with creamy fillings and covered it in more creamy icing and crackly sugar. It stood in the galley 'like a work of art' said Klaus.

I was speechless when I looked at that cake. But before we were allowed to eat it, we had to go to the beach so Dad could record his programme.

Klaus, Ivan and I climbed over the lifelines and slid from the boat into the dinghy. Omi hesitated. She'd never had to climb into the dinghy before. We'd always been tied up to a quay.

'Come on!' we said.

'*Mami*, I'll help you,' offered Dad, taking her arm.

Gingerly, Omi lifted one leg. With a bit of a push Dad managed to get her on to the other side of the lifelines. Then she lowered herself down. As her foot touched the dinghy she pushed it away so she was hanging at arm's length from the boat.

'Help,' she whispered in Hungarian. '*Segitseg.*'

'Klaus,' yelled Dad, 'hold the dinghy near the boat. Or else Omi'll fall in.'

Ivan and I looked at each other and tried not to laugh. Omi was holding on desperately to the lifelines, and she wouldn't let go. Klaus pulled the dinghy alongside and Omi plonked herself down heavily. She caught my eye then and winked.

Once we were all in the poor dinghy was laden right down.

'I can barely row,' complained Klaus.

The *meltemi* was blowing and the little choppy waves came over the side.

'My bottom is getting wet,' said Ivan.

'All our bottoms are getting wet.'

At that point Klaus dropped one of the oars. He had to jump in and swim for it.

Ivan and I were building a sand castle when we saw a Greek patrol boat pull up alongside *Aventura*.

'Uh-oh,' said Klaus. 'Hope it's not bad. Any prisons around here?' and he peered theatrically off into the distance. He had heard about our adventure at the Turkish prison island. Ivan and I giggled.

Dad appeared in the cockpit and talked to the soldiers on board. They looked at us on the beach.

'We go back,' Omi said.

'Omi, it'll be okay,' said Klaus.

'You'll have to get back on board,' I said to Omi.

'Okay,' she said determinedly.

By the time Klaus had struggled to row us back against the wind, the patrol boat had gone. Omi reached up and clutched at the lifelines and tried to haul herself up. Then she got stuck. Klaus tried to push her onto the boat, Dad tried to pull her, but she was too heavy. She started laughing, and then she couldn't move at all. The funny thing was, no sound came out. But her whole body was shaking. And in the end we were all laughing.

'Those officials just wanted to check our papers,' said Dad when at last we hauled Omi on board and stopped laughing. 'We're very close to Turkey. But I didn't want them to see the tape recorder! I had to quickly hide it, in case they thought I was a spy.'

'Can we have lunch now, *please*?' I pleaded.

'Oh sorry, Doina, I forgot. It's your birthday!'

Mum had let me choose my favourite dish, which was 'eggs stuffed in tomatoes', and that was followed by the amazing cake, which tasted even more incredible than it looked.

'Omi,' I said. 'You're a much better baker than a sailor.'

'Mulţumesc,' she said. 'Thank you, Doinitsa.'

* * *

In this part of the world Greece and Turkey were very close together. We took a trip over to Turkey for the day to visit the ruined city of Ephesus. This, I thought, was more impressive than Troy. The ruins were the biggest we had seen so far: temples and theatres and marble avenues.

'This amphitheatre could hold 25,000 people.' Mum was reading from her guidebook as usual.

I leapt onto the stage and sang and danced. Omi sat in the front row and clapped. Klaus ran to the top of the rows of seats and Ivan leapt up after him. It was a long way and they looked pretty small to me up there.

'Try saying something,' suggested Mum. 'The acoustics should be good.'

'Can you hear me?' I whispered and Klaus and Ivan waved back.

From there it was back to Greece. Omi was getting the hang of getting in and out of the dinghy by now. Dad said you wouldn't think that she had never been on a boat before.

The Red Ensign flag that flew off the back of *Aventura* was getting very frayed and Mum had to keep mending it.

'It's getting shorter all the time,' she said.

In Rhodes we saw lots of yachts flying the Blue Ensign which, Ivan explained to anyone who would listen, meant that the owners probably belonged to some Royal Yacht Club.

'Why don't we take our flag down at sundown?' he asked Dad. 'Those Blue Ensign yachts do.'

'Well maybe we should. But then you'll be asking me to serve tea on deck at 4pm sharp every day! I've noticed some of those yachts do that as well.'

'Ivan,' Mum interrupted. 'Daddy is trying to get some jobs done and you're supposed to be doing your schoolwork. Stop getting distracted.'

'But Mummy,' I joined in. 'Can't we have tea at four like they do?'

'No! Now get on with your schoolwork. I'm not very happy with your behaviour.'

It was true that Ivan and I weren't always very keen on school. There were more interesting things to see and do outside.

'Life isn't a permanent holiday, you know!' Mum said for what seemed like the umpteenth time. 'I'll be calling in UNESCO soon.'

'What's UNESCO?' we asked.

'The United Nations for Eradicating Spoilt Children. Now shush.'

* * *

The summer weeks passed as we sailed down the southern coast of Turkey. There were lots of tiny coves to anchor in, ancient ruins no one visited other than us, and golden deserted beaches. Dad taught Klaus how to spear fish and we lived off fish and octopus every day. I wasn't very convinced that Mum was right. It felt like a permanent holiday to me.

A Visit to Israel

BY NOW WE had made it to Larnaca in Cyprus. There were lots of soldiers walking about the streets.

'UN peacekeepers,' Mum explained to Ivan who was asking about them.

'Are they UNESCO?' I said excitedly. 'Are they here for us?'

Mum looked confused.

'You know, the United Nations for Eradicating Spoilt Children!'

'No, silly. I just made that up. They're here to keep the peace between Greece and Turkey. Cyprus is divided between the two countries and it is very tense.'

Boatloads of refugees were arriving in Larnaca from Lebanon.

'I heard that a guy arrived with a million dollars in his suitcase,' Dad told us. 'The refugees are coming here, and the gunrunners are going back to Lebanon. We could put *gunrunning accepted* on the stern of *Aventura*. That might get us some offers.'

'I hope, Jimmy, that was a joke.'

Ivan and I made friends with some children on the boat next to us. They were from Belgium and we invited them on board to play.

'We live in Lebanon but there's a war going on there now,' the children said. 'We're waiting to go home.'

'When will you go back?' I asked.

'When peace comes.'

I nodded my head and then we didn't talk any more about it. What they said made sense to me. We got on with our games.

* * *

A current pushed us northwards as we sailed towards Israel, so we made landfall too close to the Lebanese border. As we approached the coast under sail a fast navy patrol boat appeared, full of men carrying guns. They pointed the guns straight at us.

'Stop!' they shouted. 'Follow us into port.'

Dad turned on the engine and tried to keep up as they shot off fast towards the land.

'Maybe you shouldn't have made those jokes about gunrunning,' said Mum.

'It'll be fine.'

They escorted us into the port of Haifa and ordered us to anchor in the middle of the harbour.

'But it's too deep!' Dad protested. 'I don't think I've got enough anchor chain.'

'Just do it,' said the officer in charge who looked especially big and fierce.

Dad said nothing and went to prepare the anchor.

The boat was boarded and searched by men wearing great clumpy boots. Mum looked in despair at all the dirt on the deck. Ivan and I tried to squeeze out of the way. Omi was not bothered by all these men in uniform. She was used to it, from Romania. She went below and starting fiddling about in the galley. I guess she thought we would all be hungry.

The officer in charge peered into the cabin to see what was happening, and sniffed the air. Omi was making one of her specialities, a dip made of aubergines, cooked and mashed with garlic and mayonnaise.

'What is that?' the officer asked in good, clipped English.

'*Salate de vinete,*' she said, offering him some spread on bread.

'*Oy! Vinete!*' He took a piece and a smile grew all over his face.

'This is just like my mother used to make.'

It turned out he was from Romania originally. The search was stopped and Dad was taken to the various offices he needed to visit in order to complete formalities for clearing into the country.

We soon left the commercial port of Haifa where *Aventura* was dwarfed by all the shipping. It took ages for Dad to haul up all the anchor chain. The chain was stored in a locker at the bow, and access was through our cabin. Dad fed the chain smoothly down into the locker but sometimes it got stuck and piled up in a knot.

'Chain's stuck!' he yelled and ran into our cabin, threw aside all the toy animals that were piled up on their shelf, and opened the chain locker. A strong smell of salt water, wet metal and residues of whatever had come up from the sea bed, flooded the cabin, as he pulled at the chain to unblock it.

I could never understand how the sea could be so pleasant when you looked at it, and swam in it, and how disgusting it smelt when it was confined to that locker.

Tel Aviv had a new marina, so was more used to yachts. Susie arrived with her family and showed us around. Former neighbours of Omi's from Braşov owned the most popular cake shop in Tel Aviv. We visited and were told we could eat anything we wanted. Another friend ran an amusement park where we were allowed to go on any ride. People gave us clothes and food, and Israel seemed to me like a sort of paradise. Though sometimes I did remember the gun boat and the stern faces of the men on board.

Inland we went, to Jerusalem. I saw Jews praying standing with their faces to the Wailing Wall, and in Bethlehem, Christians prayed on their knees at the place where Jesus was born.

We floated on the salty water of the Dead Sea, or rather, everyone did except me; the salt stung the sore patches of eczema on my skin. Klaus floated happily on the water and waved his hands and feet. I tried to paddle at the edges but cried because it hurt so much.

* * *

On our return Susie came to the marina with her daughters Lili and Mayah, and her sisters and their children. Dad had promised them a trip. They arrived with bags stuffed with food and lots of jokes.

'Shall we take our passports? Will we ever come back?'

We motored out of the marina. There was no wind: the sea was an oily calm.

'I feel sick,' said Lili and she began to cry.

Within minutes all of our passengers were green with sea sickness and every bucket and bowl was in use. The children cried and the adults moaned and Ivan and I looked on in disbelief. Very soon Dad gave up and turned round. Our big expedition had not lasted very long.

Back in the marina, our guests quickly recovered and started to laugh heartily about their adventure as they laid out all the food in the main cabin. I went with Dad to check in with the port captain. When we returned all the food had been eaten.

* * *

Each time my parents mentioned their plan, that we were going to sail from Israel on to Egypt, everyone said they were mad. Israel was at war with Egypt and it was forbidden to travel from one country to the other.

But they didn't listen.

Dad had asked the officials, when we cleared into Israel, not to stamp our passports. So there would be no evidence we had visited.

Now Mum sat on the floor of the main cabin, with piles of food around her, presents of tinned fruit and other goodies. She started peeling off the paper labels.

'Why are you doing that?' I asked.

She held out a label to me. 'Look, all the writing is in Hebrew. That is such a big clue that we have been to Israel.'

She took a black marker pen and wrote Grapefruit on the top of the tin. Then she started on the next one.

'Don't mix up the tins!' I laughed. 'What if you write the wrong thing on them and we open one, but it's not grapefruit but beans or something!'

She laughed too. She sat there for hours, re-labelling. All this food we had been given, could not be wasted. Those tins, once she had carefully stored them in the spaces around the boat where we kept our food, could last us a long time.

'We'll be eating *falafels* for years,' she said.

Pyramids and Punctures

WHEN WE LEFT ISRAEL, Dad set a course as if we were sailing to Cyprus. Only when he thought we had gone far enough, and it was safe, did he turn the boat towards Egypt.

As we approached the land, the sea turned muddy and brown from the outflow of the great Nile river.

In Port Said a big fat Egyptian official clambered on board and spread himself out in the cockpit. He smiled at us children.

'I hope you like Egypt,' he said, patting Ivan on the head.

We smiled back. I was sure my smile looked really fake but he didn't seem to notice. I kept thinking to myself, *don't say anything about Israel, don't give us away.* It would have been better to have forgotten all about it, but it was the only thought in my head. The adults were talking, the official was asking questions, and all seemed quite friendly.

Then Ivan said to me in a clear voice, 'This port is a bit different. Remember when we were in Ha...'

He was just about to say Haifa. The syllable he said dropped into a sudden silence in the cockpit. Mum turned pale and Dad glared.

'Sorry, what?' asked the man, still smiling.

'Nothing,' Ivan said.

We scuttled below to our cabin, and sat there on the bunks facing each other, half scared, half trying not to laugh. Finally, I said in a fierce whisper, 'What if you had said it? What would have happened?'

'I couldn't help it.' He looked like he was about to cry.

I wasn't finished yet. 'We could've gone to prison. Or *worse*.'

I didn't really know what worse was but it sounded good. Ivan burst into tears and ran for Mum.

The Egyptian clearance formalities passed without any problems and the official left the boat. Then Ivan was teased, and we laughed at how close we had come to trouble.

Dad was used to trouble from Romania. When he was a young man, he told us, he had to bend the rules to make a living. That came in useful now. He and Mum scrimped and saved, so we could afford to visit the sights of Ancient Egypt.

When we took the overnight train to Luxor they paid for two sleeping compartments that had two bunks each. They didn't get tickets for us children. Ivan and I shared with Klaus and Omi. Every time someone knocked on the door we had to hide in case it was the train guard coming to inspect tickets.

At least the compartments had iced water on tap.

'Fantastic!' we all said.

Because Egypt was hot. Really hot. It was August and the heat was almost unbearable.

'What do you reckon? 40 degrees maybe?' said Dad.

'More,' said Mum.

As soon as we got the Luxor hotel we all took showers but we were all baking again straight after.

The heat did not stop us going to visit the Valley of the Kings. We took a tour with an old Egyptian guide.

'I remember when they opened up Tutankhamun's tomb,' he slurred, smiling and showing one yellow tooth. 'I was there when Carter came and found all the treasure.'

'He looks old enough,' Mum murmured to Dad. The guide patted her hand and winked.

'I think he likes you,' Dad said.

Underneath the rocky hills were the tombs built for the Egyptian kings and queens. Our guide led us away from the main entrances, where the other tourists were headed.

'Come this way,' he said, smiling again at Mum, and leaning on the arm of the young man who was his helper.

A steep set of steps led down into the ground. The guide waved a hand to the young man who took out a mirror. 'He stay here, give us the light.'

Down we went into the darkness. At the bottom we waited, seeing nothing. The guide called to the young man, who had stayed at the top of the steps. He held the mirror up and it caught the strong light of the Egyptian desert sun. A white beam poured onto us and past us, and hit the walls.

Suddenly there was colour and life. All the walls were painted with animals, humans, and figures that were a mixture of the two.

'That was how they lit the tombs, thousands of years ago,' Mum whispered to me. 'Candles or lamps would have been too smoky, ruined the paintings.'

When we came out of the cool tomb I felt the sun beat down on my head without mercy, like the Great Eye of Ra we had seen painted on the walls. Back at the hotel we begged the staff for more water to drink, but as fast as they put water to chill in the fridge we drank it. I never seemed to stop feeling thirsty and my head ached. We went out for something to eat but all I could manage was one slice of tomato.

'I feel ill,' I complained. I knew that I was ill, because normally I could eat anything.

Mum felt my forehead.

'Maybe you have a touch of heat stroke. We'll take it easy tomorrow.'

Heat stroke! I felt quite proud of myself then, like a real explorer. But we did not take it easy for long. We visited a camel market in a horse and carriage and watched the Nile at sunset, as the *dhows* with their lateen sails sailed downstream. We returned to Cairo and visited the Museum, the mosques, and the bazaar. We went to the bus station to get a bus to the pyramids. The buses were so packed that people climbed in and out of the windows to get on and off.

After three hours of trying we still hadn't got on a bus.

'Look at your mother and the children,' Mum said to Dad. 'They're exhausted. I'm exhausted. Let's take a taxi.'

Dad found a taxi that would drive us to Giza and then on to the pyramids at Saqqara. Ivan and I got to ride a camel outside the Pyramids of Giza.

Half way to Saqqara the taxi had a puncture. The driver pulled over to the side of the road, in a small village. We found ourselves surrounded by a crowd of young boys. It was funny to start with, as they stared and grinned, but then they began to press closer and there were so many of them, we didn't like it very much. They pushed us and tried to pull our hair and reach into the taxi and grab things.

Dad stood there, his arms folded, looking, then suddenly grabbed one boy by his ear and pulled. The boy cried and struggled, Dad let him go and glared at him. I knew that glare, and it was scary. Dad was a big, strong, hairy man. The boy rubbed his ear and retreated to a safe distance. All the other boys backed off too.

'Just looked to see who was the ring leader,' said Dad. 'That worked.'

The puncture was fixed and we made it to Saqqara, more ancient than the Gaza pyramids and yet less visited. Afterwards we had to walk to the cafe and our lift back. That meant cutting across a corner of the desert. We walked through the sand, our throats dry, heads down, desperate for water. The desert stretched grey and flat for miles to the distant horizon.

However much I loved the stories of Ancient Greece and Egypt, however much I had lived with the tales of gods and heroes for the past two years, there was only so much I could take. I felt as if I had spent my entire life trudging through ruins in the burning heat. My head felt like it was on fire and I was always thirsty. Everywhere I looked were bits of broken rock. My legs ached and I sat down on a lump of stone and glowered at my parents. Mum, as usual, was looking at the guide book and reading bits aloud to anyone interested. Dad was darting about taking pictures. Omi, Klaus and Ivan were slowly walking on.

'I've had enough!' I yelled, folding my arms. 'I hate ruins and I don't want to see *any more!*'

My parents turned in surprise. And burst out laughing.

'Too much culture for you – how many children of your age can say that!' they said. They were so proud of themselves, *and* they thought I was hilarious. Sometimes, they were *really* annoying.

But actually, later on they agreed with me.

'We've crammed a lot into this summer,' said Mum. 'I've had enough of ruins too. In fact, being at sea is quite restful.'

We were three days out from Alexandria. Omi was going to leave us in Greece and go to England and stay with Granny for a while. Dad was rushing to get a batch of programmes finished for her to take.

'They need a programme to broadcast this Sunday,' he said. 'So the race is on!'

We battled through a gale to get to Greece. Omi rushed off, and soon after, Klaus left too. *Aventura* was ours alone again. I liked visitors but I preferred it when it was only us on board.

In Greece Ivan had a little birthday party before we left for Malta. Mum made a cake and his favourite song was played at the end of Dad's programme. We knew then that Omi had made it safely to London with the tapes.

Ivan's actual birthday was at sea. We were sailing west, leaving the Mediterranean at last.

Atlantic 1976

Bucket on a rope

The Canary Islands

'DO YOU DESIRE my dinghy?' the man from the yacht next door said in a strong French accent as we moored in the harbour of Santa Cruz de La Palma, in the Canary Islands.

Two blonde children, a girl and a boy, were on the foredeck of the other yacht. They stopped their play and watched us. The girl lifted a hand and waved. I waved back.

'I don't desire it, but I'd like to borrow it,' replied Dad, smiling.

The man helped Dad take the lines ashore, then stood in his dinghy alongside *Aventura*, holding onto our lifelines.

'When you are ready, come have a drink. My name is Erick.'

Erick had a broad, ruddy face, creased with laugh lines around his blue eyes. 'There is my wife, Muriel.' A slim blonde woman greeted us from where she had appeared in the cockpit.

While Mum tidied up and Dad went ashore to clear with customs and immigration, Ivan and I studied the boat opposite. She looked very different from *Aventura*, low and slim in the water. A red, white and blue flag hung from her stern.

'French,' said Ivan. 'Wooden hull, I think. And a yawl.'

'How do you know that?'

'That mizzen mast is further back than ours.'

The French yacht was called *Calao* and that evening, as the adults had drinks in the cockpit, we children sat on the foredeck.

'*Moi* Sidonie,' said the girl. She held up six fingers. She pointed at her brother and held up three. '*Lui*, Fabien.' Fabien looked at us and then shot off down the deck, his chubby little legs running as fast as they could. Then he turned and ran back again. While I tried to talk to Sidonie, he kept this up.

I said our names and held up fingers too. I thought about the French I had learnt. *Qu'est-ce-que c'est? C'est un chien. Qu'est-ce-que c'est? C'est une table.* Not much use to start a conversation.

Sidonie beckoned. '*Viens*.' We clambered down below, past the adults in the cockpit. Erick was telling a story in a mixture of French and English and when it ended they all laughed loudly.

Sidonie and Fabien shared the forward cabin like us. She pulled out a collection of toys to show us while Fabien hurled himself onto his bunk.

'*Regardez*,' she said. Her toy animals were well loved and tatty; I thought ours were definitely superior in looks and personality, but I didn't say anything. She made one of them dance and she laughed. When she laughed she made a funny gurgling sound, and that made Ivan and I laugh too.

* * *

We stayed on the island of La Palma for a while, and Granny paid us a visit from England. She had rented an apartment ashore to stay on after we left, in order to enjoy the winter sunshine.

'Isn't this wonderful?' she said, turning her face to the sun. 'England is so gloomy now, grey and dark.'

Granny was quite different from Omi. She got on and off the boat quite easily, and she had let her hair go grey, without trying to dye it any strange colours.

Now she handed over a thick pile of letters. She already knew most of our news, because Mum wrote to her almost every week.

'We miss your puddings, Granny,' I said.

'I miss custard,' said Ivan.

'Ivan,' I said, while the adults talked. 'Do you remember, there was a TV advert in England, before we left, for golden syrup pudding?'

'No.' He shook his head.

'Well there was, and when we go back , the first thing I'll do is eat one.'

'I will too, with custard.'

* * *

'I love this,' said Mum as we visited the island's fruit and vegetable market. 'Everything grows here, and it looks such good quality. In Greece it was hard to even find a tomato.'

She and Dad spent so long choosing fruit and vegetables that Ivan and I thought we would go mad with boredom. Back on the boat it was no better as they spent hours storing everything away. We needed a lot of food for the Atlantic crossing.

'Come on, let's find Sidonie and Fabien,' I said to Ivan, desperate to escape. The four of us piled into the dinghy and rowed to the beach. The volcanic sand was quite black, and we heaped it into piles and pretended they were erupting volcanoes.

Back on the boat, every shelf and space was filled with carefully laid out fresh produce. Nothing was allowed to touch anything else so it wouldn't bruise or ripen too quickly. There were tomatoes of every colour, some very green and some just red and ripe to eat. Tins were stored in lockers and under bunks. Dry food was put into glass jars.

'We'll have fresh-baked bread all the way,' said Mum, putting away an extra large bag of flour.

Granny gave us one of her home-made Christmas puddings.

'Enjoy it wherever you end up for Christmas, and think of me!'

Dad also bought new lures for fishing and he talked to Erick about the best way to catch fish out in the ocean.

'I'm going to trail this off the back of the boat,' he said, showing us a little lure that looked like a colourful fish, with a big hook attached. He had a reel of fishing line that he fastened to the wooden aft rail. 'Fresh ocean fish – that will be great!'

Aventura was brought alongside the dock so the fuel tanks could be filled with diesel, and the water tanks with fresh water. A few extra jerry cans of water were lashed to the deck.

'You realise we can't waste a drop of this,' Dad told us. 'That's all the fresh wa-

ter we'll have. There'll be nowhere to get any more.'

It was actually quite hard to waste water on the boat. The taps had to be pumped by hand to get the water out, and that was much harder work than just turning a handle like you did in a house. The galley had two taps, one for fresh water and the other connected straight to the sea. Sea water was used for washing up when we were away from the polluted waters of port, and at a pinch you could use it for cooking, like boiling pasta; that helped save the precious fresh water for drinking only.

* * *

The evening before we were due to leave, we went out with Granny for a last treat.

'Have anything you like,' said Dad and Mum as they ordered a bottle of wine for themselves.

I decided on the best dessert on the menu. Chocolate cake. Ivan chose icecream.

'I hope you'll be safe,' said Granny, as we waited for our order to come. 'It's a long way.'

'We've got our liferaft, Mother,' Mum assured her. 'All checked and strapped on the foredeck.'

'What about storms?'

'That's why we're going now,' said Dad. 'Did you notice how many other yachts are getting ready to cross, like *Calao*? That's because it's November, the best time of year to go. The hurricane season will be finished by the time we get to the Caribbean. And the trade winds should be beginning so we'll get steady winds behind us, the whole way over.'

'How do you know that?' I asked disbelievingly. In the Mediterranean we had never known where the winds were going to come from next. Mostly they came too strong or not at all.

He smiled. 'Sailors have known about the trade winds for hundreds of years. That's why they're called the trades, they were used by trading ships, in the days before steam and diesel. Sailors have always followed the same route at the same time of year to cross the Atlantic, starting with Columbus. In fact, if you pick the right seasons, you can have the trade winds blow you right around the world.'

'How far is it though? How long will it take?'

'About two thousand seven hundred miles. And you know *Aventura* is not very fast. I reckon – about three weeks. Maybe more.'

I really hoped those magic trade winds turned up, but this was forgotten as my cake had arrived. I ate it slowly, savouring the moist chocolate. I knew it would be a long time before I ate anything so sweet and delicious again. Ivan watched me. His icecream still had not come. I lingered over my cake, enjoying his look of envy.

But then the waitress appeared, bearing before her on a tray what looked like a small replica of a Columbus caravel, and she placed it in front of Ivan. The adults cheered. My mouth fell open, and Ivan's eyes grew wide. A glass dish was piled high with several flavours of icecream, and wafers and biscuits had been used to make masts and sails. There was even a Spanish flag on top.

The few mouthfuls of cake left on my plate now looked forlorn.

'Ivan,' I said. 'You can't eat all that. Let me help you.'

'Leave him alone. You made *your* choice,' said Mum, sipping her wine.

Ivan picked up his spoon.

'I can eat it,' he said.

And he did. All of it. However many times I offered to help him.

Across the Atlantic Ocean

MUM AND DAD were up at first light, and by the time I was out of my bunk they were ready to cast off the lines.

'See you in America!' cried Granny, waving from the shore.

'Hey!' shouted Erick. 'We'll see you on the other side.'

'Okay,' said Dad. 'Where?'

Erick thought for a second. 'How about in Martinique, for Carnival!'

'Fine,' said Dad. 'We'll be there.'

'*Bon voyage!*'

The fenders were pulled onto the deck and stored in the lockers under the cockpit seats. The warps were coiled and put away.

'We won't need those for a while,' said Dad.

As we left the shelter of La Palma, a breeze blew up from behind. Mum turned off the engine and *Aventura* wallowed in the choppy sea with only the mainsail up. Dad hauled up the genoa.

'Tidy all the sheets in the cockpit, please,' he told us.

I watched as the green mountains of La Palma grew smaller and smaller until they disappeared below the horizon. We headed southwest. Dad said we'd hit the trades if we went that way. The wind came from a different direction every day. Sometimes it didn't even bother to blow at all, and we had to motor, the sea as calm as when we'd been in Santa Cruz's protected harbour.

'I'm getting fed up with this,' Dad complained, as he changed the sails yet again.

'How far have we gone?' Ivan and I asked.

'Time to find out. I'll take a noon sight.'

He took his sextant out of its wooden box.

'I'm not looking directly at the sun,' he explained, perching himself on the top of the wheelhouse. 'There's an image of it created by mirrors and smoked glass. Here, look for yourselves.'

Ivan and I peered into the black viewfinder and saw a green spot waving about all over the sea and sky. I couldn't imagine how Dad could keep it steady enough to get a reading.

'Take this,' he said to me, handing me a stopwatch. 'Press it when I say now.'

He planted his feet firmly on the lifelines to steady himself, then twiddled the dials on the sextant to align the image of the sun with the horizon. When he thought that he had the reading he called out 'Now!' I quickly pressed the start button of the stopwatch, while he ran down below to the navigation table. He noted down the exact time, and what the scale on the side of the sextant read, and I told him the time on the stopwatch, the few seconds which had elapsed since his reading. Then he set to work with the Nautical Almanac.

I could not make head or tail of the great long lists of figures that were in the

almanac, and the complicated calculations that he had to do. I did sort of understand how finding out the angle between the height of the sun and the horizon would help you find out where you were – but how to work it out, that was a complete mystery to me.

Ivan loved all the numbers and stood close by, examining all the calculations Dad made. When I looked at those numbers my head swam, but I waited eagerly, because I knew there would be that moment of magic when Dad had an answer, the longitude and the latitude, when he took his pencil and ruler, and drew a small cross on the chart. That cross was always a little bit further west than the cross from the day before.

* * *

Finally, after a week at sea, the wind settled from behind.

'I think I'll try the twin foresails today,' said Dad. He dropped the mainsail and hoisted the two genoas. Each sail was fixed to a pole that pushed it away from the boat and helped fill it with wind. The sails stretched out either side of the bow like two white wings. An ocean swell lifted *Aventura* up, and then with the wind's help she surfed her way down the other side.

The sky was bright blue with a few puffy clouds passing by.

'Look at those clouds,' said Dad. 'Typical trade wind clouds.'

'Trade winds? Have they come?'

'Maybe... perhaps too soon to tell. But it looks promising.'

'How far have we gone?' we asked yet again and he took his brass dividers and held one of their sharp points against the pencil mark from the day before, moved the other one to today's, and measured off the distance between the two on the scales along the side of the chart.

'Not bad today. One hundred miles. We're doing a steady four knots.'

The following day when we gathered around the chart table he said, 'Look, we have passed the 20° line of longitude.'

'Surprise!' Mum produced two small wrapped presents from behind her back. For lunch Dad made a treat of pancakes drizzled with syrup.

After that we waited eagerly to cross the 30° line, as we knew that we would get a present. It was exciting to think there were secrets hidden somewhere on board as until then I had thought we knew every nook and cranny of the boat.

* * *

The trades really had come. The winds blew from behind at a steady rate, Dad didn't touch the sails for two weeks and the self-steering did all the work. This wasby far the most pleasant sailing we'd ever known.

The sailing was so easy, school work had to be done. We sat in the cockpit reciting our times tables and learning some new French vocabulary so we could talk to Sidonie and Fabien when we saw them again.

Mum also set us the task of making daily observations of the weather. We had a bucket with a rope tied to the handle that we threw over the side and filled with seawater, both of us tugging hard to pull it up against the force of the boat sailing on. I always worried I'd lose the bucket over the side.

Ivan held the clipboard while I dipped in the thermometer and read off the water temperature. We noted the speed and direction of the wind and read the air pressure from the brass barometer that was fastened to the bulkhead in the main cabin, made of brass as shiny as the ship's clock next to it, and the swinging oil lamp that was more for decoration than light.

When we'd finished school, and our data collection for the day, and we didn't feel like reading, 'let's play,' one of us would say. As the boat's movement up and down in the swell was quite regular, we'd discovered a new game. We stood on the floor of the tiny bathroom next to our cabin, and jumped when the bow pitched down. If we timed it wrong, we hit the floor too hard. But if we jumped just at the right moment, for a split second we felt as if we were suspended in the air and weightless, before we hit the floor again.

When we'd had enough of that, we'd pull down the pile of toy animals from where they were squashed on the triangle shelf over the foot of our bunks.

'Put your head under the duvet,' I said to Ivan.

'Why?'

'We can get to Toyland then!' We covered ourselves with the duvet.

Ivan giggled. 'Are we there yet?'

'No, you've got to make the noise.'

So we made a noise that sounded like a cross between a car and a spaceship.

'We must help Yellow Teddy,' I told Ivan. 'He's the ruler of Toyland and his enemies are trying to overthrow him. Come on, let's go!'

We were always thinking of new stories for our toy animals. One day we organised a birthday party for Johnny the Elephant. Then we had a wedding between Big Monkey and Little Monkey. After that Musical Teddy kidnapped

Betty, the one-eyed blue rabbit who was Yellow Teddy's wife, and war was declared. Ivan ranged his toys on his bunk, and I did the same on mine. A great battle started between the two bunks.

The new toys I'd got in Romania, to replace Blulaki, had become part of the family, although I never felt the same way about them. It didn't help that they were poorly made. Ducky had lost his stuck-on eyes and feet, and then just looked like two white blobs put together. It was worse for Brownie. He was supposed to be a small brown bear, but his feet and eyes were only stuck on and when they fell off he looked like –

'What is it?'

Ivan had buried his head in his pillow and was shaking with laughter.

'Poo!' he screeched. 'He looks like a brown poo!'

I wanted to protest but it was no good, he was right. Poor Brownie. He did look like a little furry brown poo.

* * *

After two weeks at sea, when we had gathered a long list of figures written down on the paper on our clipboard, I dropped the thermometer down the companionway. The glass smashed and little grey blobs of mercury went spinning across the cabin floor as if they had a life of their own. I stared at them. They were so fascinating I didn't really care that I was in trouble, and that we couldn't keep our records going any longer.

The bucket with a rope came in useful though to give ourselves saltwater showers on the foredeck. We poured the cool Atlantic over us, and used salt water shampoo to make a lather, as regular shampoo wouldn't work. Then, dry and clean, though with skin that was salty if you licked it, we would lie on the foredeck and read, or perch on the pulpit under the white sails and dream.

Ocean swells rolled underneath us, keeping the boat in constant motion like a stately dance, and on top of these long distance waves the wind flecked the sea with white foam and little wavelets. It seemed to me that *Aventura* was really

happy then, with deep ocean beneath her keel and her white sails keeping her flying ever westwards.

Mum sat on deck and hand stitched small tears in the sails with her big sailmaker's needles and leather piece that fitted around her palm to protect it. Dad checked the ropes for wear, and ran the engine regularly to charge the batteries and keep our electricity supply going. He liked to have all the equipment well-maintained and the boat generally ship-shape. He got adventurous with his navigation and tried taking sights from the stars and the moon as well as the sun. Mum cooked tasty stews in the pressure cooker, and baked bread. We had something different to eat almost every day.

'And hardly any tins,' she said proudly. 'The Canary Islands stuff has lasted really well.'

'Let me make the bread,' Dad offered one day. When the rolls came out of the oven they looked appetising enough. I took a bite. It tasted horrid.

'Ugh,' I spat it over the side.

'What!' he cried angrily.

'It tastes awful.'

Mum nibbled a piece and made a face. 'What did you do – it's really salty. How much salt did you put in?'

'I don't know.' He shrugged. 'Two tablespoons, like the recipe says.'

'That was supposed to be *teaspoons*! *Tsp* means teaspoons.'

'Well, I didn't know. I'm only a foreigner, you know.' And he tipped the lovely-looking bread over the side.

The next time Mum was to make bread, we heard her make a strange noise as she opened up the flour bag. It was crawling with little black dots. Weevils. There were so many of them it looked like the bag was moving.

The extra-large bag of flour followed the bread, into the ocean. I didn't mind too much – finding weevils in the flour made me feel more like an old-fashioned sailor.

Dad was disappointed with his new fishing lures as we hadn't yet caught a thing. 'Where are the fish?' he wondered. 'There must be plenty out here.'

The only fish we saw were the little silver flying fish that leapt out of the water, from the crest of one wave to another. One morning we found two lying dead on the deck – they must have leapt up there in the night. At least they made a tasty breakfast fried in the pan.

Meanwhile the line of pencil crosses on the chart led us ever further away from the Canary Islands and ever nearer to the Caribbean, and we waited eagerly for the latest position. We crossed the 40° and the 50° lines of longitude and got more presents, colouring books and card games to help us pass the time. There was always a special meal as well.

I felt as if we had been at sea for months. In all these days we'd only seen three ships and one yacht. I'd read almost all the children's books on board, and we were running out of ideas of what games to play with our toy animals.

Now Ivan and I scanned the horizon desperately hoping to see a smudge of green on the horizon. Clouds deceived us with their shades of grey that looked like far off mountains.

'How far now?' we asked Dad for the millionth time.

'Ssh,' he said, trying to tune the radio. A loud and cheerful voice suddenly came out of the set. It was Radio Barbados.

'There you are. Loud and clear. And two hundred miles to go.'

At last – after 26 days at sea –

'We should see Barbados today,' Dad predicted.

For hours Ivan and I stared westwards, imagining all sorts of shapes that turned out only to be waves on the horizon.

'Land ahoy!' cried Ivan. His eyesight was better than mine.

Beyond the waves, something dark that was not a cloud, a smudge that slowly turned into green. Land. Finally, land.

Caribbean 1976–77

Conch shell

A Caribbean Christmas

'I REALLY HOPE,' I said as we rowed ashore, 'that the earth rolls under our feet.'

I'd just read a book by another sailing family, and it happened to them after a long ocean passage. Other books described sailors having a funny rolling gait as a result of walking the vast decks of square-riggers. We didn't really walk anywhere on *Aventura*, just clambered from one handhold to the next – but I was still hopeful.

I jumped out of the dinghy and took a few steps, expecting I'd fall down or stagger or something, but nothing happened. The ground stayed quite still. I stamped up and down in disgust.

'Well, I'm glad it's not moving,' said Mum. 'It's nice to be on solid ground again.'

* * *

The Bouteleux family on *Calao* arrived a few days after us and dropped anchor nearby. The crossing had taken them 19 days.

'*Calao*'s much faster than *Aventura*,' Ivan said to me.

'I thought you were going to Bequia,' Dad called across.

'We had bad luck.' Erick talked in French to Dad but I found I could understand most of what he said. 'The forestay and the rudder broke. We're lucky to get to Barbados at all.'

Ivan and I rowed over to see Sidonie and Fabien. It was good to have some other children to play with again.

'*Viens*, come on,' I said. All the French I'd learnt while we were crossing the Atlantic came in useful now. 'Let's go to the beach.'

Sidonie jumped into the dinghy. Fabien climbed in more slowly. Muriel made him wear a lifejacket.

'*J'aimepas!*' he said, clenching his fists.

'He doesn't like it, does he?' I said to Sidonie. She nodded.

'Never mind.' I tried to sound sympathetic and patted his chubby knee. 'We used to have wear them too.' Fabien looked at me with his big blue eyes.

'*C'est bon.*' I grabbed the oars. '*On y va?*'

'*Oui, vite, on y va!*' Sidonie and Fabien chorussed.

As we rowed Ivan counted the number of yachts in the anchorage, and then the number of masts.

'One, two,' he said, '*trois*, four, *cinq...*'

On the beach Fabien followed me around. It began to be annoying.

'You're his mummy now!' Sidonie gurgled with laughter. '*Sa maman!*'

'I'm not,' I answered back. 'Let's play with the dinghy.'

'No, I want to make a sand castle.'

'No, dinghy. I'm the oldest and it's our dinghy.'

Sidonie slowly trailed after me into the water. Fabien had found a stick and was banging it on rocks on the beach. Ivan played with his Tonka digger, making excavations in the sand. I flipped the dinghy over and swam underneath. It was cool and dim and the air was trapped inside. Sidonie then Ivan joined me. We stayed under there for ages, singing silly songs.

Later on the boys dug holes in the sand and jumped in them, shouting. Sidonie told me that the French word for a boy's willy was *zizou*.

'*Zizou*!' It made me laugh.

'What's a girl's called then?' I wondered. There wasn't a word in English that I could think of.

'*Lune*,' she said, giggling.

'What's that?'

She looked up and there was a pale moon. She pointed. After that we lay in the warm shallows and pointed our bottoms to the sky.

'*Lune, c'est la lune*!' we shouted.

Franglais, that was what Mum said we talked, that funny mixture of French and English.

But we always understood each other.

* * *

Calao stayed in Barbados to get their rudder repaired but Erick promised they'd make it to Martinique for Carnival. We sailed to St George's, on the island of Grenada, stocked up on food and then headed round the coast.

'We'll find a nice quiet place for Christmas,' said Dad.

We soon came across a bay where lush green hills sloped down to the beach, and although there were a few houses tucked in amongst the trees, there wasn't another boat there.

'This looks perfect,' said Mum as Dad dropped the anchor.

'Mummy, look!' Ivan pointed.

A shark's fin cut the water just near the boat. Underneath we could see its dark silhouette.

'That's a good eight feet long,' Dad estimated. I felt rather scared then. I'd just been thinking of jumping into the water.

'Don't swim!' a man had appeared on the beach and was shouting to us. 'There are hammerheads here and they're breeding!'

Later on we found out from the people who lived onshore that the sharks came to this bay every Christmas to breed.

'The only bay they come to, on the whole of Grenada. And we managed to pick it. Never mind. Children, help me make a Christmas tree.'

It was so hot, it didn't feel much like Christmas to me. But I helped Mum make a tree out of green paper that she stuck to the bulkhead in the main cabin. Ivan and I cut some decorations out of silver paper and put them on the tree.

'Not bad,' said Mum when we'd finished.

I looked at the paper tree and for the first time, I felt a bubble of excitement in my stomach. Christmas was coming. And there would be presents tomorrow morning. I had no idea where Mum had managed to hide them on the boat, but after the surprises we had crossing the Atlantic I knew she could.

The morning came swiftly. The presents were there, under the paper tree, in their coloured wrapping paper. We waited for our parents to get up – Mum had to have a strong cup of coffee before she was ready – and then we gathered in the cockpit. Ivan had a Meccano set and I had a little makeup bag with a bottle of nail polish which I'd asked for.

'Maybe if you paint your nails,' said Mum, 'you might stop biting them!'

I got a Barbie doll as well. I examined her closely. She was so pink and shiny, with her shiny outfits, and her tiny feet that fitted tiny high-heeled shoes. A doll. Well, I supposed I might play with her.

Ivan had an Action Man and a plastic shark to go with it. We had books too, and a shared present of a cassette player that could record onto blank tapes.

'What a lot of presents. You're very lucky,' said Dad, and Mum nodded in agreement. 'If we'd lived a long time ago, Ivan would have just got a wooden toy made by me, and Doina a doll sewed by Gwenda.'

I rolled my eyes. They always had to say things like that.

'This is our present from Granny.' Mum pulled a huge fishing net out of a bag. She spent the morning sewing on the weights and floats. Meanwhile Dad took out of a locker a pile of ropes and bits of wood and started to put the pieces together.

'What is that, Daddy?'

'I bought it in La Palma. It's a rope ladder.'

By lunchtime he had finished. He fixed it on the main mast and it ran all the way up to the spreaders.

'This will be really good for keeping a look out when we go through the reefs,' he said to Mum.

'Can we go up?' I asked. I slowly climbed up and Ivan followed.

'Careful!' called Mum as I hoisted myself up onto the main spreaders. The deck seemed very far below and I held on tightly. My blood thumped in my ears. A vivid image of me falling came into my head but I tried to push it out. I swung onto the other side of the mast and sat down on the spreader while Ivan came up and joined me on the other side. Our feet dangled about twenty feet above the deck.

'This is great. You can see really well from up here.'

'Look at the water. You can see the colours, where it's sandy, and where the rocks are.'

'And the sharks.' I pointed to where two black silhouettes cruised slowly round the boat. Their heads ended in a blunt hammer shape.

'Let's come up here every day.'

'This is the best present!'

That evening we ate roast chicken and Granny's pudding. Dark and fruity, it brought back memories of cold Christmases back in England. We did not miss the cold.

Dad put out the new net.

'Let's hope we catch something for breakfast,' he said.

In the morning when he hauled it in, two fish were caught in the mesh. They were about a foot long, with thin bodies, grey skin, and little curved mouths under their flat heads.

'They look like baby sharks,' I said.

We cooked the baby sharks for our Boxing Day lunch. They were very tasty and tender.

The next day we left. We'd had enough of the sharks and wanted to find a place we could swim. Besides, we'd eaten their children.

Lessons of the Caribbean

WE LEFT GRENADA and made our way through the little islands of the Grenadines where the beaches were white and the waters were blue and clear. We caught lots of fish in the new net. Many of the islands were uninhabited and the only way they could be reached was by yacht.

The new rope ladder came in useful now that we had to navigate our way through the coral reefs. Dad climbed the main mast and stood on the spreaders. From up there he could clearly read the colours of the sea, the bright blue which meant a safe sandy bed, the dangerous yellows and browns of coral heads lurking just beneath the surface.

I stood on the aft deck. I had an important job.

'Five degrees to starboard,' Dad called. 'Ten degrees port.' I repeated these messages to Mum at the wheel. She was under the wheelhouse and couldn't hear Dad. She kept one eye ahead and the other on the echo-sounder which told her what depth was under the keel.

There were coral heads scattered on either side. Dad did his best to guide us through but despite his best efforts, we grazed the side of one. The boat shuddered and a horrible cold shiver ran through me. As we inched forwards, unbearably slowly, I began to pray silently 'Please God, please let us get through safely. Please. If we get through, I will believe in you, I promise.'

'This is good!' shouted Dad. 'We'll anchor here.'

He climbed down quickly and let out the chain in a great rattling rush. The anchor sank down and buried itself into the sand. He leapt into the water with his mask and snorkel to check it was well dug in. Then it was our turn to swim. I had forgotten my fear by then and my promise, in my delight at looking at what was underneath the water. Individual fishes of every possible colour swam gently around coral heads, while great packs of silver ones flicked themselves this way and that. A fat reef shark, about the same size as me, cruised slowly past without bothering to notice us humans. It was well fed on those reef fish. I was a bit scared though.

Ivan was still not a strong swimmer.

'You know what,' said Dad one day. 'I'm setting you a challenge, Ivan. Swim all the way round the boat without stopping and I'll buy you... what would you like?'

Ivan looked blank.

'I dunno.'

'A hamburger?' I suggested.

'Yes, a hamburger.'

'Deal!'

After that he struggled hard to get better at swimming. By the time we got to Port Elizabeth on the island of Bequia, he was nearly there.

Ivan and I sat on deck and watched a couple of charter yachts careering around the crowded anchorage narrowly missing other boats. As I watched one yacht try to disentangle itself from another, I realised that we weren't beginners any more, who got sick and rammed pontoons like on our very first voyage. 'You can't buy that experience over the counter,' Dad liked to say. 'Not even under it.'

Ivan jumped up. 'I'm going to try again.'

I called Dad and Mum. Ivan lowered himself into the water from the dinghy and set off round the stern.

'Come on,' we shouted as he swam determinedly up the side of the boat.

'I can't,' he gasped when he was half way. His head was barely above the water and he looked as if he was going to sink.

'You can!' we yelled back. I crossed my fingers and willed him on. He turned around the bow and kept going. At last his outstretched fingers touched the dinghy. Dad jumped down and hauled him into the dinghy and Mum wrapped him up in a towel. He had made it.

'So come on, young man,' said Dad. 'I promised.'

Ashore, the bars and restaurants were busy with people drinking and eating. When my parents saw the prices on the menu they were not so happy. However, we had hamburgers and cool lemonade for us, and beer for the grownups. But we felt a bit out of place.

'Look, a place you can swap books,' Mum said to me afterwards when we went for a stroll. 'You could exchange some of yours. You keep complaining you've nothing to read.'

'But do I have to give away the ones I really like?' I asked, thinking of well-loved ones, like the set of Narnia books I'd received for my seventh birthday back in London.

'You've got no choice, really. You've finished reading all of those twice over at least, and you want some new ones. We have to try and keep the weight down.'

It was true that we had a lot of books on board. There were the six volumes of the *Children's Encyclopedia* that we referred to whenever we had a question. And as well as the crammed bookshelves in the aft cabin, and the shelves above our own bunks, there was the secret place at the end of the quarter berth in the main cabin. It wasn't really secret but it was so small and dark it felt like that. I crawled in there with a torch because there was no light. The air always smelt faintly of diesel, because the engine was in the compartment next door. There were lots of cubbyholes, crammed with books. I rummaged through, hoping that this time I might find a treasure, a book I hadn't yet discovered.

In Bequia I swapped Narnia for a series of books on the adventures of Nancy

Drew, an American girl who went about solving mysteries. I read them quickly. They were okay. But they didn't really live in my imagination like Narnia did.

Silly books like Nancy Drew I might read in a day. I was a fiddly, picky sort of a person. I picked my nose and picked my scabs, chewed my fingernails, despite my new nail polish, and one day, absent-mindedly starting tearing strips off the corner of the book I was reading and chewed the paper.

Mum gave me a book about the history of the Caribbean and I read about the original Arawak and Carib inhabitants who were pretty much wiped out by the incoming European settlers, from Columbus onwards. They couldn't cope with the diseases these new people brought, who took over their islands and stole their wealth. But the white people did not stop there. Africans were shipped over to work as slaves and create riches for the white people on sugar plantations. Those slave ships had crossed the same Atlantic that we had just sailed over.

Dad had started to follow the trail of Africa through the Caribbean after he recorded an African song in Barbados. He sent the recording to someone he knew in the African Section of the World Service.

'Some more freelance work for the BBC would be great,' he said.

'It would definitely help our finances,' agreed Mum. 'The Caribbean is so expensive.'

On the island of St Lucia he tried to follow up leads about African music, drums, secret ceremonies and poetry.

'This freelancing hasn't been very successful so far,' he complained. 'I seem to be spending money, not making it!'

'Well at least we've seen some interesting things,' Mum said wisely.

We visited the workshop of an artist who had painted a fresco of a black Christ for a local church. I preferred his Jesus to the one in the illustrated children's Bible we had onboard – I loved to look at the illustrations but I knew there was no way he would have been so blonde and blue-eyed.

I read my parents' copy of *Roots*, just recently published, about one American's story of his African ancestors. The scene where Kunta Kinte tries to escape his slavery and is brutally recaptured and has half his foot cut off, stuck vividly in my imagination.

I observed the places we travelled through, listened to Dad's stories, and tried to make sense of it.

We anchored off Pigeon Island in the north of St Lucia. Dad wanted to take photos of *Aventura*, the only yacht in the anchorage, so we climbed the hill to a ruined fort at the top. Ivan clambered onto an old cannon. I found a fluffy seedhead on the end of a long dry stick, and started to dance about.

'Film me, film me,' I cried to Dad. 'Look, I'm a fairy! I'm a fairy!'

I'd learnt a lot about the world but I was still a nine year old kid.

Auntie Beeb

IN ST KITTS Dad came back excitedly from the post office where he'd gone to check for mail.

'Look, a telegram!' he said. 'It's from Network Africa. They've used some of my pieces. They want more!'

That set him off on two days of interviews.

'I need some quiet for editing all this together,' he said as a dinghy puttered past with an outboard engine that sounded like an angry fly.

The rest of St Kitts was closed to yachts but Dad had made lots of friends during his interviews, and we were given special permission to anchor in another bay. The bay was deserted apart from a few pelicans.

'I'll get up early tomorrow to start recording. But first I'll go spearfishing.'

'I'll go too,' said Mum. 'I want to take a look at the fishes.'

One of my ears was hurting so I didn't want to swim. Mum thought I'd got an infection because of all the swimming. She gave me some pencillin from the medicine cabinet which seemed to help a little bit.

'Kids come and look at this!' we heard Dad shouting.

The dinghy was full of lobsters. Dad was grinning from ear to ear.

'I do love lobster...' Mum began. 'But maybe that is a bit too much. How are we going to eat them all?'

'Perhaps I did go a bit mad,' he admitted.

'Two barracudas followed us,' Mum said to me. 'That was rather scary. I thought I'd swim for the beach but one of them followed me. So I stuck next to Dad. He had a gun and a knife, after all! How's your ear, by the way?'

'A bit better. It still hurts.'

Mum boiled the lobsters in the pot until the shells turned from brown and green to bright red. Lunch was a feast of lobster and mayonnaise. The meat was tender and sweet and nourishing.

* * *

The soft sounds of Romanian came winding into my sleep. Dad had got up really early and started on his recording, reading aloud from the script he'd written.

I crept quietly to the door into the main cabin, rubbing my eyes, and watched him editing the tape. He laid the magnetic tape on a block of wood, cut out a piece with a razor blade and carefully taped it back together with a tiny sliver of clear sticky tape. Then he played the tape back to check the splice was okay. In this way he could edit out mistakes, and mix up recordings of his script with music and interviews.

After breakfast Ivan and I wondered what we could do. We weren't allowed on deck or in the main cabin because we made too much noise. We slunk back into the fo'c'sle.

'Let's record something,' I suggested. Ivan dug out the cassette recorder we'd got for Christmas from under a pile of animals.

'Give it here,' I said, grabbing it from him.

'But I want a go,' he said.

'In a *minute*. Me first.' I pressed the record button.

'This is the news,' I said in a posh voice.

'Do it properly.'

I pressed the stop button. 'What? You messed that up now.'

'You have to do the beeps.'

'Alright,' I answered irritably. But I knew he was right.

Beep, beep, beep, beep, beep, beeeeeeeeeeeeeeeeeeep.

This is the BBC World Service. It is 2000 Greenwich Mean Time. Here is the news. A bomb has exploded in Beirut but only one person was injured. The bomb was in a supermarket. It was in a Golden Nuggets cereal packet.

Hallo I'm Rag Doll, I squeaked in a high-pitched voice. *Now I'm going to have my very own request show. Dear Raggy, I request 'Come quickly I'm dying.' I am 19 and I want a penfriend. I like cars and planes. Carrots Petersen, 24th Avenue, New York, USA. Come quickly is sung by Little Monkey.*

Little Monkey's voice was even squeakier and screechier than Rag Doll's.

Come quickly I'm dying
Come quickly I'm ill,
Soon I'll be buried,
In a grave, in a coffin
Soon you'll only have me as a skeleton
Come quickly I'm dying,
Come quickly I'm ill
Come quickly I'm dying,
Come quickly I'm ILL.

After Rag Doll had 'played' several songs (I sang them all, with Ivan making suitable noises in the background) it was Ivan's turn.

This is the broadcast for Toyland and here is the news. Scientists on Spetak Island have discovered a new food which is good for long voyages because it contains little space and has a lot of vitamins and energy. Also it cannot rot so you could carry it on forever without it going sour.

Next I'm going to tell you some useful tips for sound effects. To make a footsound, you take a hardback book and a tube from some cooking foil and then you tap it on the book like this. Here is a demonstration.

- Joe! (steps getting louder)

- Quiet!

- He's approaching!

- Hide behind that barrel

- I will (steps getting quieter)

- He's going

- He's gone, Joe

We soon filled up the blank tapes we had, so we recorded over them again. We imitated the BBC World Service as accurately as we could. After all, Auntie Beeb was our daily companion, and she paid our way.

Sailing in Company with *Calao*

DAD WAS A MAN of his word. And so was Erick. They had arranged to meet in Martinique for Carnival, and when we got to Fort-de-France, the familiar low white silhouette of *Calao* was there to greet us.

Carnival was like no other festival we had ever seen. On the first day, Fat Monday or *Lundi Gras*, weird wedding couples paraded in the streets, tall men in veils and bridal dresses alongside short female grooms in suits. The second day, Mardi Gras, everyone was dressed in red, even the onlookers. There was loud music, drumming, singing and dancing, and we pushed our way down the crowded streets. We laughed to see the comical brides, and we were amazed by the red clothes people wore. Each day the dancing got a little bit wilder, the music a bit louder.

On the third day, Ash Wednesday, all the costumes were black and white. The whole town was dressed up, even the tiniest babies. Some people were armed with bags of flour and water, and they pelted us until our clothes were white and soggy. A group of people dressed in black and white wheeled on a huge effigy of Vaval, the Carnival king, who was to be burnt. I was crushed in the crowd as more and more people poured into the streets and I nearly let go of Mum's hand.

* * *

Dad and Mum were sat in the cockpit talking about their plans with Erick and Muriel. Sidonie and I were down below drawing and I was half listening to the adults as well.

'We're heading for the Turks and Caicos which are pretty remote,' said Dad. 'And they say the charts aren't always accurate. Why don't we sail together?'

'It's nice to have company as well,' Mum added.

'After that we're going to head up the east coast of the States. We might even go up as far as Maine, as we have friends up there.'

The Bouteleux family had been planning to head next for the Pacific, through the Panama Canal.

'Well, we could postpone going into the Pacific,' Erick discussed it with Muriel. It was decided. The two boats would sail in company. I nudged Sidonie and grinned. We had slept on each other's boats and we spent all our time together. We were firm friends now.

* * *

In St Thomas, part of the US Virgin Islands, Mum took me to the doctor. It turned out I had a 'swimmer's ear' infection and he gave me some drops.

At least the drops soon made my ear better.

In San Juan, Puerto Rico, Erick and Dad set off to find somewhere good and cheap for provisions.

'There won't be many shops where we're going,' Dad explained. 'We'll have to be pretty much as self-sufficient as when we crossed the Atlantic.'

He returned with Erick hours later.

'We found this amazing wholesalers,' he said excitedly. 'It was really cheap.'

'How much did you buy?' Mum gasped.

There was a huge pile of supplies on the dock – tins, boxes, and a bulging sack.

'You can't buy individual items. Only by the dozen. And we can split it with *Calao*.'

'But it's just too much.' Mum picked up a large square tin. 'What's in this? *Bay leaves!* There's enough in there for *years*.'

'*Et c'est quoi exactement*? What's *that*?' asked Muriel, pointing at the sack.

'Cabbages,' said Erick. '*Les choux, mon choux!*'

'We'll split it,' said Dad cheerfully. He and Erick were very proud of themselves and nothing the mums said made any difference.

'It's going to take months to eat those cabbages,' said Mum.

'What about this? *Et ça*?'

'Pork and beans, just what it says on the label. A real bargain.'

Mum and Muriel gave up. It was utterly impossible to argue.

'Looks like we're going to be living on cabbage salad,' said Mum.

'At least we won't get scurvy,' I said, trying to be helpful. 'Captain Cook discovered cabbage would keep it away, didn't he?'

We Nearly Lose *Aventura*

AVENTURA AND *CALAO* sailed downwind towards the Ambergris Cays. *Calao* was always a little bit faster than us and she pulled ahead.

Dad stood on the spreaders to see the way through the reef.

'The sun's against us now,' he called down. 'It's hard to see the way.'

Calao picked their way through the coral heads and got into the lagoon but just then a cloud came over the sun and the surface of the sea went grey.

'It's okay, go on,' cried Dad from the mast.

At that point there was a heart-stopping crash. *Aventura* hit one coral head, then another, bounced off, and came to rest on a cluster of heads. Mum tried to go astern, then ahead, but we were stuck fast.

Dad shot down the mast, grabbed his mask and jumped overboard. Immediately a strong current took him. He tried to grab at the coral but it broke off in his fingers.

'Jimmy be careful!' Mum's voice was weak and trembly. Finally he managed to stand on the coral and hold himself upright against the sea.

'Keep her full astern,' he yelled and then plunged under the water.

'Oh god,' said Mum. She revved the engine as hard as she could.

The swell came rolling up to break onto the reef, and each time it pushed the boat up and then let her down again with a sickening thud. I was so afraid. Not for myself, but for the boat. She could be bashed to pieces. The waves pushed her up and down, bang after bang, and the hull tilted awkwardly to one side. It was so wrong. *Aventura* was like an animal in a trap, desperate and struggling to get out but not knowing how.

Dad tried to lead an anchor astern but he couldn't walk against the current. Erick anchored *Calao* as near as he could to the reef and swam back to help. Together they managed to put the anchor down.

'I'll go onboard and winch it in,' Dad yelled. The rope broke. They set the anchor again, and then took another anchor out with a halyard attached to the top of the mast, to try and heel the boat over to get her out.

I was no use. Everyone was busy. Even Ivan was in the cockpit trying to do something useful in his own small way. I ran below to our cabin and grabbed an old plastic box which contained all my treasures, a wooden Russian doll, a few shells. If the boat was going to be wrecked, I wanted to take it with me. I sat on the floor of the main cabin, clutching my box and waiting for the end.

'The tide's coming in,' I heard Dad shouting. 'We'll make it.'

With all the pushing and pulling and the tide turning in our favour, *Aventura* started to move. Dad cut loose the anchors and the boat somehow bounced her way across the reef, pushed by the waves. She fell into the calm waters of the lagoon and floated upright, finally herself again.

As soon as the anchor was down, Dad dove to inspect the hull. Amazingly there was no damage other than a few scratches and a tiny chunk out of the front part of the hull. He sat in the cockpit wiping his face with a towel.

'It could have been much worse,' he said. 'I didn't tell you, but when I was on the reef, I looked underwater and saw the boat was moving towards a huge hole. If the keel had got stuck in there, we really would have been finished.'

We sat there in silence for a while. We had been so close to losing – everything. Around us the lagoon waters seemed peaceful, but if I raised my head I could see where the ocean waves were breaking white over the reef. That white seemed sinister to me now.

I knew then that the boat was more than just a vehicle to take us from place to place, and she was more than a house – I almost felt as if she was alive. I couldn't bear to lose her.

Erick and Dad wasted no time catching some fish. Dad hoisted the bos'n's chair up on the main halyard for us to swing on.

'We'll try some spinnaker flying this afternoon,' Erick proposed.

Erick anchored *Calao* by her stern, so the bow pointed downwind. He hoisted the spinnaker, a huge blue sail that was used in very light winds. *Aventura* didn't have one. A canvas seat was slung between the two bottom corners. Muriel went first and the wind caught the spinnaker and lifted her into the air.

'Me next, me!' we children shouted.

At last it was my turn.

I swam out and sat myself in the sling, using my arms to push the sail as far apart as I could. Then I waited for the wind to catch the sail. A gust came, and the sail lifted up, full of wind, and I was lifted too, high above the water. Up I went, and then down, up and down, according to the whim of the wind.

Again and again the great sail lifted me out of the water and into the air so I felt as if I was flying above the sparkling sea.

'You had one of the best rides,' Dad said afterwards. 'Because you're lighter than the adults.'

We cooked the fish on the beach over a fire.

'What can we have with the fish?' Sidonie and I asked.

'Well, cabbage salad of course!' said Muriel. We all groaned. We were getting tired of cabbage and there were still plenty in the Puerto Rico sack.

'Well, if you're tired of cabbage, there is always lobster.'

'Oh no,' we cried, 'not lobster *again*.' That was all we had eaten for weeks.

'Okay,' said Erick. 'So let's open that can of pork and beans.'

The next evening we went to *Calao* for dinner. It felt like a special occasion. The can was huge, big enough for eight people, and the photograph on the front looked very appetising.

'Yum,' I said.

'*Miam*,' said Sidonie.

Muriel opened the can ceremoniously and tipped it into a pan.

'So where's this pork then?' she said. '*Où est le porc?*'

She poked around with a wooden spoon but there was no pork to be seen, only a mass of beans. There was a chorus of disappointment. Sidonie and I were the loudest.

'*C'est pas vrai!*' said Erick disappointedly.

We ate the beans anyway.

'*J'ai trouvé quelque chose!*' cried Sidonie. 'I have found something!' She pointed to a tiny piece of meat in her plate. We all cheered.

'So, back to lobster and coleslaw tomorrow then,' said Dad, rubbing his hands.

'That's the last time you and Erick do the shopping,' Mum and Muriel agreed.

* * *

For two weeks we cruised the outer islands of the Bahamas and saw no signs of human habitation other than a few ruined houses. Some of the islands weren't where they were supposed to be on the chart, and many of the reefs weren't on the chart at all. We saw a lot of wrecked cargo ships.

'It feels like the end of the world,' Dad said. 'I can't really believe we're so close to America.'

'I think I'll be glad to get out of this wild area for a while,' Mum admitted.

'America here we come!'

The Americas 1977–78

candy corn

America is Big

'SOON WE'LL BE in America, and then we'll eat so many hamburgers we'll get sick of them,' Ivan and I told each other several times a day, as we chewed our way through yet another cabbage salad.

In Fort Lauderdale, our first landfall in the United States, an American called Carl came to see us. He'd met my parents in Romania. He drove up in a car bigger than Ivan and I had ever seen, with a huge square bonnet and shiny chrome all over that made it look a bit like a space rocket.

'It's a Cadillac,' Ivan told me.

'Last time I saw you,' Carl said to me, 'you were only one week old! You've grown a bit since then!'

I smiled self-consciously.

'Romania, what a dump,' he went on. 'The only good thing about it was meeting you, Jimmy.'

'I remember that amazing car seat you sent us,' Mum said. 'It must have been the most high-tech baby seat in the world.'

Carl took us to the Fort Lauderdale Yacht Club which according to Mum was very 'posh and exclusive'. The inside of the Cadillac was just as incredible as the outside, with every surface covered in creamy leather. Ivan and I were astounded by the electric windows that went up and down at the mere push of a button.

The yacht club was okay and Mum said our table manners were perfect. But Ivan and I were more interested in trying a hamburger. Of course we had eaten them in the Caribbean but this was going to be the real thing.

Mum and Dad grumbled but in the end they took us to a fast food restaurant. The lights were bright, the walls and furniture as colourful and plastic as my Barbie doll in her best outfit. Ivan and I could hardly wait. The burger came wrapped in a piece of paper, warm in my hands. I unwrapped it excitedly. Inside there was a limp yellow bun, made of bread perhaps but like no bread I had ever seen, and sandwiched between it a thin slice of grey meat.

I took a bite. The bread stuck to the roof of my mouth and the meat tasted as grey as it looked. I put it down and looked at Ivan, pulling a face.

Dad grinned. 'Maybe lobster wasn't so bad after all?'

* * *

The supermarkets in America were as astonishing as the cars. Even Mum was impressed. We walked down one aisle, shelves of bread stretching off into the distance.

After a moment Mum complained. 'There *is* so much but it's all the same, look at this bread, rows of it, white and sliced. Revolting. I'll stick to baking my own, I think'.

'Forget the bread,' said Erick, when we got back to the boat. 'This is the best, *c'est super!*'

He was in *Calao*'s cockpit waving a large jar of peanut butter. Sidonie and Fabien were sitting next to him holding spoons which they dug into the jar, licking off the peanut butter with delight.

'You French are crazy,' said Dad.

'No more than you *Rosbif*,' returned Erick, getting his own spoon.

'What's a Rosbif?' I asked later.

'Roast beef – that's what the French call the English. Because they like to eat it,' Dad explained. 'Like I call Erick a Frog. Because the French eat frogs' legs. It's only for fun, because we are friends.'

I was puzzled though. I couldn't remember ever eating roast beef in England, and when I asked Sidonie if she had eaten any frogs, '*Beuch*,' she said and made a face.

* * *

'Choose your rides.' Dad gave me a booklet of Disneyworld tickets. It felt like Christmas all over again. We went on a haunted house ride where a ghost suddenly appeared sitting in the carriage with us, which made me jump. There

was a parade of cartoon characters, larger than life, and Mickey Mouse held out a white glove and shook my hand. Then we took a space ride to Mars where our seats rattled as we came back down to earth, and an underwater ride in an old fashioned submarine.

'Did you like that?' asked Dad.

'I liked the mermaids,' I said. 'And the giant squid was scary. But the fish and the lobsters were silly.'

'Not really the same as the real thing, is it?'

Everything in America felt big. At the Cape Canaveral Space Center we drove in the tour bus past the disused parts of rockets lying on their sides like gigantic fallen trees.

'They are so huge,' I said to Ivan. 'I don't know why, I thought they would be littler.'

'The moon landing was so exciting,' said Dad. 'I watched it on TV. I had just got out of Romania.'

It was only a few years since an American astronaut had landed on the moon.

'Did we see it too?'

'You were only two, and Ivan didn't, he was still in my tummy!' said Mum. 'We were living in one tiny room and we all had to sit on the bed to watch.'

Black, Brown and White

RIPPLES APPEARED ON the brown water as we motored up the river, and I stared hopefully at the muddy surface, desperately wanting to see the inquisitive whiskered face of a manatee staring back. The river water remained unbroken however, and I had to content myself with looking, yet again, at the picture in my *Book of Monsters*.

I knew there were manatees, or sea cows, lurking here among the mangroves, and the book said that sailors once mistook them for mermaids, as they raised their weed-draped heads to gaze curiously at passing ships.

We were making our way up the East coast of the USA, mostly inland from the sea, along the rivers and canals of the Intracoastal Waterway. On either side of us were thick mangrove forests where the trees reached their tangled roots into the water, and the water was always as brown as chocolate.

I looked at my book again. It was full of black and white pictures carefully drawn with pen and ink. There was a white-faced vampire, smiling as a drop of black blood trickled down his chin. I could hardly bear to turn the next page because I knew what came next. A werewolf snarling, the full moon hanging in the sky behind him. I looked at his hairy face and his clawed hands with my eyes half-open, wondering how a picture could be so frightening. No doubt I took after Mum, who when she was little had to be taken out of the cinema after the Wicked Witch in the *Wizard of Oz* reduced her to tears.

Dad was waving to *Calao*, following on behind us, that we should stop here for the night. The land looked wild and inhospitable to me, but after anchoring we went ashore. There was a strip of muddy beach strewn with empty shells from the weird horseshoe crabs that lived in these waters. Strange enough, I thought, to go into my monster book.

'Let's go and explore,' suggested the two fathers. They were both, as always, ready for an adventure.

We struggled a little way under the damp green trees, hung with trailing creepers. I didn't like it much.

'Look!' cried Dad. He had found a group of old graves.

'Early settlers,' Mum said, bending to read the dates.

'*Aïe!*' screamed Sidonie at this point and Muriel started slapping her. A cloud of mosquitoes had descended.

'I think they probably haven't tasted human being for years,' Dad laughed as we ran back to the dinghies although it wasn't that funny. I was covered in bites and they itched like mad, and when we rowed back to the boat a cloud of mosquitoes followed us so in the end we had to up anchor and leave.

American diesel was dirt cheap, and as we had to motor so much we needed lots of fuel. We stopped off at a fuel jetty in the middle of nowhere where a single pump was manned by a man in oil-stained overalls. His wife came down to take a look 'at the sailboat from England,' and then she invited Ivan and I to go with her to pick apples from her tree.

'Take these back for your Mom,' she said, giving me a bunch of roses.

Sometimes people found it hard to understand our English accents and we found it hard to understand theirs. I did like the way they spoke. The lady who gave us the apples had a drawling way of speaking, which seemed to belong to a story or a film.

'People are so friendly,' said Mum, thanking the lady and smelling the roses.

Nothing was ancient now in the little towns where we stopped – buildings bore plaques proudly proclaiming they were one or two hundred years old.

'I like them though.' Mum pointed to the old clapboard houses with their wide verandas. There was always a rocking chair outside, ready for someone to come and sit and rest a while.

'Life seems pretty relaxed down here,' Mum remarked to Dad. 'Everyone keeps saying, watch out when you go north, those northerners are so hectic!'

We walked on down the street. An elderly black woman was walking towards us on the pavement. Or rather, the *sidewalk,* as Americans say. As she came nearer to Mum, she stepped off into the road to make way.

Mum was so shocked she stopped in her tracks.

'I can't believe that,' she said. She turned and looked at the old lady who had walked on without a backward glance.

'There is a lot of history going on here,' said Dad.

I wondered what he meant. But maybe I already knew. I'd run out of children's books again and I was reading *Black Like Me,* a true story from the 1960s about a white man who took drugs to make his skin black and then travelled through the southern states of the US where the laws meant black and white people were segregated. Where you sat on the bus, where you went to school, where you went to the bathroom: that depended on the colour of your skin.

People fought hard against those laws. By the time we visited the southern states, the segregation laws had been abolished. But the old lady still stepped off the sidewalk when she saw the white woman coming along.

Skateboards and Blueberry Pancakes

WHITE FOG SURROUNDED US, so thick I could hardly see the bow of *Aventura.* All around boomed the foghorns of invisible ships and ferries. They sounded very close but it was hard to tell. We were blind, with no radar to help penetrate our surroundings. It was like sailing through a glass of milk. All we had was a handheld horn which Dad had to sound every two minutes. One long, two short. *We are a sailing yacht.* Or a sailboat, as the Americans say. Around us all the blasts were long, that meant they were under power.

A huge shadow loomed right next to us, my blood ran cold because I was sure we would be hit, the shadow receded again. Then the fog began to lift as quickly as it had dropped down, and we found ourselves right inside New York harbour, passing the Statue of Liberty. We motored past the skyscrapers of Manhattan, under all the bridges, up the river to Long Island Sound where we stayed at the City Island Yacht Club.

We travelled into New York every day. The city was hot and crowded. Mum and Dad took us on a frantic sightseeing tour. Broadway, Fifth Avenue, Times Square, Greenwich Village, the Empire State Building.

We sat in Central Park eating the packed lunch Mum had made.

'It's cheaper. Plus none of you like the hamburgers.'

I thought my feet would drop off for all the walking.

'We'll get a bus back,' said Dad.

There was a metal bar on the bus for people to hold onto and if you were shorter than the bar you went for half price.

'Bend your knees when you get on,' Dad instructed me. But the bus driver noticed.

'Stand straight,' he said in his hard New York voice.

It was embarrassing – though I should have been used to it by then. Mum and Dad tried it wherever we went, even when we queued with *Calao* to get into the Museum of Modern Art.

'We'll try and get Doina in for free, she looks young enough.'

My parents spoke to each other in Romanian, the language they used when they didn't want other people to understand what they were saying. I had heard enough Romanian to grasp the meanings of simple conversations. Unfortunately I was not the only one.

'*Buna ziua*, good afternoon.' The man at the ticket booth smiled. His Romanian was perfect. 'Okay, for once, you can go through.'

Later Dad said, 'There you are – America, land of immigrants.'

'Tomorrow is the 4th July,' Mum told us. 'The Independence Day Celebrations. There's going to be lots of free things going on. You'll love it.'

I hoped there wouldn't be any more walking. But I did love it: circus shows, clowns, Punch and Judy, parades, folk dancing, and finally, the most fantastic firework display we'd ever seen, lighting up the city sky.

Two days later I had my tenth birthday. Granny had sent me £5. I was given a blue plastic skateboard from Mum and Dad and a frisbee from Ivan. Later Sidonie and Fabien came over for cake and crisps and afterwards we tried the skateboard on the quiet roads outside the yacht club.

I decided that I wanted to spend Granny's money on books. I'd heard that there was a huge bookshop in the city that had a corner room just for children's books.

'Look, Mummy!' I had found a stall with books that were only 19¢ each.

'What is that in English money?'

'About 10p.'

'Wow. That's cheap.' Some of the books I chose because I liked the covers. Some I went for the thickness. The thicker the better.

* * *

Calao had to stay in New York to fix their engine and we arranged to meet them further north, in the state of Maine, which was right at the other end of the United States from Florida where we had begun.

Aventura swung on a mooring off Cousins Island where my parents' friends

Louise and Wally lived. Mum and Dad had met Wally in the Canaries when he was sailing on a friend's boat across the Atlantic and he'd invited us up to Maine to visit him and his wife Louise. They were older than my parents and had grown up children.

Louise took us into the woods by their house to pick blueberries, which grew in low bushes across the ground, and then she cooked us delicious blueberry pancakes. At low tide we went out onto the mud flats and dug for clams, to make into tasty chowder.

There was white, fluffy angel cake made with so many egg whites I lost count, waffles drowned in maple syrup that came from nearby trees, and marshmallows toasted at the fire. Every day there was something new to try. We told Louise the story of those grey hamburgers in Florida and she laughed.

'But I love the American food you make,' I said.

From Louise we learnt campfire songs, and an old sea shanty:

My father was the keeper of the Eddystone Light
And he slept with a mermaid one fine night
Of this union there came three,
A porpoise and a porgy and the other was me.

Yo ho ho the wind blows free
Oh for the life on the rolling sea.

One night I was a-trimmin' of the glim
And singin' a verse from the ev'ning hymn
A voice from starboard shouted 'Ahoy!'
And there was my mother, a-sittin' on a buoy.

Yo ho ho the wind blows free
Oh for the life on the rolling sea.

'What has become of my children three?'
My mother then she asked of me.
'One was exhibited as a talking fish,
The other was served on a chafing dish.'

Yo ho ho the wind blows free
Oh for the life on the rolling sea.

The phosphorus flashed in her seaweed hair.
I looked again, and my mother wasn't there.
A voice came echoing out of the night:
'To hell with the keeper of the Eddystone Light.'

Yo ho ho the wind blows free
Oh for the life on the rolling sea.

I liked this song because it was about the sea, and Ivan and I sang the chorus with gusto, as that was exactly how we felt. Also, we knew 'hell' wasn't really a word we should be using, so singing the last line always gave us a little thrill.

Calao soon turned up and we made friends with some local children and went down to the wharf to try the water. There was a half sunken wooden dinghy that we tried to stand on as it floated half submerged. The seawater in Maine was so cold we could only stay in for a minute or two, shrieking, our hearts pounding so fast I thought mine would burst.

Our new friends dared me to walk past the island cemetery on my own, at the end of the day when the long summer twilight was beginning. Trying not to think of the pictures in my monster book, I walked as fast as I could. They had said I wasn't allowed to run. I looked straight ahead, though at the corner of my eye was the flickering white of the cemetery's picket fence. I made it to the trees at the other side, feeling proud of my achievement but the others laughed and ran off. They didn't care. They were much the same age as me, but despite all my travels and the grown-up books I had read, they seemed so much older and more knowledgeable.

I followed them to the tree house where pages torn from a magazine were scattered on the floor, photographs of naked women. They laughed again and kicked the pictures into the corner.

'Oh, that rubbish. Our older brothers climb up here and like looking at them.'

I wasn't really shocked. Curious, more than anything – why would anyone want to look at naked women? I felt detached, looking on, and wondering about the world.

A Surprise Visitor

WEATHER DECIDED EVERYTHING in our life. When and where we could go depended entirely on the seasons and the wind, how strong it was, and from what direction it blew. The hurricane season was coming to an end so it was safe to go back to the tropics.

We said our farewells to Louise and Wally and headed south. We moored *Aventura* right inside the Mystic Seaport museum, next to square-rigged ships and replica workshops and houses from the nineteenth century. Mum created questionnaires for us and we spent hours wandering about.

We explored the ropewalk, the riggers shop, the pharmacy and the coopers. People dressed in old fashioned clothes and talking in an old fashioned way took the time to explain their work. Our favourite place, however, was the children's museum, and we spent so long trying on clothes from the sea chest and playing with the toys children who went to sea a hundred years ago would have had, even the woman who worked there began to be impatient with our endless questions.

But we loved it. None of the other visitors had come by boat and lived among the exhibits; they went home at the end of the day. I read *Two Years Before The Mast,* which was all about the life of a sailor on a square-rigger, and even though I knew that life was bitterly hard, I still wished I could go back in time and sail around Cape Horn on a fast clipper ship, in the days when there were no cars or planes and sailing ships were the only links between the continents.

In Newport, Rhode Island, Mum checked the post yet again. She had written to Granny asking if she would like to visit us.

'Nothing. Maybe something cropped up and she couldn't come. I'm surprised though. I thought she was quite keen.'

We took our time motoring down Long Island Sound and once again moored at the City Island Yacht Club outside New York.

The white club launch came out to greet us.

'Your wife's mother is here,' the boy said to Dad.

'Are you confusing me with someone else?'

Then it clicked.

'Gwenda, I think your mother has beaten us to it!'

It turned out Granny had been waiting for us for two days.

'Didn't you get my telegram to Newport?' she asked after all the welcoming was done.

'No!'

'I had to sleep on the couch here at the club,' she chuckled. 'There were no hotels nearby and the club people were so friendly, they let me stay the night. Only the night watchman didn't know I was there and I gave him a fright!'

Arriving in a foreign city with nowhere to stay was a big adventure for her. She had enjoyed it, however, and loved telling us the story several times more.

'I took a bus into the city and walked down Fifth Avenue,' she said. 'And I found out that skyscrapers don't worry me as much as I thought they would.'

* * *

Dad had a meeting at the BBC building downtown, and Mum went with him. The wind started to blow and Granny said there was a 'nip in the air.' Autumn was on its way.

'The Americans call it fall, Granny,' I said helpfully.

She glanced out of the porthole at the other boats.

'They do seem to be tossing about.'

'They're racing boats,' Ivan explained. 'And light. That's why they're moving.'

'I'm glad your boat is so solid. But I think I might lie down for a while. I feel a bit queasy.'

She swallowed an anti-seasickness pill and lay on the main bunk. Ivan and I felt quite alright, although the wind was blowing strongly now, and the rain lashed against the portholes. We holed up in the foc'sle on our bunks, reading and drawing until Mum and Dad came back on the club launch.

'Good news, folks,' Dad told us. 'From next year they want to make my programme weekly instead of fortnightly.'

'That is good news.' Granny was feeling better after her nap.

'Yes! More work, but more money.'

Mum was pleased too. One of the English yachting magazines were going to publish an article she had written about our trip to Israel and Egypt.

That night we went out with the Bouteleux family. We weren't going to see them for a while as they were heading back to the Bahamas to spend Christmas with Muriel's parents.

'I hope we'll be in Peru by then,' said Dad.

'Remember how you said, when you left, that you didn't have a plan?' Granny smiled. Sometimes she could look quite mischievous. 'Well that sounds like a plan to me.'

Mum laughed. 'You are right. I think, in our zig-zag way, we are committing ourselves to a round the world voyage.'

'A toast,' proposed Erick. 'We will see you in the Pacific in 1978.'

'You know me,' replied Dad. 'I can't refuse an offer like that. Cheers!'

'*Santé*!'

Not to be left out, we four children clinked our glasses together and sipped our fizzy drinks.

I Get Myself into Trouble

IN ANNAPOLIS WE hired a car and drove to Washington to see the Capitol and the White House and the Smithsonian Museums. We even spotted the President in his black limousine surrounded by police cars and motorbikes. Then we took Granny to the airport and she flew back to England.

Annapolis was a good marina so Mum and Dad were very busy with boat jobs. There wasn't much for Ivan and I to do though, after school was finished.

Near the waterfront there was a row of public payphones and one day we noticed a kid my age pushing down at the change buttons, and sometimes retrieving a forgotten coin – a nickel, dime or even a quarter that callers had not bothered to collect.

'Hey, let's try that,' I suggested.

Almost all the phones were empty but we found two that gave us a couple of coins. We headed for the nearest shop to buy sweets which we put into bags Louise had given us as a leaving present. They were made of colourful spinnaker canvas and shaped just like mini sail bags.

The next day there were no coins. Then an idea came to me. Or rather, an impulse, because it didn't go consciously through my head like an idea would.

'Come on,' I said to Ivan. I knew he would follow. I went into one of the shops on the main street, slipped a few sweets into my canvas bag, and went out again without paying. I did this in several shops, going up the street, filling my bag. And Ivan trotted meekly along beside me. No one noticed.

Back at the boat I lied, 'We bought the sweets with money we got from the phones again.'

It was easy. So the following day we went back again. First shop, okay. Then we walked into a second shop that sold little ornaments and toys as well as sweets. I had a fleeting thought that a man was looking at me.

'Look at that.' I pointed randomly at a little toy dog on a shelf, and turned away from the man, to show that I was only interested in the dog.

But the man said, 'What's in the bag?' and he took it and looked inside.

'Where did you get that candy?' He was tall and fat and wore a baseball cap. 'Where are you at?' he asked angrily. 'Where are your folks at?'

At first I didn't understand what he meant. He asked again, 'Where are you at?'

Then I realised it was his American way of saying 'Where do you live?' I said, a yacht in the harbour. I had to repeat it several times before he understood me.

'Let's go find your folks,' and he grabbed my arm firmly and marched me off down the busy street. He kept meeting people he knew and each time he showed the contents of the bag and told the story. He asked me if I had got sweets from other shops. No, I lied.

Near the harbour by chance we met Mum and Dad. When Dad heard what had happened he burst into anger and smacked me, there, right in front of everyone. It didn't really hurt, but I cried.

'You'll feel my belt when we get back,' Dad yelled.

My brain felt fogged over, but in the dimness one thought came through: *he doesn't have a belt.*

'You folks'll sort those kids out, now?' The shopkeeper was saying to Dad. He took one more glance at us. Me crying. Ivan shivering and crying and holding onto Mum's hand. The man shook his head and went back up the road. The awful road he had just marched us down.

Out of the fog, I knew: the shopkeeper was satisfied. He could see we were going to get the punishment we deserved.

Back at the boat, lots and lots of shouting. Mostly at me; Ivan wasn't blamed so much, because he'd just followed.

'Why did you do it?' Dad shouted furiously. 'Why, why, why?'

'We'd have given you money if you wanted sweets,' said Mum, who was angry too, but quiet with it. Her face was twisted in a look I knew, of disapproval and disappointment.

I couldn't answer them. Because, really, I didn't know why I'd done it. I didn't even like the sweets that much. But grownups wanted everything explained. There *had* to be reasons. Not having answers made it worse, and the shouting and the questioning went on.

'I'll smack you again,' threatened Dad. 'And it'll really hurt this time.'

'I hate you!' I screamed into his face. He looked shocked. 'I hate you!'

I ran into my cabin.

He didn't hit me again. For me, though, the shouting and being hit wasn't really the punishment. It came in the night, as I lay in my bunk. I kept going through it all over and over again. The man's question 'Where are you at?' like a jabbing finger, repeatedly endlessly in my head. The memory of being paraded through the streets flooded through me like a wave of shame. I wanted my thoughts to stop but they wouldn't. I relived every moment and it was horrible.

For many nights after that I lay there with those thoughts and could not sleep. Why, why, I asked myself, like my parents, but I could never answer.

With time passing, I started to feel better. One day I went to Dad. Since the argument, we had only spoken a few words to each other.

I swallowed hard.

'I'm sorry,' I said.

He smiled. 'Thank you for saying that.' He kissed me. 'I love you, you know, even when you do silly things.'

Later Mum said to me, 'Well done. Saying sorry was the best thing you could do.'

The storm in the family passed and we went back to normal relations again. We were strong. The sailing life had made us like that.

But I never did anything like that sweet-stealing again. Those sleepless nights burned it out of me.

* * *

We cruised through the Canals and Chesapeake Bay as the trees turned to their fall colours. In Beaufort, North Carolina, lots of yachts had gathered, ready to head south as soon as there was a decent break in the weather. I made friends with a Canadian girl my age and she told me all about Halloween. We'd never heard of trick or treating in England, but here all the children did it.

As evening fell, outside the houses along the waterfront, huge orange pumpkins with carved faces were lit with candles. With a group of other children from the yachts, Ivan and I went from house to house, knocked, said 'Trick or Treat!' and strangers smiled and gave us candy. Strange sweets we had never had before, such as yellow and orange candy corns that looked like kernels of maize. We filled up our canvas bags with so many sweets we couldn't eat them all.

We left port the next day and it was cold and grey.

'There's no blinking weather window to head south,' said Dad, 'but I'm fed up with waiting. I bet all those other yachts will still be here for days. Let's just go and hope for the best.'

We had to cross the Gulf Stream and as the strong northerly wind blew against the current, the waves lurched at us from every possible angle. I had lost my sea legs. I looked at my Halloween sweets and my stomach heaved. I tipped them over the side and watched the bright yellow and orange candy corn bobbing away behind us.

Dad turned out to be right. Later we found out that none of the other yachts in Beaufort managed to get away, and many of them had to spend the winter in the States. We, at least, were on our way to the Pacific Ocean.

King Neptune's Initiation Ceremony

SINCE THE PANAMA Canal had been dug out of the narrow isthmus that connected South to North America, it had made sailors' lives so much easier. No need to sail down to the southernmost tip of South America and fight your way around the dreaded Cape Horn, battling storms and giant seas that had spent so long rolling round the Southern Ocean they were as big as houses. Though if you sailed around the Horn at least you got to wear a golden ring in your ear.

Aventura had to have a pilot on board for the Canal transit, as well as extra people to handle the lines when we went through all the locks. The locks were huge and the water boiled up and down with the force of a giant's cauldron. The linehandlers had to really concentrate. If they let out too much rope, *Aventura* might swing out and bob like a helpless top, bashing against the concrete of the lock walls. Letting the ropes out too slowly might rip the cleats off the deck as the water dropped away. But we made the transit safely.

As we left the final lock, I sat at the bow, one hand holding the forestay and the other stretching forward into the air. I wanted to be the first to arrive in the Pacific. Ivan saw what I was doing and ran up the deck to struggle with me but I was bigger and stronger and I won, just, though he pulled fiercely at my elbow. I waved my hand defiantly as we came out of the canal into the new ocean.

* * *

Sailors have always been very superstitious. They said that it was bad luck to kill an albatross and when the crew killed one in the *Rime of the Ancient Mariner* they suffered a terrible curse.

Dad would never leave port on a Friday. It was bad luck to start a voyage on that day. And when *Aventura's* mast was first raised and stepped – which means fastened down – to the deck, a coin was placed beneath the foot of the mast for luck, and indeed we kept that mast for all the years we sailed in her, when other yachts lost theirs.

Don't whistle on a boat, they say, because it will bring too much wind. Sometimes I did whistle, in the dead calms of the doldrums, that zone of little or no wind that lies around the Equator, as we made our way down the South American coast to Peru.

Another nautical tradition was that when sailors cross the line of the Equator for the very first time, they must be initiated by Neptune, King of the Sea. In the olden days sailors might be tarred and feathered. Or even thrown overboard.

Dad's pencilled crosses on the chart showed we were drawing nearer to the Equator, but as the days passed I forgot about it. The current and winds were against us and we had a slow passage.

'Look at this sail.' Mum was sitting on deck repairing the main. 'I seem to be stitching it on every voyage now.'

'It has got very baggy. We need a new one.'

The slow sailing didn't bother me. There were lots of new books to read and things to make and draw. Dad decided to teach me and Ivan some Spanish because it would be useful when we got to South America. Only it didn't go very well because he was too impatient and shouted at us.

'I don't know how you do it,' he said to Mum in exasperation. 'I give up.'

We were sailing through the cold waters of the Humboldt current, famously rich with marine life, and we saw whales, sharks and turtles every day. At times the sea looked like it was boiling with thick shoals of fish, and hundreds of dolphins, pelicans and other diving birds came together in a frenzy of eating. Once a beautiful frigate bird flew above us and nearly landed on the mast. Dad was sure its wing span was a good six feet.

On one very hot day, Ivan and I were on deck reading while the boat slopped around in the light winds. Suddenly a strange figure emerged from the aft cabin. It was Dad, dressed as King Neptune. He had put on a *jellaba* robe he'd bought in Egypt, and for a white beard he'd draped his head in a ball of wool Louise had given me, supposedly to make *macrame* belts, though it had just ended up in a tangle. He had a card crown on his head and a wooden spoon sceptre in one hand.

'Now I will baptise you for crossing the Equator!' he roared. His beard was very black against the white wool. I giggled and ran up onto the foredeck, where he caught me and tapped my head lightly with the sceptre, before spraying me with shaving foam. Ivan screamed and ran down below crying. He thought Dad was too scary and he didn't want to be sprayed. In the end Mum did manage to persuade him out into the cockpit and he had a little bit of foam on his head.

'You're Sons and Daughters of the Sea now!' Dad proclaimed, laughing so much he could hardly speak.

A Trek Across South America

THE WHOLE CONTINENT of South America stretched before us, tempting my parents.

With *Aventura* safely moored in the port of Callao, near the capital Lima, after Christmas the plan was to go travelling inland.

Dad hired a couple of local men to look after *Aventura* while we were away.

'We'll take the train across the Andes,' said Mum. 'It's supposed to be one of the most scenic routes in the world.'

The day before we were due to leave the train was cancelled because of landslides.

'We'll have to take the bus.' Dad worked out the route and we headed off to Nasca.

'Is that it?' Mum gestured towards a rusty old heap that was already crammed full of people and bundles of luggage. There was even a parrot in a cage and a few chickens.

When we got on and sat down the other adults tried to make Ivan and I move off our seats because they didn't believe we had seat tickets. No one ever bought children seat tickets. Children always sat on the floor.

As we drove up into the Andes, outside the grimy windows I could see there was no barrier between the road and the sheer drop, which plunged down thousands of feet. I saw flocks of llamas and alpacas on high plateaus and black condors gliding overhead. There were piles of crosses by the roadsides where people had died.

At each stop people rushed on board to try to sell the passengers grilled maize cobs and a cloudy liquid also made from maize, something like a frothy weak beer.

The crush was so bad the beer woman was pushed from behind and poured a jug of beer all over my lap.

All through the night Dad perched on a seat near the driver and talked to him in broken Spanish to help keep him awake. After 44 hours we were glad to get off that bus. It should have taken 31 hours but the bus broke down twice. Dad helped them to fix the engine by making a gasket out of a bit of aluminium foil from one of his Kodak film wrappers.

A week later we heard on the news that a bus had plunged over the edge.

'I'm not surprised. There was no one like me on that bus, ready to talk to the driver to keep him from falling asleep.'

'That was a once in a lifetime experience,' Mum said. 'Which means I don't especially want to repeat it!'

In Cuzco we found a hotel and we all went to bed. Except for Dad.

'You are revelling in this, aren't you!' Mum told him.

Cuzco lay thousands of feet up in the Andes, a city of the Incas long before the Spanish Conquistadors arrived and took over. Huge Inca walls crossed the city made of massive square rocks that fitted together perfectly without cement.

It was cold. We bought woollen hats with ear flaps, and warm ponchos. We tried the local speciality, roast guinea pig, which looked like a cooked rat but tasted like chicken.

The high altitude, more than ten thousand feet above the sea, didn't bother us at all.

Colours splashed against the giant walls: the bright magenta pink of the women's brimmed hats, their full short skirts, and the big bundles strapped to their backs. Colours in the churches: gold and silver orna-mentation everywhere, and pink-faced baby dolls in glass cases, dressed in frilly frocks and diamante shoes.

'It's actually supposed to be Jesus,' whispered Mum, as we watched an old woman bend and kiss the glass. Toy tanks, sports cars and tiny dolls had been left like offerings at the feet of the doll.

We saw a religious fiesta where a hundred men staggered out of a church under the weight of the wooden frame of a statue of Saint Sebastian, his naked body pierced by many arrows. Men danced wearing woollen head coverings with only holes for their eyes and nose that made them look like bank robbers but were in fact protection from the bitter mountain cold of winter.

From Cuzco a train took us up the Urubamba Valley to the ruined city of Machu Picchu. We spent the night in a tin shack.

'We'll beat the tourist groups that way,' explained Dad, as Ivan and I complained about getting up in the cold at 6am. 'And the afternoon rain. Haven't you noticed how it's only sunny in the morning?'

'Are you going to look for Paddington Bear?' Mum asked Ivan with a smile. He was wearing his favourite top, which had a picture of Paddington on the front. We kept teasing him about this, because the top was starting to look rather tatty, but he never wanted to take it off. Of course, we all knew that Paddington came from Darkest Peru.

We did beat the crowds to Machu Picchu. Ivan climbed the hills, but bears were nowhere to be found. It didn't matter much as he just liked climbing. I was more interested in the Urubamba River that ran alongside the train track, through what they called the Sacred Valley. I'd never seen such wild water before, a torrent of brown liquid whipped up and churning as it sped away down to the sea.

* * *

Trains, more buses, and even hitch-hiking to make our way across the continent. Dusty towns at the borders of countries, midnight waits on station platforms,

Cochabamba, Lake Titicaca. This last, one of the highest lakes in the world, had a name that Ivan and I could not say without giggling. *Caca* was our silly baby word for poo.

On our way to the lake on the train, rattling through the night, disaster struck. A woman selling jumpers – 'chompas' she called them – spread her wares over our seats, and when she had gone we realised that our bag of toys was gone too. We carried them in a shiny black holdall made of leather. Dad rushed down the train but the woman had vanished.

'It was a nice bag,' said Mum. 'She must have thought it had valuables in it.'

I tried to imagine the woman's face when she found there were only toys inside. Did she throw it straight out the window? That made me cry, tears down my face, staring out the window at the rushing night. Poor Brownie and Ducky, lying abandoned somewhere by the train tracks. And also, the diaries we'd kept of the South American trip so far, my drawings of the mummies, the stone walls, the Jesus dollies. I didn't have the heart to start another.

In Las Paz, capital of Bolivia, there was another fiesta going on. There were stalls selling miniature fridges, cars and food, and we saw people clutching wads of toy money that looked just like the bank notes you'd find in a Monopoly game.

'Why are people buying all these things?'

'Because they want to get them in real life,' Mum explained. 'The priests are going to bless the small things, and people hope then that in the future they really will get a car or money.'

As replacement for our lost toys we were bought a little bear each and some salt dough figures, brightly painted and coated in shiny varnish.

Crowds pressed around us and policemen in green uniforms, their faces as flat as stone, pushed me and Ivan with batons. The government recruited the police, we were told, from remote parts of the mountains, and they had no sympathy for anyone let alone children.

* * *

Another carnival! We had crossed a whole continent, and were in Rio, looking again at the Atlantic Ocean as we lounged in the sand on the famous Copacabana beach. The Carnival tickets were really expensive but Dad managed to persuade the press office to give him one press ticket to the first night of the carnival procession.

'Being a BBC man is useful,' he said. He met a BBC TV crew inside the office and with their help he got us in too.

The parade started late in the evening. Ivan and I sat down on the pavement near the journalists' section and waited; it was already past midnight and we were dead tired. My legs itched unbearably; I had slept under the open window at the hotel and woke to find my legs covered in mosquito bites. I counted them; more than thirty.

At last the dancers appeared. There were about a thousand people in each samba group. They wore glittering costumes of silver and gold, covered in sequins and lace. Some of the costumes were so large the people wearing them could hardly move, but some dancers wore nothing more than tiny gold or silver bikinis.

Men and women passed us, dancing in a way I had never seen before; they were lost in the dance and their bodies moved in perfect time to the rhythm from the armies of drummers coming up behind.

Ivan and I watched, fell asleep, woke again, watched and slept as the warm night passed in a dreamy whirl of colour and music. Afterwards, in the light of dawn we walked to the hotel through the crowded back streets, keeping close to each other. Dad kept his seaman's knife at the ready.

Maybe the joyful carnival made up for the hard life many people lived outside; the day before we had seen on the busy freeway a young boy knocked down, and not one car stopped, but rather steered round the dark unmoving shape on the asphalt.

There was a fancy yacht club in Rio Harbour and a round the world yacht race had just arrived. Dad's powers of persuasion couldn't get us into the club, but we could still walk along the quay and look at the yachts. Most of them were at least twice as big as *Aventura*.

'That is some machine!' Dad was looking at *Pen Duick VI*, sailed by the famous French sailor Taberly. 'When we were still in the Med, he was winning the single-handed race across the Atlantic.'

'*Aventura* is far more comfortable though,' said Mum. 'Look at that steering wheel. The helmsman is going to get a faceful of water, every wave that hits the boat. Give me my wheelhouse any day.'

The race was only stopping in one or two places as it went around the world.

'I'd much rather take my time,' Mum said. 'Slow travelling is the best.'

* * *

We went to see the spectacular Iguaçu waterfalls which crashed through the jungle; I could see three countries at once from the viewing platform: Brazil, Argentina and Paraguay.

That night was spent in the worst place of all our South American trip, a dirty hostel in Asunción, Paraguay. We arrived there late and it was the only place Dad could find. Mum woke up and saw a huge rat crawling across the rafters.

'That's it,' she said to Dad. 'I have had *enough*.'

No more travel overland. No more roughing it. Next day we bought plane tickets back to Lima.

* * *

I was glad to get back to our beloved *Aventura*, as far removed from an ocean-going racing yacht as could be. She was laden down and slow, but at least she was comfortable.

We had plenty of stories to tell the cruising sailors who had stayed behind, but they had a bigger story and we were thankful then that we had been away on our land journey. While we were gone the authorities discovered illegal drugs on one of the yachts, and as a result rounded up all of the other yachties in the anchorage, put them in jail for a day and searched their boats. When the innocent sailors were released, they returned to find their boats in a mess and all their valuables gone. *Aventura* was the only one to have been spared. There were children on the boat that had the drugs; I don't know what happened to them.

It was time to go. To leave behind the dangerous land, and head west into the welcoming ocean, where there was not a speck of earth for thousands of miles.

Pacific 1978

Easter Island
bird Statue

Our Second Ocean Crossing

'DID YOU KNOW that the Pacific is the largest ocean in the world?'

I'd just read that in our *Children's Encyclopedia*. Ivan shook his head.

'Well, it is. It takes up about 30% of the *total* surface of Planet Earth.'

We were looking at the chart. There was an awful lot of white, which was the sea, and one little brown dot in the middle of it.

'That's Easter Island,' Dad put his finger on the dot. 'Where we're going next.'

'I find it incredible,' said Mum, 'that people managed to find that tiny bit of land a thousand years ago and settle there.'

Dad nodded. 'They must have been amazing sailors.'

Mum had given me a book to read, *The Voyage of the Kon Tiki*, about a man who thought the mysterious Easter islanders must have sailed west, like we were doing, from South America, and so he built a huge raft and sailed to Easter Island.

'It's an interesting theory,' she said. 'But I wonder. I can't help feeling they came the other way, from what is now Asia. I'm reading about how the Pacific islanders had canoes that could travel long distances over the sea. They were very good at navigating. They made themselves charts of the stars using white shells

and they could read the shapes of the waves and the signs of sea birds to find out where the nearest land was. No one has found that the South Americans were great at sailing. But I hope we'll see for ourselves.'

For the long voyage from Peru to Easter Island a young American called Alan joined our crew. Mum and Dad had made friends with him in Callao. He had done lots of sailing and because the anchorage was supposed to be so bad at Easter Island that the boat couldn't be left unattended, Mum and Dad thought having an experienced crew on board would be useful.

Aventura was really laden down. Alan had brought his surfboard with him. Plus there was all the provisions, and our new South American souvenirs: ponchos and gourds, jumpers and wooden flutes.

'I'll have to close off one of the cockpit drains.' Dad had noticed that the water was coming up into the cockpit, the boat was so low in the water.

This time the trade winds were with us from the start of the voyage. The sailing was so easy, Ivan and I got to take day watches for the first time, while the adults slept. The self-steering was on and all we had to do was take an occasional look around the horizon. It was an empty part of the ocean; we never saw another vessel of any kind.

I sat on the aft deck, which was raised above the rest of the boat, rather like a poop deck on an old fashioned ship, and if I looked back I could see the bright flash of the fishing lure following us, deep within a wave rising behind the boat.

Alan had made the lure out of scraps of colourful material. He was keen to catch some ocean fish and he'd said our bought lures were no good.

I looked forward to the twin foresails and it felt as if I was being carried by a great white bird, its spread wings full of the wind's breath which lifted the boat up as if to pull her into the sky. *Aventura* was a thing of grace and beauty then, not a heavy overladen lump.

Suddenly a new noise burst into my thoughts.

'The line!' cried Ivan, jumping up and letting his book fall to the floor. The reel was spinning fast and the line was running out at a terrific speed. The noise woke both Alan and Dad.

'Something big!' yelled Alan excitedly. All of a sudden the line went slack.

Dad put on some gloves and slowly pulled in the line but there was just a disappointing limp bit at the end, no lure at all.

'That was definitely big,' they agreed. Out went a new lure. They sat in the cockpit and chatted for a while then headed back to their bunks. In a minute the line started rushing out again with a great force and they were back on deck. Even Mum put her head out from the aft cabin, yawning and rubbing her eyes.

Alan took the gloves and started hauling in. Something was splashing and thrashing in the sea. He hauled the line to the side of the boat.

'Keep it taut...'

A huge fish hung there for a moment before Alan gave a great heave and swung it quickly into the cockpit. It thrashed wildly on the floor, its red blood speckling the white fibreglass. It was big – about the same size as me. I watched it gasping, its gills opening and closing. It was drowning in the air.

'A *mahi-mahi*,' said Alan.

The fish was beautiful. Its scales shone green and gold, and then, at the moment it died, flared into many different colours, from yellow to red, to silver and blue.

'Look,' said Ivan, pointing to where another fish swam just beneath the surface, twisting this way and that.

'Maybe that was its partner,' said Dad. 'Wondering where its mate's gone.'

'We can't be very sentimental,' Mum added. 'We haven't got a fridge, so this is the only way we can get fresh meat.'

I did feel a bit sorry for the fish which had lost its mate. It followed us for hours. What did it think of us, seeing the underside of our hull speeding through the water? But then again, the thick white steaks lightly fried in the pan were very good. That one *mahi-mahi* fed three adults and two children for days.

* * *

Mum insisted that Ivan and I start school again. It was difficult after our weeks off travelling. I sat and looked at the text book but my head felt heavy and I could hardly pick up the pencil. I didn't seem to have one clear thought in my head. The pencil lead broke and I threw it down in disgust.

'Oh school,' I snapped. 'Why do we have to *bother*?!'

Mum frowned. 'You two are such hard work. You know what you need. You

need to go to school again. Have a bit of competition with other children your own age.'

My eyes lit up and I forgot my bad mood. I would *love* to go to school.

'Where could we do that, Mummy?'

'I've been thinking about it. We might make our way down to New Zealand. Later on, after we've sailed through the Pacific. We need to find somewhere safe to spend the hurricane season anyway. But nothing's really decided yet. We'll see. Now you need to get on with your work.'

That was easier said than done. I couldn't help thinking about what she'd said.

'Kids, come and see this,' called Dad.

Ivan and I scrambled to take a look before Mum could stop us. Any excuse to get out of school for a minute.

Dad was standing at the aft rail, adjusting the self-steering. He pointed down to where the shaft of the self-steering cut into the sea. A tiny striped pilot fish was swimming merrily along in our wake.

'I guess he thinks we're a whale or something, and he's expecting to get some tasty leftovers.'

I watched the little fish for a while and then went back to my reading. Later on I looked; it was still there. Such a tiny thing seemed to have no trouble keeping up with us. The next day a killer whale surfaced nearby. Water shot out of its blowhole with a great whoosh. Then it dove and came up again right by the stern, rubbing its smooth back on the self-steering rudder. There was an ominous crack; the whale vanished.

'Great,' Dad looked over the side. 'A steel bolt. Broken.'

Soon after we discovered the pilot fish had gone too.

'Defected!' chuckled Alan. 'He must have gone off with that whale.'

* * *

Sea creatures like the whale and the pilot fish were not the only animals to have discovered *Aventura*. One evening Ivan spotted a little brown insect scuttling across the bulkhead.

'What's that!' he shouted. 'And that!'

Cockroaches.

'Life in the tropics, eh!' Alan laughed. 'Must have come aboard as stowaways in some fruit.'

The cockroaches were not big, smaller than my thumb.

'I've seen much bigger ones... this size.' Alan held his thumb up, it was about five times bigger than mine.

Ivan crouched near the bulkhead and kept very still.

'Can we keep it as a pet?' he asked Mum when he had caught a tiny one.

'Oh please,' I said. 'We can put him in a jar.'

'Well...' She wasn't very keen.

'He'll probably die anyway,' said Dad.

'What shall we call him?' I asked Ivan.

'What about Roger?'

So we wrote 'Roger' on a label and put it on the jar. Roger scuttled about but by the end of the day he was dead.

'Maybe he didn't have enough air.'

'Or didn't like being a captive.'

'I knew a yacht once that had a pet gecko,' said Alan. 'Good for keeping the cockroaches down.'

'No pets, thank you,' Mum said firmly.

I didn't mind the cockroaches too much until one morning, when Dad brought me a cup of cocoa and I took a sip only to find something soft in my mouth. I peered into my mug, where half a cockroach was floating about. I spat the other half back. After that I often lay in my bunk at night wondering if they came and crawled over us when we were asleep. I was sure I'd seen a big one like Alan had described, out of the corner of my eye, lurking in the shadows of the cabin.

* * *

Days and days passed at sea. The adults had to steer by hand now the self-steering had been broken by the whale, and they were getting tired.

Ivan and I stayed in our pyjamas all day, or just our underpants if it was really hot, and we didn't have to wash unless we felt like a shower from a bucket of sea

water thrown over us on the foredeck. Our new toys, the little bears bought in Bolivia, Bingo and Bungo, joined in the games. Our friend Louise from Maine had wrapped up some little presents for us, which we received each time we crossed another 10° line of longitude.

At last it felt as if Easter Island was drawing nearer and then Ivan and I kept our eyes peeled for any sign of land – a green branch, a stray bird. The Polynesian navigators had the skills to read the signs. But we didn't.

At dawn on March 13th the island rose out of the sea, just where Dad had predicted it would. After 19 days and more than 2,000 miles of ocean, he had found this little speck of land using those magic numbers and the ever-reliable sun shining in the sky.

Easter Island Adventure

EASTER ISLAND WAS not a great place to visit by yacht. As expected, there was no protected harbour and *Aventura* had to anchor in the open roadstead off the main settlement of Hangaroa, rolling uncomfortably in the big ocean swell.

'I don't like it,' said Dad. 'The weather's unsettled. We'll have to take it in turns to go ashore.'

Alan helped him inflate the dinghy, and fit the Seagull outboard engine to the back. I sat on deck and looked at a line of grey stone statues that stood on the shore. I wondered why their faces were turned away from the sea.

Ivan was watching how the fishing boats struggled to head out to sea from the shore, where great breakers rolled in and crashed on the beach.

'Look at that one,' he said. The little boat tried to rise over the incoming waves

but the bow went up too high and it flipped right over.

Dad motored off in the dinghy, clutching the precious bag of ships' papers and passports. At times he disappeared behind the waves and we held our breath, but he always recovered again, and made it safely ashore.

By the time he came back to the boat the sky was darkening and the wind changing direction.

'The wind is blowing onshore,' he said. 'We'll have to move.'

We rounded the island and anchored off the eastern end, next to the extinct volcano which was the site of the quarry for the stone statues. Alan, Mum and Ivan went ashore, while Dad and I kept anchor watch.

'What's it like?' I asked Ivan enviously when they returned.

'Well, there's a big old crater...' he said but his words, as usual, weren't very satisfying.

Next day, when it was our turn to go, the wind had turned right round again, and we had no choice but to sail back to the town anchorage. I wasn't happy. But you couldn't argue with the wind.

Dad managed to find a man who would hire two horses for us to make the trip to the volcano.

'He only wants six American dollars,' he said. 'Seems reasonable.'

'But I can't ride!' I cried. I'd never been on a horse before.

'You'll be fine.'

In the morning we headed for the shore in the dinghy. The waves were big and I was scared. I looked at Dad. He was never afraid. Once, I had asked him why.

'Because I'm a fatalist. Which means, you have to take things as they come. That's a good attitude to have as a sailor. The weather and everything around is unpredictable and you have to be ready to deal with it.'

My mind stuck on the word *fatalist*. What did that mean? I remembered when Dad had shown Ivan and I the bullet scar on his leg. He got that when he was eighteen and tried to escape from Romania one night by swimming out to a foreign ship anchored off the coast. At first the Swedish captain was going to take him, but someone had spotted him swimming out and the alarm was raised. So Dad had to leave the ship and swim back to the shore. A guard shot at him and the bullet grazed his leg. He dived deep, and swam away, and managed to get to the beach safely.

Now, he revved the trusty Seagull as fast as he could and raced for the shore. I looked behind to see great sea swells towering above us, gathered over thousands of miles, ready to break to pieces on this bit of rocky land, and break whatever happened to be in their way. The motor strained to outrun the wave which kept rising up, curling and whitening with foam. The dinghy rose and rose and I gripped the side. Yet the wave was not quite ready to break; somehow we managed to surf down it, slip out of its grasp and make it to the beach.

The first thing we saw on shore was the wreck of a Japanese yacht.

'Someone told me it was left at anchor with no one onboard and it was pushed onto the rocks.' Dad peeled at the layers of fibreglass poking from the great hole torn in its side. 'This hull is so thin – *Aventura* we know is good and strong.'

I waited for Dad to collect the horses. There was a small square surrounded by houses, and in the centre was one of the mysterious stone statues, its white eyes staring, its body short and squat. I sat next to it on the plinth. Some tourists passed by and talked in loud American voices.

'Take a picture of the statue, look, with that little local girl sitting there.'

I was very tanned and my hair was dark brown and tangled. I was wearing a crumpled cotton dress and my feet were bare and tough. I suppose I didn't look much like a tourist. I sat swinging my legs and stared at them solemnly, as if I didn't understand. But inside I was laughing.

I enjoyed our ride. The horses were placid enough, though rather skinny, and every time we stopped they gorged themselves on the yellow grass which was pretty much all that grew on the island.

The extinct volcano Rano Raraku was a grass-covered bowl, and across its slopes were scattered countless statues. Some were finished, standing, others only half carved out of the grey rock. It was peaceful: there was no one else there and all I could hear was the rustle of the yellow grass. I wandered about, touched the rough surface of the statues, looked into their blank eyes.

I remembered all those other strange, old places we had visited in the past three years: Delos, Pompeii, Knossos and the Valley of the Kings.

'Fantastic,' said Dad, taking photographs and cine film to his heart's content.

'Yes.' I couldn't share what feelings filled me up; they were my own, private.

The horses happily grazed. When it was time to go, we mounted and headed for a gap in a stone wall but they refused to go on. We dismounted and Dad led my horse through by its bridle. I held it and waited for him. But his horse was nervous; I could see the whites of its eyes. Dad tugged harder, and suddenly the bridle broke and the horse bolted.

It galloped wildly away along the side of the hill, bucking against the weight of our things on its back. The camera bag was bouncing up and down where it was attached next to the saddle, and as I watched the cine camera bounced to the top and went flying off through the air in a slow arc before banging onto the ground.

Eventually the horse ran out of steam and halted a little way off where it again cropped mildly at the grass, allowing Dad to go and take what was left of its bridle. But the camera was broken. And we couldn't find my jumper anywhere.

'The old guy swore that bridle was alright,' Dad told me after taking the horses back when we got to the town. 'But I'm sure it was already broken this morning. He was drunk, anyway. I think he'd bought a bottle of firewater with those six dollars.'

It was time to set off back to the boat. A few people watched us go. Here came the first wave, beginning to curl into a breaker. Up and up our little dinghy rose, the bow went higher and higher. We made it!

At least Dad and I had good stories to tell, about mad horses and American tourists, when we were gathered round the table that evening clutching our plates and trying to eat, while the swell rolled the boat to and fro.

'I guess you're our little Polynesian girl now,' said Mum. I was rather proud.

* * *

Alan left us, taking the plane home, and we had several days with weather so settled that we dared go ashore all together for one last exploration.

'We're going to visit another volcano, Rano Kau,' said Mum. 'We can walk there from the town. Everyone has heard of the Easter Island statues, but what about the birdmen of Orongo? They're just as mysterious.'

Up the slopes we climbed, through the long grass, where a fierce insect stung me hard on the leg. On the edge of the deep green bowl of the ancient crater, we

came upon low stone huts built high above cliffs that fell steeply down to the sea. This was the village of Orongo. Little islets lay below, their rocky slopes alive with white birds. There were many carvings engraved onto the flat surfaces of the rock around the huts, strange figures, with bodies of men and heads of birds.

'Here are paper and pencils – you can draw them,' Mum said, opening her bag.

'Hey, teacher,' teased Dad. 'Always well prepared!'

She ignored him and sat beside us.

'The tradition was this,' she explained. 'Men of the island came and lived in the dark huts once a year. They performed a ritual of swimming to one of the islets. Each wanted to be the one to get the first egg of the nesting season. But no one really knows what the bird-man figures mean.'

When Ivan and I had finished drawing, we tried to peer into the low entrances of the huts. There were no windows. I plucked up courage to crawl into one on my hands and knees. The darkness was complete and I felt the air of Orongo was crackling with mystery, just like the rest of the island.

By the Wind Sailors

STRANGE THINGS WERE floating on the surface of the calm sea.

Dad was sleeping down below. Mum manoeuvred the boat around while Ivan and I got a little beach net with a handle and managed to scoop one up.

The creature was small, no more than five centimetres long and three centimetres wide. It had a dark blue base that was soft like a jellyfish, and raised on the top was a transparent, hard structure. Underneath was a hole covered in tentacles.

'The mouth, I think,' suggested Ivan.

I searched through the various books we had on sealife.

'This is it!' I pointed at a picture. 'It's a By-The-Wind Sailor. Or a *Velella velella*. They're a sort of jellyfish. And they use that thing on top like a sail. They go sailing all over the tropical parts of the ocean. And the sail points from southeast to northwest, it says here. North of the Equator the sail points the other way.'

'What a clever little thing!' said Mum.

'What do they eat?' asked Ivan.

'Plankton. They sting them with their tentacles.'

We dropped the little *Velella Velella* back into the ocean and watched it bobbing up and down over the waves. There were lots of them now, everywhere we looked, sailing slowly over the oceans and nibbling as they went.

A Welcome on Pitcairn Island

I CAN'T SEE where the dinghy can get ashore,' said Dad, staring at the sheer cliffs of Pitcairn Island.

'A nice sheltered anchorage would be lovely.' Mum gave a tired sigh. 'And a chance to sleep the whole night through.'

'Looking at that coast –' Dad shook his head '– we won't be staying here long.'

It had taken us two weeks to cross the twelve hundred miles of ocean that separated Pitcairn from Easter Island. As I watched the island draw nearer, I thought about the people who lived there. In that fortnight at sea I'd had plenty of time to read the books we had onboard about Pitcairn and its history.

Two hundred years ago the crew of a navy ship the *Bounty* had mutineed against their captain, the infamous Captain Bligh. Bligh was turned off into a little boat with a few loyal men, and the mutineers sailed to Tahiti, took some Polynesians on board, and set off to find somewhere to hide, because mutiny was punishable by death. They ended up on Pitcairn, and the descendants of those sailors and their Polynesian wives still lived there. Pitcairn was a perfect hiding place, in those days not even plotted correctly on official charts, and once the *Bounty* had been burnt and sunk offshore, it was years before they had any further contact with the outside world.

We anchored in Bounty Bay.

'Somewhere underneath us,' said Mum, 'are the remains of the *Bounty*.'

As Dad had predicted, there was no shelter at all and the rolling back and forth was awful.

A big inflatable was launched through the huge swells to meet us.

'We don't get many yachts visiting,' said one of the young islanders. 'They mostly go from Panama to Tahiti. And ships only come once or twice a year.'

They invited us ashore. Dad wasn't very keen to leave the boat.

'The wind is quite light at the moment,' he decided. 'Perhaps we can risk it.'

'We can keep an eye out,' the man said. 'We'll whisk you back if the weather changes!'

We climbed on the back of motorbikes to drive up the hill to what they called the 'town'. The island was very hilly and there was not one flat place that could be made into an airstrip. Pitcairn could only be reached by sea.

Mum and Dad were taken on a motorbike tour and we spent a day at school with the island children. There were only eight of them at school, and two of those were in fact children of the teacher, who had come from New Zealand. The island

children had the same family names as the mutineers, like Christian and Brown; it was like meeting characters from a story.

I did like going to a real school, and wished it could be for more than a day. Ivan and I told them about our travels so far and the teacher got us all to read out some poetry.

After that the Pitcairn children took us to swim in rock-pools that were filled by the ocean crashing onto the shore. There was a girl my age and she showed me how to collect passion fruit to make some juice. Ivan went off with the boys, throwing frisbees and climbing trees. They spent about an hour trying to lasso a goat.

Then we all perched up a banyan tree and talked. When they remembered, the Pitcairn children talked to us in regular English, but when they spoke to each other I found it hard to follow what they said. It sounded like a bit of Polynesian, and a bit of English, but it was the oddest sort of English. I felt as if I was listening to a bunch of old sailors who had sprung off one of those square-riggers I so loved. It was old-fashioned and sea-salty, rather drawly like the accent of Cornwall where Granny lived.

'Ye bastard,' one of the boys said to another boy. I would never say a word like that but it didn't sound like an insult when they said it.

That evening we were all invited to an island celebration. It was someone's birthday and they were having a feast. Only about sixty people lived on Pitcairn and they were mostly related to one another, so everyone turned up at the party. Afterwards we slept ashore with Mum, but Dad went back to *Aventura*. One of the islanders had been telling him about a yacht that was wrecked here a couple of years before. He didn't want to take any chances.

The next day we had to leave.

'There was something special there,' said Mum, as we watched the green hills slowly sink below the horizon. 'I wished we could have stayed longer.'

'Yes, they get so few visitors no wonder they welcomed us,' agreed Dad.

'No, more than that,' she insisted. 'There is a definite spirit of friendliness, and I'm sure it has something to do with the Pacific. Remember when I dropped the ripe watermelon at the market on Easter Island? Everyone burst out laughing. They wouldn't do that in South America. Silly things were met with stony silence there.'

I remembered the unfriendly adults on the Andes bus, the maize beer poured into my lap, and the stony-faced Bolivian policeman. I was pretty sure she was right.

A Month in the Gambiers

FOR THE FIRST TIME in weeks *Aventura* was safe in a calm protected lagoon. We had made it to the island of Mangareva in the Gambier Islands and anchored off the main settlement, Rikitea.

'I don't think you can stay,' said the local *gendarme* who'd come to welcome us. 'Yachts aren't allowed to visit without prior permission.'

'But my wife is so tired,' pleaded Dad. 'Can't you see if they'll let us stay for just a little while, until we are rested?'

'*D'accord*. I'll radio Papeete.' To our surprise he grinned and winked. 'It may take some time for the reply to come through.' He held out his hand and Dad shook it.

'Welcome to Mangareva,' he said. 'My name is Manu.'

Another man had come with him.

'And I am Lucas, the mayor. *Bienvenu*.'

After they had gone, I asked why we couldn't stay.

'The Gambiers are in French Polynesia, and are a part of France,' Dad answered. 'And the French are conducting nuclear tests on Mururoa Atoll which is quite close. They don't want visitors.'

Lucas offered to take us on a tour of the island by jeep.

'Can we buy some fresh fruit and vegetables?' Mum asked.

'Oh no,' he said. '*Mais non*.'

She looked very disappointed.

'You won't be able to buy anything,' he burst out laughing. 'Because everyone just helps themselves!'

We drove to the end of the island and there were fruit trees everywhere, laden with grapefruit, oranges and lemons. Piles of fruit lay rotting under the trees.

'Wow,' said Dad. 'I've never seen grapefruits like this before.' He picked one up. It was as big as my head. When the thick green skin was peeled off it tasted sweet and wonderful.

On the way back Lucas pointed out a huge church, the size of a cathedral, built of coral slabs, that stood on the hill above the town. We visited the island priest, who gave us vegetables he had grown in his garden, and he told us that the cathedral was the idea of a former priest who had it built in the nineteenth century.

'Thousands died building it,' Dad told us later. 'He was a maniac. I have to say the current priest is quite pleasant.'

'Would your children like to go to school?' Lucas asked Mum when he took us back to the boat. As well as mayor, he was a teacher at the island school.

Mum glanced at me to see if I had understood what Lucas had said. My French was pretty good by then. Of course I had understood.

'Oh yes,' she said. 'They would *love* to go. They get fed up with having their mother as a teacher all the time!'

I woke up very early on Monday morning, and was ready long before seven o'clock, which was when the school day began. Lucas took us first to meet the headmaster. When I saw all the children staring at me I felt quite shy and hid behind Mum. Lucas took Ivan off to his class. He went quite happily, and I was left with Jacques, the headteacher.

'She's a bit worried about it all being in French,' Mum said.

Jacques smiled. 'That's no problem. All these children here learn French as a foreign language too. They speak Mangarevan at home you see.'

My initial shyness did not last long, and I quickly made friends. School only lasted for the morning, before it got too hot. We ate in the canteen and then were free to do as we pleased. We sat on the low branches of fruit trees, and the girls taught me to juggle using small unripe fruit.

'How did it go?' Mum asked when I eventually made it back to the boat at the end of the day.

'It was just the best. And I've got homework to do!' I sat down to do some French grammar exercises.

'Homework?' Mum raised an eyebrow. 'And you're pleased about that? What about you, Ivan?'

'I've got a best friend already!' he declared.

'I have to say you both look like you're in Seventh Heaven. Who would guess that children would think going to school was such a great thing to do!'

Although all the lessons were in French I found I could understand most of it, even the Maths. We had dictations to copy down every day – they were quite hard. But I didn't mind any of it. I just liked being in a classroom, being with other children.

Mum and Dad had only meant to stay for two weeks but they were enjoying themselves so much, socialising with all the islanders, that in the end we stayed a month.

'I'm feeling so much better now,' said Mum.

'You look it,' said Dad.

'That's a compliment, I suppose.'

'What about this fishing trip idea?' he said.

'Are you changing the subject?' she laughed.

'What fishing trip?' I asked.

'You know Manu said that the fish in the lagoon can't be eaten,' explained Dad, 'because they're poisonous...'

'But why?' I interrupted.

'No one knows exactly. Maybe when the reef was blasted to make a safe passage for the ships, somehow the coral didn't grow back in the right way and the fish ate from the reef.'

'The problem is,' explained Mum, 'as Manu told us, you just can't tell from looking at a fish if it's poisonous or not. Cooking doesn't make it go away.'

'What would happen if we ate any?' Ivan wanted to know.

Mum started to explain at great length.

'You can tell,' joked Dad, 'that she's a pharmacologist!'

'Very funny,' she said. 'I do find it interesting. Let me answer Ivan. You would get sick and numb, all tickly and prickly. It damages your nerves, so if you touched something cold, it would feel hot. So it wouldn't be very nice to eat an icecream!'

'The fish outside the reef are safe,' Dad went on, 'so I offered to take Manu and Lucas on a fishing trip on *Aventura*.'

The trip was arranged. I stayed onshore with Mum and Ivan at the house of the chief gendarme, and his daughter showed me how to feed the pigs. We tipped a mixture of slops and kitchen scraps into their pen and while we were scratching their hairy backs we heard that the fishermen had returned.

Aventura's cockpit was covered in blood and full of fish: a *mahi-mahi*, a king fish and even a large shark. They had only landed it because Manu had a special 'whistling' lure that he did not want to lose.

That evening under the big breadfruit tree in the garden of the *gendarmerie* we gathered to eat the fish. Ida, the chief gendarme's wife, had prepared *poisson cru*, which was raw fish 'cooked' in lemon juice and served with coconut cream. I didn't think I would like it but it was very good.

'Your permission has come at last!' cried Manu, turning up on the quayside the next afternoon and waving a piece of paper.

Dad took the paper. 'But it expires tomorrow!'

Manu shrugged. 'I can get an extension.'

He radioed for a week's extension, and we began to think about farewells. Our friends Wally and Louise were coming to join us so we needed to get to Tahiti.

On the day we left, our friends hung shell necklaces around our necks.

'This is the Polynesian way of saying goodbye,' Ida told Mum. 'These will not fade, not like the flowers when you arrive.'

Manu gave Dad his special whistling lure and the jaws from the shark they had caught, well scrubbed. The jaws were hung on the bulkhead in the main cabin.

There were presents of grapefruit, lemons and oranges and stems of green bananas, which Dad stored in the aft cabin. After we had motored away from the quay, and waved goodbye over and over to the little group standing there, I put my head through the companionway to take a look. I counted two hundred oranges, about the same amount of lemons, and twenty coconuts. I tried to count the bananas but I lost count after I reached three hundred.

'Mum,' I said.

'Mmm,' she said, not really listening. We had to get out of the lagoon before nightfall, and the pass through the reef was narrow.

'Mum, that is a lot of bananas.'

'It's okay,' she said. 'They're green. They'll ripen slowly.'

We had four stems; on each stem was about a hundred bananas. Mum, unfortunately, turned out to be wrong. They all ripened at once. A thousand mile passage to Tahiti. Bananas all the way.

Fried bananas, banana fritters, banana cake, banana bread. We ate bananas for days on end, and there were still more.

'You've always loved bananas,' Mum said. 'Ever since you were a baby and I mashed them up for you with milk and sugar.'

'But now we're surrounded by bananas,' I cried. 'I can't bear *another banana*!'

The Most Beautiful Islands in the World

WE HADN'T SEEN a single other yacht for months, and now we were one yacht of many, moored stern-to on the waterfront of Papeete on the island of Tahiti.

Papeete was a bustling city, expensive but useful. Dad got the cine camera mended, bought a new steel bolt for the self-steering, and we took on provisions and spare parts. The life raft was checked and the emergency supplies inside were replaced. We visited the spot on the island where Captain Cook observed the 'transit of Venus', and the Gauguin art museum too, although we were rather surprised to find that the museum had only copies and not one single original painting, even though some of his most famous work had been painted in French Polynesia.

Wally and Louise arrived on standby tickets from America.

'I remember the songs you taught us,' I said to Louise. Without much prompting Ivan and I sang *The Ballad of the Eddystone Light*.

With our guests onboard we cruised to the other islands that made up the Society Islands along with Tahiti. We didn't mind leaving noisy Papeete behind.

Moorea was really beautiful, the place you would imagine in your dreams if you had to picture a perfect tropical island. Coral reefs enclosed a lagoon of emerald and turquoise waters lapping at a strand of pure white beach, hung over by coconut palms. Beyond the beach, dark green slopes rose up to jagged volcanic peaks like gigantic broken teeth.

From there we sailed to Huahine and Tahaa. *Aventura* anchored near the beach. The turquoise water was so inviting that Ivan and I had our masks and flippers out and were ready to go when the anchor had barely touched the ground.

I let my grip on the boat go and dove below the surface, without a splash. Once I was right under, I kicked hard with my legs, determined to reach the white sand I could see about fifteen feet beneath me. I breathed out air to help me sink, and the bubbles danced past me up to the surface. My lungs began to feel tight the further I went down and I wondered if I would make it. I stretched out my hand towards the sand and with one last effort touched it before I turned and swam upwards, fast, breathless. With my last bit of breath I blew out the water from my snorkel, sucked in a mouthful of sweet air, and then floated, looking all about.

In every direction the plains of sand stretched off into the blue misty distance. There was the underside of *Aventura*, the deep, strong keel, painted with blue anti-fouling paint, but shaggy with months of sea-growth: long strands of green weeds and hard white barnacles. From the bow the thin strand of the anchor chain fell steeply down to the sand in a heavy curve and snaked off along the sea bed to where the anchor was safely dug in.

I hauled myself hand over hand down the chain to reach the bottom faster. Then I turned and looked up at the waves. They looked funny upside down, or was it inside out, like a moving silver sky.

I spent hours in the water with my mask and snorkel. The world I knew beneath the surface of the sea was where I felt at home.

The only bad thing was Dad couldn't get any fish. He even went out at night with a torch, but nothing.

'Completely fished out,' he said. 'I guess we were spoilt in the Caribbean.'

We took Wally and Louise in the big dinghy to the nearest reef where the underwater life was a riot of colour. The corals were shaped like gigantic brains or delicate fans. Angelfish went by with their long ribbons of tails and parrotfish with funny hard beaks pecked at the coral. Tiny bright blue and orange fish hid among the sea anemones.

Ivan was quite good at snorkelling now. Mum, however, was so buoyant she couldn't get down more than a couple of feet.

'I just can't dive,' she complained, trying to reach a shell she'd seen.

There were so many beautiful shells to be found, cowries, tritons and augers. We consulted *Seashells of the World* regularly, and our collection grew. The boat was full of smelly shells, suspended over buckets of water, trying to draw out the animal by tempting it with water.

I was fascinated by the cone shells that had spectacular geometric patterns, but which fired a poison dart that could be fatal to humans. We only took ones where the creature inside had died already.

There were other dangers on the reef. The stonefish, for example, which disguised itself as a grey stone, and would sting you with a terrible venom from its spines if you trod on it by mistake. We never walked barefoot on the reef. I'd read a vivid description of a sailor getting stung by a stonefish, fortunately not fatally: Robin Lee Graham, who only a few years before us, on his little yacht *Dove,* became the youngest person to sail around the world single-handed.

I read that book several times over and really envied him. I loved the idea of sailing on my own across the sea.

* * *

Louise and Wally were easy-going visitors. But one day as I jumped into the main cabin from the cockpit, a book in my hand as usual, Wally said to me in a rather exasperated voice, 'Can't you put something on!'

What did he mean? I wondered as I went on into my cabin. It took some thinking on my part to understand. I was not as flat-chested as a boy any more. I hadn't given it a great deal of thought until then. We didn't bother much with clothes on the boat; it was so hot I spent most of my time in a pair of underpants. Most of the time there was no one around to see us anyway. My strongest feeling, as I pulled on a T-shirt, was one of complete surprise.

Even if my body was changing – I was nearly eleven after all – I didn't feel any different from the girl who had left to go sailing three years earlier.

* * *

Louise and Wally went home from Bora Bora. Ashore the palm trees nodded, and the green slopes rose to amazing mountain peaks. I could see why it was called the most beautiful island in the world.

A Hollywood film was being shot on location on the island and Alex, who owned the yacht club, told Dad that they were looking for white men to be extras.

'I'll go and see what it's all about,' he said. 'We could do with a bit of extra income.'

'What sort of extra do they want you to be?' asked Mum.

'No idea.' He shrugged.

Later that day Ivan and I were reading in our cabin when we heard the dinghy come back and Dad climb aboard.

'Oh my goodness!' cried Mum.

'What?' We ran into the main cabin. When we saw Dad we screamed and ran away. His hair had been cut short, and his black beard completely shaved off.

Slowly we crept back. I knew it was Dad standing there and grinning. At least, my brain knew that, but all my senses were telling me he was a weird stranger. His smooth face looked all wrong. We tried to look but each time screamed and hid our faces again.

'I didn't expect this!' He laughed loudly. 'They want me to be a US Navy sailor. All I've got to do is sit around until I'm needed and then dance with the best dancing girls on the island. Food's good too.'

'Okay,' said Mum. 'My logical side says good, we can do with the money. But my other side isn't so keen on those girls!'

But she was smiling.

I was glad when the few days of filming were done and he started to grow his beard back again. Soon his face was back to normal. But he had earned more for one day's dancing than he would get for a week's worth of his BBC programmes.

* * *

'Your birthday soon, Doina,' said Mum. 'There are quite a few kids on yachts here. We'll invite them over. I'll even try and bake a cake.'

'And I'll dress the boat with flags,' piped up Ivan.

'Excellent work, Flag Officer,' said Dad.

'Aye aye sir!' Ivan replied smartly.

The cake came out lopsided, and burnt on one side, but the party was great. There were a collection of children of different ages, and everyone sang as I blew out the eleven candles. For presents I had a colour aerial photograph of Bora Bora and a dress made of a dark blue fabric Mum had bought in Papeete. It was patterned with white hibiscus and frangipani flowers, and outlines of Tahiti's distinctive figure-of-eight shape.

A week later Bora Bora celebrated the French National Holiday, with a festival of canoe races, song and dance competitions. Men ran 200 yard races laden down with huge stems of bananas, others raced to husk fifty coconuts in the shortest time, and women competed to weave a basket the fastest out of dried pandanus leaves.

The dancing was the best though. I saw the Polynesian *tamuré* for the first time. The girls and women who danced had thick black hair curling down to their waists, flowers tucked behind their ears and long grass skirts that sat low on their hips. Their hips moved from side to side in time to the fast beat of the drums, while their upper bodies remained still, and with their hands and arms they painted graceful movements in the air. The rhythm went right through me in a way I'd never known before.

'No wonder the *Bounty* crew got to Tahiti and refused to leave,' Dad had a twinkle in his eye. 'How could a downtrodden Limey sailor resist those girls?'

Out in the lagoon, a tourist boat motored slowly past full of holidaymakers trying hard to dance the *tamuré*. I felt far removed, and superior to those white strangers, moving their bodies so awkwardly.

I managed to persuade Dad to spend a dollar on a grass skirt and on the boat I tried the *tamuré* myself.

'Not bad,' said Mum. Ivan sniggered.

'*Shut up!*' I yelled.

* * *

We walked along the coastal road that followed the thin strip of shore encircling the island between the mountains and the sea. There was no traffic. I took off my flipflops to feel the hot gritty tarmac under my bare feet. The others dawdled, I walked ahead, to be on my own.

Suddenly I felt like running down the empty road. I was wearing my new blue dress. I tucked it into my pants and began to run, leaving the family behind. The warm air was like a kiss on my face, and the contact between my bare soles and the ground seemed to give speed to my legs. I was surprised how fast I went, and how easy it was. I had never run so fast before, I had never even liked running. Now I felt light and my feet barely seemed to touch the ground. Far away from the others, round a bend they disappeared. I was alone – I ran fast, fast – to catch the wind gusting down the green island valleys. To beat the waves, the white breakers crashing onto the encircling reef. I felt as if I could keep going forever. I felt full of everything: the dance, the sea, of being newly eleven years old.

I never quite ran like that again, but I always remembered that feeling.

Going Out in the Cook Islands

'WHERE NEXT?' was our question.

'West, it has to be.'

'What is west?'

'The Cook Islands. We're heading for the island of Aitutaki.'

We were getting used to making a long ocean passage between each Pacific country. Schoolwork was now about the history and myths of Polynesia, which covered a huge triangle of the Pacific Ocean stretching from Easter Island to Tonga, New Zealand to Hawaii.

'Sorry, you can't stay,' said the Aitutaki agricultural officer. We had just arrived, having braved the narrowest reef pass ever, and tied to a broken down dock. The man was smiling but firm. 'The boat has to be fumigated against pests, but I've run out of fumigation spray. I'm sorry, but we can't afford to have any foreign pests like fruit flies coming in and destroying our fruit trees. That's the rule.'

'Will these do?' said Dad, showing him some fumigation tablets that we used

against cockroaches. Fortunately the officer approved. The hatches were sealed and the tablets set alight. A thick grey smoke poured into the air. The companionway was closed with a wooden board that slotted into place and padlocked to the hatch cover. We set off on a walk round the island while *Aventura* filled with smoke.

'Would you like a lift?' an elderly man asked, stopping in his pick up truck which was already filled with a bunch of island kids. 'I'm Father George.'

'Oh I've heard of you!' said Dad. 'Do you still have your books?'

For fifteen years Father George had welcomed sailing yachts to the Cook Islands and helped them as much as he could, on the main island of Rarotonga, and now on Aitutaki. In return they filled his guest books with beautiful drawings, poems and dedications.

After our tour, having thanked Father George, who promised to bring his latest book for us to sign, we returned and opened the boat hatches. The smoke had mostly vanished, leaving a chemical smell that stayed for a few days. Unfortunately, the fumigation did not seem to have got rid of the cockroaches. We still had those.

Someone recommended we try what they called a 'Roach Motel'. The 'motel' was a clever trap. There were little doors with flaps all round, and in the middle was a space where you could put some tempting food. We left it out overnight when the cockroaches were busiest and in the morning it was full of them. Because the flaps only opened one way, they were trapped. It looked revolting to see them crawling over each other.

'Easy to get rid of them now,' said Mum, taking off the lid, or roof I suppose, of the 'motel' and throwing the guests into the sea.

'They're swimming back!' cried Ivan, who was looking over the side. The little brown insects had reached the boat and were climbing up the hull.

'Heck,' Mum said crossly. 'We'll have to squash them after all.' She started squishing each cockroach as it reached the top. Their yellow insides came out and smeared all over the white fibreglass.

'Oh Mum, yuck,' we shouted.

'You've got to leave the motel in the sun,' Dad told her later. 'That's what he said. Just let them burn to death.'

'Can't be worse than squashing them.'

* * *

On our island tour we had spotted a poster advertising an 'Island Night' with singing and dancing at the only hotel on the island.

'Let's go,' said Mum. 'I would enjoy going out for once! We used to go out all the time in London.'

She painted her nails, brushed her dark hair, and put on a long dress that left her tanned arms and back bare. I thought she looked very nice. Dad didn't say anything, just whistled.

Mum found a clean dress for me and tried to comb my hair. I cried out as she pulled at the tangles.

'One of these days I will cut it off!' she said crossly. 'Either that or you actually try to comb it yourself occasionally!'

'Behave properly,' Dad instructed us on the way to the hotel. 'I want to see proper table manners.'

Before the show started Ivan and I sneaked outside, bored with sitting at a table being good and listening to adult conversation.

A billy goat with curved horns was tied to a palm tree; there were quite a few goats on the island, cropping the grass. It seemed like a good idea to chase it round the tree so its rope got shorter and shorter until it couldn't move. Eventually the goat had enough and turned around, lowered its head and charged us with its horns. That was a bit scary, and we ran back inside.

After the show, which had drumming and dancers like Bora Bora, there was music for the guests to dance to. My parents took to the floor in a slow waltz.

'Can I try?' I begged Dad. He took me for a twirl and showed me how to move my feet.

I tried to persuade Ivan to be my partner.

'Come on, let's dance together.'

'No, I don't want to.'

'Come on, please.'

In the end he gave in and off we went. After a minute he put his hands round my neck, and hung all his weight on me. We collapsed to the floor in a heap and Dad pointed to the table, frowning. We were banned from the dance floor. I fumed; I had got the blame, though as far as I could see it was all Ivan's fault.

* * *

Father George brought his guest book to the boat.

'I don't get so many entries now,' he said sadly. 'Not many yachts come this way.'

'Doina, you're the best at drawing,' said Mum. 'Better than scribbling in your own books.'

It was true. I had developed a habit of drawing ladies with long hair and pouty lips on the blank end papers of my reading books. I suppose it was better than tearing strips off the pages and eating them, though I still did that on occasion if I was being absent-minded. In Father George's book I drew *Aventura*, and the four of us waving. A dolphin swam in the waves and a cloud of wind blew out big puffy cheeks, sending us on our way.

In the end it was the tide which sent us on our way. *Aventura* shot out of the narrow pass like a cork from a bottle of champagne. The keel hit the sand a couple of times, but with the engine and the strong tide pushing us we ploughed on through and came out into a sea like a boiling cauldron of angry water.

Tonga and Fiji – Back on the Beaten Track

'I'M GOING TO meet a princess,' announced Dad soon after we arrived in the Tongan capital Nuku'alofa.

Mum raised her eyebrows at this but his smile told her he was pulling her leg.

'For an *interview*,' he continued. 'Princess Pilolevu is the daughter of the King and she's the director of the Tourist Board. I've got an appointment to see her.'

We had already seen the white Royal Palace, a Victorian building near the sea front, surrounded by neat green lawns.

'We visited French Polynesia, that's part of France,' I said to Mum. She was working out a list of questions for us to answer about Tonga and its culture. 'And then the Cook Islands used to be a British colony, but are now independent. What about Tonga?'

'Good question,' she said, putting down her pen. 'Tonga is the only kingdom in the Pacific, and it is ruled by an ancient royal family that has always kept its independence. I remember when Queen Sālote came to England for the Coronation. I was thirteen and we went to watch it on a neighbour's TV. Everyone loved her because she sat in an open carriage in the rain smiling and waving.'

'Can we go to see the Princess too?' I asked hopefully.

'Not when it's work,' she answered. 'And don't sulk about it. I've these questions for you and Ivan. You can start by drawing the wooden totems that are outside the Tourist Board.'

After our drawings, and the interview, were finished, we walked through Nuku'alofa, where we saw smart policemen wearing hats with turned-up brims, white gloves, and blue uniform skirts, or *lavulavu,* the traditional dress for Pacific men.

'They might be wearing skirts,' observed Mum, 'but they look scary enough. You wouldn't want to mess with them.'

'Bligh did lose one of his sailors here,' added Dad. 'Even if Captain Cook named Tonga the Friendly Isles. These days they're not warriors. Good at rugby though.'

In the market were baskets full of oranges, papayas and melons on sale for twenty cents, but one thing really made our jaws drop.

'Are *those* what I think they are?' asked Dad, pointing at some dark green shapes that were the size of melons.

'Avocadoes, only five cents each.' The woman sat behind the stall smiled. She was a big lady, like many of the Tongans, and a tatty pandanus mat was tied round her waist. We had seen lots of Tongans wearing these mats which we had found out were a sign of mourning and respect for the dead.

'I must be dreaming,' said Dad. 'My favourite. Even cheaper than Peru. And we thought *they* were cheap.'

We bought several avocadoes. They tasted heavenly. Mum tried one little spoonful. She liked avocadoes but they made her ill, so she had to sit and watch us.

'Rather these than bananas,' I said.

'What if you had to eat 200 of them?'

'Oh Dad,' I groaned, 'don't remind me!'

* * *

After our long detour to Easter Island and Pitcairn, we had slotted back into the usual route yachts took through the Pacific. Mum and Dad changed their plans umpteen times but in the end we ended up in Fiji like most other yachts. The Fijian archipelago lay at the centre of the Pacific and its capital, Suva, was a great gathering place for sailors. There were at least fifty yachts anchored off the Royal Suva Yacht Club, which organised barbeques and other social events, and there was always a mess of kids to play with.

'Fiji is a real mix, thanks to its history,' explained Mum, as we settled down to a morning of schoolwork. 'First there are the native Fijians whose Melanesian ancestors sailed here hundreds of years ago. Melanesia means 'black islands', and

Melanesians are darker-skinned than Polynesians. There are Indians also who came during the days of the British Empire, mostly as cheap labour to work on the sugar plantations.'

We arrived in Suva in time to see the Hibiscus Festival with its Pacific singing and dancing. Ivan and I liked the International Coconut Tree Climbing event best. The children in Aitutaki had tried to teach us to climb palm trees. We weren't anywhere near as good as they were, and couldn't manage to learn the knack of gripping on with our feet to shin up the tall trunks. Now we watched in amazement as young men from Tonga, Samoa and other islands competed to be the fastest to shin up a sixty foot coconut palm. The winner made it in a few seconds.

Back on *Aventura* we looked at the mizzen mast.

'I reckon we could climb that,' I said to Ivan.

'Yeah. I reckon we could.'

I pulled myself up onto the boom, put my arms around the mast and started to push up with my feet. I managed to get a good grip on the metal and with a lot of effort I got to the spreaders and hauled myself over.

'Come on. You can do it for sure.'

Ivan puffed and pulled. He made it to the spreaders. We sat one on each side and dangled our legs down. We were about fifteen feet above the deck.

'Good view from up here,' I said.

Mum came into the cockpit.

'Shh,' I said. We stayed really quiet while she looked all around.

'Doina?' she called. 'Ivan?' Suddenly she heard a giggle and looked up.

'You're *there*!' A smile appeared on her face. She called Dad up from the cabin and he went back for his camera.

'Stand up!' he said. So we stood on one leg and waved the other leg around while he took a picture.

After that we often climbed the mizzen mast. It was too small to take the weight of an adult. Good; it was our mast.

* * *

'The boat's bottom is really dirty,' announced Dad. 'She needs a good clean.'

The parts of the hull which had been underwater for months were covered with green weeds and hard barnacles. All that growth slowed her right down.

'We can't afford a boatyard – we'll have to dry out. There's a good five foot tide here and a place where we can do it.'

At high tide *Aventura* was moored to some wooden pilings. As the tide went out the keel settled onto the sea bottom, but Dad had tied her on well so she stayed upright.

We only had a few hours before the tide came back in so we all had to work fast. With metal blades we started scraping at the hull. The weed stank, and slimy bits trickled down my arms. Pale little creatures that had hitched a ride on the boat for the past few months scuttled out of sight. I chiselled away at the hard barnacles that were clinging on for dear life, crushing their shells and flicking them off. I felt sorry for the big ocean creatures of the deep, like whales, that got barnacles growing on their skin. They must hurt a lot.

Scrape, scrape, my hands above my head, smelly, aching. When the worst of the growth was off, we cleaned it all with a scrubbing brush and let it dry.

Then we had to wait for the tide to come in and out again before painting. We used anti-fouling paint that was supposed to slow the growth down. The paint was blue, and its smell made my head spin. Ivan and I got a lot of paint on ourselves as well as the hull, and when the job was done, and we had to be cleaned up, agony! Mum daubed us with white spirit which made our skin sting and our eyes burn.

* * *

Way back in Easter Island Mum and Dad had met an Englishman called Tom who said we should visit the British colony of the Ellice Islands which were going to become independent this year. According to Tom the celebrations really would be worth seeing.

We weren't even sure where the Ellice Islands were until Mum remembered the Gilbert and Ellice Islands from her childhood stamp-collecting days.

We met Tom again in Fiji. It turned out that he was Her Majesty's High Commissioner for the Ellice Islands, and also, that a Princess from the British Royal Family was coming to the independence celebrations.

The decision was made: we were going to sail six hundred miles north of Fiji to the Ellice Islands. Because of the Princess, Dad managed to get commissions from two English newspapers and he decided to buy himself two new Nikon professional cameras, with a whole range of lenses, from one of Suva's duty-free shops.

'My old camera was really no good,' he said. 'I need something of professional quality, if I want to take decent pictures. But they are expensive.' The cost of one camera was about two month's salary.

'I'm certainly tired of sending off rotten photos with our articles,' agreed Mum. 'I just hope they pay their way.'

'They will. I know it,' he replied.

* * *

As we headed north, away from Fiji, nice and fast now the bottom was clean, I kept scratching my head because it itched horribly. Finally Mum checked my hair and found it was crawling with lice. And Ivan's too. By now we were en route and far from any shops, so she laid out some newspaper in the cockpit and doused our heads in paraffin from the hurricane lamp. I howled: the paraffin stung far more than the white spirit had. But the lice couldn't bear it either, and they leapt off my head like a bunch of sky divers to land on the paper below.

'That's it,' Mum said as she rinsed my hair through and tried to comb out the tangles. 'Your hair – this time it's going to get cut!'

In the end I had to wait until we returned to Fiji. I had my first proper haircut in a hairdressers and all my long dark hair was cut off.

'Why are you smiling?' said the Indian lady who was cutting my hair.

'I can't help it,' I told her. Everytime I caught sight of myself in the mirror I grinned, because I looked so odd with short hair. I liked it though. I regarded myself now as a bit of a tomboy. Girls with long hair were silly. They probably played with dolls and spent most of their time crying.

The Birth of a New Nation

'I'M SURE WE should be able to see the islands by now,' said Dad, peering at the horizon. 'My fix shows we are only a few miles away.'

We all stared at the horizon, but there was nothing there but sea.

'Hey, what about there!' cried Ivan, jabbing with his finger. We all looked and thought we could see a black dot. Then another dot appeared.

'They must be palm trees,' Dad dug out the binoculars. 'Yes, they are. No wonder we couldn't see anything until now. If the island's no higher than a palm tree it wouldn't be visible from more than a few miles away.'

Mum altered course and we headed for the dots, which slowly turned into green feathery fronds, and brown trunks appeared underneath them. We motored through the reef pass and across a large lagoon to the main island.

The capital of the Ellice Islands, Funafuti was just a small town and as we walked down the dusty main street everyone greeted us with a cheery *'Talofa'*.

'Let me see if I can get an interview with the Chief Minister,' Dad said enthusiastically. 'He'll be Prime Minister after independence.'

At the Government offices they said the interview could take place straight away so we rushed back to the boat for the tape recorder. Ivan and I stayed on board to do some schoolwork.

But it was too hot to concentrate, the air was so heavy and humid. I put down my book and wiped my face.

Outside something began to hammer hard on the deck.

'Rain!' I said.

We ran onto deck and stood there, feeling the welcome coolness on our skin. I felt a sudden urge to jump into the sea. After the rain, it was as warm and smooth as syrup. But salty. The rain squall passed, but another came just after – so we stood on the deck, and then jumped in the sea all over again.

In a gap between squalls we saw Dad rowing back, as fast as he could, Mum trying to protect the precious tape recorder. They made it a moment before the rain started pouring down again.

'Was the interview good?'

'Oh yes. But quick – get all the buckets, anything!'

We put out every available receptacle, buckets and saucepans, and within seconds they were full. The islands relied on rain for their water supplies so we needed to collect our own. Dad blocked the scuppers that normally drained any water off the decks into the sea, and unscrewed the cap that led into our fresh water tank. Down poured the rain, and within half an hour the water tanks were filled with 40 gallons of rain water.

'You two next,' said Mum when Dad had finished and the rain was still falling hard. She shampooed our hair and we stood on deck and let it all rinse off. Then she washed all the clothes. And still it rained.

'These islands don't have much,' said Dad, when the rain stopped as abruptly as it had begun. 'The Minister was telling me. No resources. There are nine islands and half a million miles of ocean. They'll sell the fishing rights to Japan and make money that way. They get revenue from postage stamps too.'

'And some aid from the UK,' said Mum. 'But it's true, they have so little – just sand and sea and coconuts.'

At this point we heard some lovely singing drifting across the water and we looked out to see a boat laden down with people, singing in beautiful harmonies as they came ashore.

'They do know how to enjoy themselves, though!' she laughed.

'That's the inter-island ship,' said Dad, 'bringing people from other islands, for the celebrations.'

Soon after an Australian survey ship arrived to mark the reef pass with buoys and then the lagoon began to fill up with navy warships.

'That's the Australian guided missile destroyer, and the American's a destroyer too,' Ivan told me. 'The New Zealander's a frigate and the two Fijians are both minesweepers. There's a French one too, not sure what that is.'

When the ships all dressed themselves from bow to stern in flags, Ivan's satisfaction was complete.

'They have done it in the correct order!' he cried excitedly. 'We have to do that too.'

He and Dad set about arranging our set of code flags to be hauled up the forestay and backstay. Not haphazardly as they had done in Bora Bora for my birthday, but properly, because we were the only British vessel in the lagoon. There were four other yachts, but not one flying the Red Ensign.

'Amazing,' said Dad. 'We are the only vessel flying the British flag, *Aventura*, with her Romanian captain!'

Funafuti's main street was crowded now with people from other islands and navy sailors in their spick and span uniforms. The island was only a few hundred yards wide and there wasn't much space for all the visitors. Half of the island was taken up by the grassy airstrip. Most of the time the strip was used as a football pitch, but when planes landed the goal posts were taken down. We went to watch a Hercules transport plane land, rolling out of its big belly a shiny new fire engine for airport safety and a car for the Princess.

On the day that the Princess and all the VIPs were due to fly in, Mum decided we ought to look a bit smarter than usual.

'Is there anything reasonably respectable in here?' she said despairingly, searching through my clothes. 'Why do you have to stuff it into your cubbyholes like that? Everything is so crumpled.'

'Nothing fits me anyway,' I complained, as she held up a dress. 'That one is far too small.'

She stopped and looked at me appraisingly. 'You're right. You really have grown an awful lot these last few months. You'll be as tall as me soon enough! When we get back to Suva I'll get you some new clothes.' She shoved a top and skirt at me. 'This will have to do today. And *please* brush your hair.'

Crowds of people had gathered at the airstrip, dancing girls and singers. Dad was busy with his new cameras. High Commissioner Tom was there, looking smart in a tie, shorts and long socks. The Chief Minister invited Ivan and I to sit down next to him, in the shade out of the blistering sun. He was a broad-faced smiling man. I looked curiously at him, not having seen a real politician up close before. He was dressed in a skirt of plain dried pandanus, overlaid with pandanus

strips coloured and decorated with patterns specific to his clan. A garland of flowers was on his head and his feet were bare. I guess he didn't look much like a typical politician.

The Princess, slim and dark, stepped off the plane to be greeted by the dignitaries. A girl put flowers around her neck and gave her a fan and she walked down the main street, which was now carpeted with pandanus mats, in the shade of a large umbrella held by another girl, with the Chief Minister by her side.

There was a big feast in the *maneapa*, the open-sided meeting house, its floor laid with finely-woven mats, the pillars decorated with palm fronds and flowers. Everyone had to take off their shoes and sit cross-legged, which was the traditional style. That was no problem for the VIPs who had come from other Pacific countries, but Mum whispered to me some of the Europeans were 'creaking a bit' when they sat down.

When I say feast I really mean it. Long lines of banana leaves had been laid out, laden with piles and piles of food. Roast suckling pig, lobsters in their red shiny shells, baked fish, starchy root vegetables like taro and pulaka, crispy slices of fried breadfruit, leafy greens in coconut milk, rice, potatoes and sweet ripe yellow bananas. There were green drinking coconuts that stood upright in little pandanus baskets.

It was a fine feeling for us to be included in the celebrations, on the VIP list and sitting next to politicians and diplomats.

Afterwards the Princess was taken by launch out to the New Zealand warship where she was to stay. On the way one of those sudden rain squalls drenched her.

'She's ill,' Dad told us the next day. 'Apparently she's going to remain on board, and she may miss all the festivities.'

'Could be an interesting angle for your news story,' suggested Mum.

She was right; several more newspapers got in touch with Dad, wanting reports on the sick princess.

That afternoon there was a special event at the Philatelic Bureau. A commemorative book of stamps had been produced and each VIP was presented with a copy in a special binder.

'We ought to get one really,' Dad said to Mum. 'After all we are the only British ship in the lagoon.'

The people handing out the stamps were embarrassed and gave us our own set. Dad had been joking but he was overheard by an Australian journalist. The story of the British yacht and the Romanian captain representing Britain's naval might made it onto the front page of an Australian newspaper.

Meanwhile the Princess stayed onboard the New Zealand frigate and wasn't seen. Mum and Dad had made friends with one of the officers and he invited us to tour the ship. We had to tiptoe past the door of the Captain's cabin where the ill Princess was resting.

Equally exciting though was the ship's navigation room. It was dimly lit so the sailors' eyes could read the screens better, and full of instruments including radar which showed us a ghostly green pattern of the island and other ships at anchor, including *Aventura,* a little dot on the screen.

Every day, princess or no, the islanders celebrated. There was feasting in the *maneapa*, followed by dancing. The men, cross-legged on the floor, beat large wooden boxes with their bare hands to create the rhythm, the singers filled the air with sweet harmonies.

Each island had sent their best troupe of dancing girls. Colourful flower wreaths crowned the dancers' heads and they wore bodices embroidered with tiny shells and colourful pandanus skirts. Necklaces of long pandanus strips fell over their shoulders and their brown skins glistened with coconut oil.

No wild swinging of the hips like in Bora Bora – all the passion and expression now went into their hands and faces. Their bodies barely moved, other than a brief turn of the waist or a dip of the head, and they told stories with subtle gestures from their fingers and wrists, punctuated by the flash of a white smile or a raised eyebrow. They wove their hands into intricate patterns in the air, turning and curving as light as birds. Back on *Aventura* I held out my arms and tried to make my fingers flutter in the same way. Ivan giggled, just like he had on Bora Bora when I tried to dance the *tamuré*.

'Go away!' I yelled but he continued to grin at me. He was so annoying. I turned and stamped off to our cabin and flung myself on the bunk. There wasn't anywhere I could go to be alone, I fumed to myself. My irritating little brother was always there.

* * *

At midnight, 31st September 1978, the Ellice Islands colony ceased to exist and the independent nation of Tuvalu was born. The Union Jack was lowered and the Tuvaluan flag raised in a solemn ceremony. Fireworks burst over the lagoon, and the American destroyer set off a 21-gun salute.

'I met someone,' said Dad the next day. 'From the Gilbert Islands.'

'Where is that?'

'North of here. Anyway, *they* are becoming independent next year... And he's invited us.'

'That would mean another year in the Pacific...' said Mum.

'Yes!' we children cried.

The Floating Darkroom

AVENTURA WASN'T JUST laden with books. There was a film projector stored under one of the bunks that could play the Super 8 films Dad shot as well as a collection of old black-and-white Charlie Chaplin and Laurel and Hardy films.

'One of these days I'll organise a film show ashore,' he often said.

As well as that, we had all the equipment that was needed to develop and print black and white photographs. Dad had bought it in New York because he was fed up with his prints being spoilt when he sent them away to be developed.

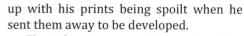

'I've taken so many pictures here,' he said. 'We ought to get some printed, to give to people before we leave.'

First he developed the films in a special canister that was sealed from the light.

'If any light gets in before the films are developed,' he explained to Ivan and I, 'all the photos will be ruined.'

'Is it okay for the light to get them now?' I asked when he pulled out the film at the end of the process.

'Yes, it's safe now.'

He held up the film and I could see negative images had appeared there.

'Now we have to get our darkroom set up,' he said, pegging all the films up to dry.

As evening fell Mum pinned material to all the portholes in the main cabin so not one speck of light could get through. Dad set up a red electric bulb that he was going to work by.

'Red light is safe,' he said. 'You always use it in darkrooms.'

'Only this is a dark cabin!' Mum laughed. 'Now, you children stay there and don't get in the way.'

Ivan and I stood at the doorway to the main cabin so we could watch. Dad had dug out the enlarger from under a bunk and now set it up on the chart table. Next to it, on the galley, was a line of trays, each filled with a different chemical. He switched on the enlarger and put in a negative. He seemed to fiddle around for ages, and I could see there was a picture projecting onto the board below, but it didn't look like much. At last he seemed happy.

'Pass me a sheet of paper,' he said to Mum.

He placed the photographic paper under the enlarger, switched on the light, counted for a few seconds, then placed the paper in the first tray.

'I'm developing this now. Just watch.' He took some plastic tongs and swished the paper about. Ivan and I craned our necks to see. Suddenly, black marks began appearing on the white paper, like magic. I saw an eye, and another, then a nose, and a whole face appeared. Hair, arms, flowers – a dancer came to life on the paper.

'Quick, into the stop bath, before it over-develops.' He picked up the print, let it drip for a moment, then put it gently into the next tray. After that it went into the fix, 'to fix the print forever,' and finally it was washed in water.

Ivan and I watched this process over and over until we started to yawn and we took ourselves off to bed. The printing kept going, until late into the night. When we woke the next morning the cabin was festooned with photos pegged up to dry.

'Those dancers were my favourites,' said Mum, pointing at one of the photos.

'Yes, definitely. From the island of Nukulaelae,' agreed Dad. 'We'll take them some prints as a present.'

In the encampment of the Nukulaelae islanders they were cutting up turtles for food. There was lots of blood, the chunks of flesh were red with it. Somehow, I don't know why, I had expected turtle meat to be green. The dancers loved their photos. One man gave Dad a turtle shell that was cleaned out, patterned on the front and shiny and brown.

'My name is Tinirau,' he said. 'And you must come one day and visit our island.'

'Thank you,' replied Dad. 'We would love to.'

However, now the hurricane season was on its way and we had to head out of the zone.

Just outside the barrier reef, as we left Funafuti behind, we hooked a big tuna. Manu's whistling lure always worked well. Dad expertly hauled it into the cockpit. A lean brown ocean shark followed close behind.

'They are the really dangerous ones,' said Dad. 'Not like the well-fed reef sharks.'

When the bucket of guts and the tuna carcass were thrown back the shark pounced, crazy with the smell of blood. The sight made me shiver all over.

New Zealand 1978–79

cone shell

Camp and Lisa

I HAD TO get used to the idea that summer in New Zealand began in December, because we were in the southern hemisphere now. We settled down in the town basin at Whangarei on the North Island for a long stay, and for Ivan and I that meant one thing: school.

I joined Form 1 at one of the local middle schools. I was secretly rather pleased that I was going somewhere different from Ivan, who was going to a primary school. Even better, in a couple of weeks when term ended my class were going on a three day camp.

School wasn't bad. The other children were welcoming and I wasn't teased. I liked the lessons on Maori culture, especially when we got to draw traditional designs such as the curling patterns of waves. I read book after book from the school library and auditioned unsuccessfully for the school musical. The teacher asked me to sing to notes she played on the piano. I tried, but I had no idea how to do that. Mum and Dad loved to listen to music but could not sing or play at all.

Afterwards, Dad said, 'Why didn't you tell the teacher you've been on a boat, and haven't had any music lessons?'

I couldn't tell him the reason – that I was too shy to tell the teacher. After all, how could he understand that, when I think he had never had a shy moment in his life? I knew Mum would understand me better – she'd once told me that when she was at university she was too terrified to ever raise her hand in a seminar to ask or answer a question.

So I watched the school choir's rehearsals of *Joseph and the Amazing Technicolour Dreamcoat*, got to know all the songs perfectly well, and sang them to myself on the boat.

I spent the fortnight before class camp making lists of what I was going to take.

'Thank heaven you're going tomorrow,' Mum exclaimed. 'I don't think I can take any more of you rehearsing packing and unpacking your rucksack!'

* * *

'Hi,' a girl said to me as we set out for a hike to the beach on the first day.

'Hi.'

I'd seen the girl before but never talked to her at school. She was as tall as me, but very thin and pale-skinned. She had bright blue eyes that stared at me in a way I found rather fascinating.

'Are you half Maori?' she asked, chewing on a fingernail. I shook my head.

'I like your hair.' She pointed to where I'd had it cut short in Fiji. 'I'm Lisa. Wanna drink?'

She held out a flask.

'What is it? Juice?'

She laughed and wouldn't say.

'No thanks.'

She took a swig herself then held it out to me. I tried to look into the flask but I couldn't see inside. I noticed Lisa staring at me again with those blue eyes. I felt a bit like I was a scientific specimen.

But I was thirsty, so I slowly tipped it up and a few drops touched my tongue. It tasted disgusting and I spat it out. It was milk.

'Yuck, it's horrible. But that's odd – because I like milk.'

Lisa studied me for a moment more.

'Come on,' she said suddenly as if nothing had happened. 'We're going swimming.'

We jumped around on the rocks by the sea. I had grown a lot and my old swimming costume was too small. I tried to hold the thin nylon material in place over my chest but if I let go it just would not stay put. The rest of the class was there. The boys laughed and pointed. They could see everything.

I stopped jumping and sat on the rocks.

'Get lost!' Lisa yelled at them.

'No!' they shouted back.

'Bloody boys,' she said, sitting by me and grinning.

That evening Lisa and I made a fire with two other girls and nearly burnt off our eyebrows when we poured the remainder of oil from a frying pan onto the flames.

When it was dark everyone gathered in a circle around the fire and told scary stories. Lisa told a gruesome one about a madman beating a man's head against the windscreen of a broken down car, with his wife and daughter trapped inside, on the lonely forest road... She was good at telling stories, with all the bloody details.

I really enjoyed that camping trip. And I'd made a friend too.

Before term finished, there was a disco at school and we had to dress in 1950s clothes.

'Can you help me, Mum?' I asked.

'I expect so! I was a teenager then. Now you make me feel ancient.'

She made me a cotton dress with a flared skirt. Lisa met me at the disco. She had backcombed her hair so it stood out on her head. I wanted to dance but I felt too shy. Lisa stood by me at the wall and giggled.

The disco ended sooner than planned because a boy had an epileptic fit and lay on the floor choking on his tongue until one of the teachers saved him and called for the ambulance. I tried not to stare as it didn't seem fair on the boy, but I couldn't help but be interested.

Soon after the disco, the school finished for the long summer holidays.

I'd hoped to spend some time with Lisa, but Mum and Dad already had the holidays all planned out; somewhere nice for Christmas, and then an overland trip with the two grandmothers who were coming out to join us in January.

'Guess I'll see you when I get back,' I said to Lisa.

'Yep,' she said. 'Guess you will.'

The Grandmothers Visit

GREAT BARRIER ISLAND was a short sail from Whangarei and we spent Christmas there, anchored in a sheltered bay. The water was rather cold for swimming so Ivan and I camped ashore on the beach in our old tent. We woke to find that our feet were wet where the rising tide had come in during the night.

On Christmas Day we went for an afternoon stroll. I felt sharp pains in my stomach, which got worse the further we walked.

'My stomach is hurting,' I complained.

'It's part of growing up,' Dad said mysteriously.

I had no idea what he was talking about.

Back on the boat that evening I lay on the aft deck almost doubled up in pain. The wooden deck was cool and comforting, and I stared at the familiar strips of teak dried out to grey and the thin black lines of caulking in between. Pain coursed through my abdomen in waves. Just like a sea, coming and going through my body. What was happening?

The next day I started to bleed. I went and told Mum and she produced a packet of sanitary towels from a locker in her cabin and a little book for me to read about what happens to girls when they hit puberty.

'I expected it,' she said.

Well, I hadn't: but it seemed this event was a surprise to me only.

* * *

Omi was going to travel to England and spend Christmas with Granny, and then they would fly out together.

'Nusi is really looking forward to it,' Dad said. Nusi was what they all called her though her real name was Ana. 'She has had to wait two years before they let her have another passport to travel abroad.'

'Daddy,' I said, then hesitated.

'Yes?'

'What about our grandfathers?' I asked. The story I knew seemed rather hazy.

'When the communists took power in Romania at the end of the war,' Dad explained, 'they asked my father to join them but he refused. He was working for the Romanian king at the time so I guess they thought he was an important person to have on their side. They threw him into prison. He died there eventually.'

'And what about your Dad?' we asked Mum.

'He came from a Welsh mining village,' Mum said. 'He met Granny when he walked to London from Wales in the '30s to try to find a job. Then he signed up in the first days of the Second World War but they stupidly sent them off to France with no equipment and he slept in the mud. He got really ill and he never properly recovered. He and Granny were supposed to be moving down to Cornwall to start a B&B when he had a terrible accident and broke his back. He died soon after.'

'I wish I'd known them,' I said. The words sounded mild when they came out of my mouth, but the feeling I had was fierce.

In spite of what they'd been through, Granny and Omi were generally rather cheerful souls.

'What a great time we've had,' said Granny chirpily when they arrived after their long haul flight. 'We had a Romanian-English dictionary between us and we got on fine.'

'How you've grown,' they told me and Ivan. I hugged them both and smelt the faint lavender of Granny's favourite soap and Omi's familiar perfume. We hadn't seen them for two years, and they looked exactly the same as I remembered.

Mum and Dad had made a temporary swap with some New Zealand friends, *Aventura* for their car, an old-fashioned black Wolseley that was vast and comfortable inside.

We piled in and set off through the North Island to Auckland and Wellington, then down to the South Island, where we saw glaciers and bubbling mud pools,

tame *kua* parrots and massive tree ferns that seemed to come straight out of a prehistoric forest. Money was saved as usual by making Ivan and I hide on the car floor so as to pay for less people in the campsites.

'I swear that this car consumes more in oil than it does petrol,' said Dad, as he fixed another leak.

We had several punctures as well, but that could not prevent our enjoying our trip.

'I love the fact I actually have to put on a jumper,' said Mum. 'We've had so much tropical heat.'

'I do like New Zealand,' remarked Granny. 'It's a bit like England.'

I hadn't really thought much about England until then. I remembered bits of London, the school, the shops in the high street, the park, but not what reminded Granny, not green fields and sheep.

* * *

When we got back to Opua, where *Aventura* had been left, Dad couldn't start the engine. The car-boat swap didn't seem such a brilliant idea anymore.

'The batteries are completely flat,' he grumbled. 'And it looks like the starter motor is broken. We'll have to sail back to Whangarei.'

We anchored for the night and then discovered the gas bottle was completely empty. Granny and Omi couldn't even have a cup of tea.

'Fine,' said Dad. 'I'll go ashore and make a fire. Let's go fishing for our supper!'

He was cross that the boat had not been looked after as well as he'd looked after that car.

However, having our supper on the beach in the dark, grilled fish and water boiled for tea on the open fire, made up for it. Omi and Granny would soon be taking the long flight home, and we didn't know how long it would be before we saw them again, or even where in the world that would be.

'Here,' said Omi, as the time came for goodbyes. 'A present from both of us.' She kissed me and left lipstick on my cheek.

Granny put a small object wrapped in tissue paper into my hand. It was a Maori tiki figure made from bright green jade. I thanked them and hugged them and put it round my neck.

A Whole Term at School

BY NOW I had begged for a new swimming costume, and in it I easily won the Junior Breaststroke Championship in my school's swimming races, which qualified me for the county under-12s swimming event.

For a treat we went to a place that served the most fantastic milkshakes I had ever tried, so thick the straw stood up straight in the glass. Milk was good in New Zealand and the ice creams superior to anywhere else. Once Dad bought a big tub and bet us we couldn't eat it all for supper. Mum said 'Rather a glass of wine for me,' as she watched us tuck in and finish the whole lot.

Every day after school I trained hard for the county race at the Whangarei town pool, which was just near the harbour.

The day before the race, the cramps and the bleeding started again.

'What about the swimming final? I won't be able to do it now!'

Mum and I went into town to look for mini-tampons so I could swim. Fortunately on the day of the race I felt fine. I was confident too: swimming was one thing I knew I could do. I won my heat easily which put me into the final. I was up against girls from twelve other schools. Some of them looked much bigger and

stronger than me. I swam as fast as I could but came second.

'Doina, never mind,' said Mum afterwards. 'The girl who won was much bigger than you.'

'But I looked round half way through.' I was very disappointed. 'That was a mistake.'

I kept on swimming though, and hung out at the town pool most days after school. I often met Lisa there. We went and had tea at her house, with her mother who was as thin as Lisa and smoked without stopping, her face was tired, but she was nice to me.

One day at the pool Lisa picked a couple of discarded cigarettes off the floor.

'Try this,' she said, lighting them with a lighter she pulled from her pocket. I tried it: I didn't like the taste of the smoke very much and it made me feel dizzy but I kept going.

Lisa puffed away. 'I shot my brother, you know.'

'No!' I said, trying to copy her grown-up gestures in holding the cigarette.

'I did. It was an accident, of course.'

She screwed up her blue eyes as she tried to draw a puff of smoke from the tiny bit of cigarette and then opened them again and stared at me defiantly as she exhaled. I really didn't know if she was telling the truth or not.

After some days of picking up fag ends we bought a small packet of cigarettes in the shop near the harbour. The shopkeeper did not challenge us when we went in and said it was for our father.

Sometimes she and I went to the cinema, and because we looked older than our ages we managed to get into films I wished afterwards I had never seen. The one about a grizzly bear killing people was horrible but I could cope as I didn't think there was much chance of meeting a bear anywhere. The one about the hordes of killer spiders did make me afraid of dark corners for a while but that eventually passed. It was the film about the killer shark that really got to me. I wished I'd never seen it. The film shark was obviously fake but it still really scared me.

There were a few boys that we saw hanging around the pool. One in particular we often saw looking at us, but he never said anything. He was Maori and had a thick mop of hair and a screwed-up face.

'Ugly-Mug,' Lisa called him. I thought that wasn't very fair, but then Lisa was like that.

'I reckon Ugly-Mug likes you,' she said. 'Do you like him?'

It was a new feeling to have someone interested in you like that.

'I don't know,' I said. I really didn't. It never came to anything anyway.

Then I managed to leave our half-finished packet of cigarettes in the public

toilets near the swimming pool and I remembered only when it was too late. Lisa was rather cross but I was relieved; I hadn't ever really liked smoking much.

I met a boy called Chris who trained regularly at the pool. He was pale and skinny and didn't look up to much but he was a good swimmer. Lisa and I challenged him to arm wrestle, and beat him everytime. He invited me over to his house, along the waterfront from the harbour, and his parents were polite and asked me questions about my travels. Afterwards he and I messed about, tickling each other, and he put his arms around me and kissed me. I kissed him back, but too hard, and I cut his lip against the braces he wore on his teeth.

I didn't see Lisa so much after school now as I was spending time with Chris. Then it rained solidly for three weeks and I didn't see anyone at all. Winter was on its way.

By now *Aventura* was in 'tip top condition' according to Dad. She'd been hauled out of the water and thoroughly cleaned, painted and varnished. There were new steps going up the main mast, to make reef navigation much easier. She even had a new mainsail. Dad had ordered a fibreglass dinghy and every day he went to the yard to inspect it with Ivan. It was Ivan's favourite topic of conversation.

Knowing our plans for the coming year would take us far off the beaten track again, Mum stocked up on good quality New Zealand tinned butter, powdered eggs and tins of cabin biscuits.

'I feel like I'm back in my childhood in the war,' she said.

Dad had also made contacts with Radio New Zealand and was going to send them reports from the Pacific places we visited. He was always on the lookout for a story, and sometimes they landed right in his lap.

A replica of the *Bounty*, the ship whose remains we had anchored over in Pitcairn, was launched while we were still in Whangarei. Although the replica had a steel hull and an engine, her rig was identical, and when they held the first sea trials for her, we went out in *Aventura* and Dad took lots of photographs. The old fashioned sailing ship, with her three masts, square sails, and great big Ensign

flying off the back, looked pretty impressive as she made headway through the grey seas.

March turned into April and it was time to leave New Zealand and head back into the Pacific. My classmates gave me a leaving present of a small box whose lid was made of native New Zealand woods. I managed to stand up and say 'thank you very much' in a faltering voice and then I sat down and looked at the box. The names of the wood were written on the lid – *rewarewa, kahikatea, totara, taraire, pukatea, matai* – lovely words that I repeated silently in my head.

I wasn't really emotional, because goodbyes were easy for me, but somehow my speech came out as if I was upset. Afterwards I felt as I had been acting.

The box was a perfect replacement for the plastic icecream tub that held my treasures, the box I had held onto so tightly when I thought *Aventura* would be lost on the Caribbean reef.

I said goodbye to Chris and then Lisa.

'I made that story up, you know,' she told me, biting on a fingernail. 'About killing my brother.'

'Oh.' I was amazed that someone could lie so well and so calmly.

'See ya,' she said, as if she didn't care, and she set off down the quay. I watched her go. I didn't really know what to make of her.

As we sailed north in a gale, sick as dogs because we had lost our sea legs completely, school and Lisa began to seem far away. Our old boat life was returning, just the same as ever. I wondered if it wasn't simpler away from the towns, with their horror films and cigarettes and other temptations that made you feel bad about yourself or just plain scared.

Pacific 1979–80

Betel
face'
madang

Tongan Boy

HIS ARM RESTED as heavy as wood on my shoulders as we sat together on top of the tall stone arch. A long time ago the ancient Tongan kings had this limestone hewn into blocks that were now stacked up rough, grey and pitted.

He was a Tongan boy, a few years older than me, and crew on the boat moored next to *Aventura* in Nuku'alofa harbour. His fellow crew had decided on a trip around Tongatapu island on a hired pick up truck.

'Come along,' they said to us.

'We've jobs to do,' said my parents. 'But Ivan and Doina you can go if you like.'

We stopped first to look at trees thick with colonies of flying foxes which flew up into the sky in great black clouds.

'Those belong to the king,' a woman said to me, 'and no one is allowed to hunt them.'

From there we visited the blowholes on the wild southwest of the island where

the sea pounded a flat rocky shelf along the coast and burst up through holes in the rocks in towering white plumes. After that came the visit to the arch.

'Climb up there, for a photo,' someone said to me. 'Sione, you too.'

I climbed up and sat on the grey stone. So did Sione.

'Put your arm around Doina!' they said, laughing. He looked at me without smiling and I looked back. He put his arm on my shoulders and let it rest there. It felt very heavy. The picture was taken and we both climbed down, without saying a word to each other.

'Don't worry about them,' said the woman who had told me about the foxes. She was younger than Mum and had a kindly face. 'They're just teasing.'

After that I was aware of Sione's presence; he often looked at me, but said nothing.

As the day drew to a close the group stopped for a meal. They had arranged with some Tongans to prepare a traditional oven, a pit dug into the earth and filled with hot stones, where they cooked food wrapped in banana leaves: suckling pig and fish, sweet potato and yam. There was beer too.

Nearby us a group of Tongans were laughing and talking loudly. They were men, at least I thought they were. Their hair was long, they talked in high voices and had gestures like women. I found them rather fascinating.

Some of the sailors in our group drank too much beer. The drunk ones started dancing, now with each other, and now with some Tongan women. A fight started between a Tongan man and a sailor who had been dancing with his wife. There was much shouting and the kindly woman grabbed my hand and Ivan's and led us back to the truck. Other people shouted it was time to go. Sione was there too.

On the ride back he sat beside me, quite close, so his arm lay next to mine, just touching it. That ride seemed to last a very long time, in the open back of the pickup, over the bumpy roads, in the warm night air. All I could think about was the touch of his arm. I kept very still, and talked to Ivan, reassuring him, as if nothing else was happening at all.

The following afternoon, I wandered off by the harbour wall to look at the mudflats. I climbed onto one of the boulders there and sat looking at the mud. I wanted, for some reason, to be on my own. I didn't feel like talking to anyone. Little crabs that had scuttled away when I approached, began to creep slowly back out of their mudholes. I watched them closely and stayed as still as possible. I began to be aware of this stillness, and how I was looking at the world. I felt as if I could remain there for hours, just be a pair of eyes, and take it all in.

But just as the crabs had gained the confidence to poke their eyes from the mudholes, Sione leapt down in one great bound onto the rock next to mine. The crabs vanished and then he could not understand why I was cross with him.

I could not stay cross for long. He himself was such a novelty to me. I never expected him to understand anything about the crab-watching and I did not even bother to try and explain.

'Hallo,' he said in a low voice.

'Hmm,' I said. Normally I could talk to other people easily, but my words had dried up. He said nothing more, just looked at me. I looked back and then stared again at the mud, but it wasn't the same, it was false now to be looking like that.

Then I wasn't sure I wanted to stay there alone with him and scrambled back up the bank.

That evening Ivan and I were invited to see Sione's boat, which was a big old-fashioned thing, with wide decks and rope ladders into the rigging. We sat in the roomy cabin with the rest of the crew who were young Australians and Americans, and sipped lemonade, listening to their music, their jokes and stories. When I talked to other adults I felt confident; that came of spending so much time with them, when children on other yachts were so few and far between. But with Sione, who didn't know much English, I didn't know what to say at all.

He passed me a scrap of paper and when I returned to *Aventura* I unfolded it. He had scribbled *I want you I need you*. The words had to have come from a song, I thought, he couldn't have made them up, and anyway, how can anyone want or need anyone else?

At the end of the next day, when he had finished his jobs on the boat, he came up on deck and talked to me. I found out that he was fifteen. He sat on his boat, and I sat on the edge of our wheelhouse with my feet on the lifelines.

There was a canvas awning slung over the main boom, which protected the cockpit from the sun and the rain when we were in port. We'd got it in New Zealand. It made a little tent on top of the wheelhouse and Ivan and I liked to sleep up there, pretending to camp.

'Let's sleep on the wheelhouse tonight,' I suggested to Ivan.

When everyone else was asleep I stayed up with Sione. He took hold of my hand and we sat there quietly, me on my boat and he on his. Once Dad got up, because he had to check everything was alright. He saw us but didn't say anything and I thought that was strange.

On the night before we were due to leave Sione and I sat together on the foredeck on his boat, his heavy arm around me, and his head bent close to mine. He tried to kiss me but I turned my face away; I hadn't the courage to find out what it would be like.

Playing with *Calao* in Vava'u

IN THE ANCHORAGE in Vava'u, the northern part of the Tongan archipelago, a familar boat was anchored off the shore.

'*Calao*!'

'Hallo!'

'*Salut les rosbif*!'

'See, we made it,' called Dad. 'We got your letter in New Zealand and here we are!'

'Jimmy, impeccable timing. We've only been here a few hours. Come over when you're ready and have a drink.'

'Doina, how much you've grown!' exclaimed Muriel as we clambered into *Calao's* cockpit.

'She's nearly as tall as me,' said Mum.

'A young lady, *une jeune femme*.' I smiled awkwardly.

Muriel gave us children drinks and when I said, '*Merci,* Muriel,' she laughed.

'*Mon dieu*! You speak French with a Tahitian accent now.'

'Come on,' said Sidonie, and we ran onto the foredeck. I didn't think she'd changed that much. Next to Fabien, who was only six, I did feel older and taller. He was just as chubby and blonde and little as I remembered, though he didn't seem so keen now to run up and down the deck.

'What shall we do?' I wondered. We talked in our old mixture of French and English, though there was more French added in now.

'Let's climb the mast,' Sidonie suggested.

'I don't want to,' said Ivan.

'Can I?' asked Fabien.

'*Non*, you're too little. *T'es trop p'tit*,' Sidonie told him firmly.

He stamped his little foot.

'Let's go,' Sidonie said to me. 'Brothers are so annoying!'

Calao's mast had little metal steps like on *Aventura* so it was easy to climb, but her mast was higher. Soon we were perched on the spreaders 25 feet above the sea. The adults in the cockpit below seemed very small.

'We could jump,' I said. The water looked tempting and being reunited with *Calao* had made me feel a little crazy.

'You first then. But I bet you won't.'

'I will too.'

My heart was pounding in my chest and my knees felt wobbly. I swallowed and launched myself into the air.

Wham! I hit the surface of the water hard and plunged underneath, my hands and feet smarting from the impact. I swam to one side and saw the adults staring. Erick was wagging his finger at me. Before I could register properly what my parents' reaction was, down came Sidonie.

She hit the water with an almighty crash, disappeared, and then came up spluttering and crying.

'*Aïe, aïe*, my legs hurt.'

'What were you thinking?' chorused the adults when we climbed back onboard. 'You could have hit the deck and killed yourselves!'

Sidonie and I looked at each other and grinned sheepishly. It had seemed like a

good idea but we didn't try it again, it hurt too much.

We went down below to their forecabin. Sidonie sang me a song she'd learnt during their time in the Marquesas, less of a song than a few words, and we didn't have a clue what they meant: *tu tu eh manu ta*. We danced the *tamuré* and Ivan and Fabien yelled *eh eh eh*.

I tried to teach them how to juggle like the girls in Mangareva had taught me, until we were told off by Muriel for dropping the fresh fruit.

Muriel asked if we wanted a snack, *un goûter*, and we stopped our play for sandwiches and glasses of milk. Fabien took such big gulps he ended up with a white moustache which made us laugh. We made up a song for him.

Mon petit mari
Il dors dors dors
Avec son longue barbe
Il snore snore snore
Quand il se leve
Et il se lave
Son longue barbe disparu!

My little husband
He sleeps sleeps sleeps
With his long beard
He snores snores snores
When he gets up
And he washes
His long beard disappears!

Muriel said the French wasn't very correct but we didn't mind.

'Can we go to the beach?' I asked when we'd finished.

'Okay,' said Mum, 'You are the oldest so you are in charge.'

'Great. Do I have to be?'

'Yes, you do!'

We jumped into our new fibreglass dinghy. Fabien squashed himself into the bow, I sat on the seat in the middle and Sidonie and Ivan at the back.

'Remember when Dad had to rescue us in Greece,' I said to Ivan, 'and he lost his tooth?'

'Yeah. We were rubbish at rowing then.'

'Let's row together. Try to go as fast as you can!'

Ivan and Sidonie put their hands on the oars, I pulled and they pushed.

'Ho heave ho,' Ivan and I sang, and Sidonie and Fabien joined in. 'Pull together ho heave ho.'

We went really fast. It was much more fun than the old inflatable which wouldn't go at all.

On the beach the boys gathered stones and bits of wood and amused themselves drumming while Sidonie and I practiced our dancing. Some local children came along to watch. They crept towards us and a boy grabbed Fabien's stick.

I stopped dancing and stared at the children. They stepped closer.

'Let's go back to the dinghy now,' I suggested.

One of the children threw the stick but it missed. I took Fabien by the hand and we ran for the dinghy and rowed away as fast as we could, leaving the children to watch us from the beach. Sidonie shouted at them then laughed her funny, gurgling laugh.

'We could sail instead,' Ivan suggested hopefully. He loved the new dinghy; he'd spent all his time in Nuku'alofa sailing around the harbour.

We put up the mast and centreboard and Erick helped Sidonie and Fabien get their Optimist ready and then we sailed the dinghies round the anchorage. We invented a good game, which was to catch the wind and pick up speed, and as the dinghy was sailing briskly along, one of us would shout 'now!' and we would jump into the water and let the dinghy go wherever she wished. Then we'd swim to her and haul ourselves back in like seals.

The next day we wanted to play with *Calao* straight away but Mum said we had to do school first.

From across the water we heard Muriel shouting 'Fab-*ien non!*'

'Muriel is just starting him on school,' Mum explained.

'I don't think he likes it very much,' commented Ivan.

'Well, he is only six.'

'He probably doesn't know what school is,' I remarked. 'He was too little when they left. All he knows is life on a boat.'

'They are doing a French correspondence course,' said Mum. 'I had a look at it. It's quite formal. They get the work by post and send back their homework.'

'They get homework!' I wondered if I would like that. 'Why don't we do a correspondence course?'

'Well, I trained as a teacher so I could teach you myself. And your school in London gave us lots of books. Anyway, time to get on with your own work. Erick has said we can have a go at spinnaker flying later.'

* * *

Work had really picked up for Dad now, and he was filing regular reports for English programmes on the BBC World Service and Radio New Zealand as well as writing for the *Pacific Islands Monthly* magazine. He had even got his very first cover photo. A letter came that *PIM* were going to use one of his photos of the replica *Bounty* on their cover.

'Actually on the cover,' Dad exclaimed. 'Can you believe it!'

'The cameras have started earning their money!' said Mum.

There was always something interesting to find out.

'I'm off to interview someone about a pig farm,' he announced. 'It's a cooperative and apparently they're using methane gas from the pig poo for cooking fuel.'

When he returned we could see him rowing from the shore with some difficulty.

'What on earth is in that dinghy with him?' exclaimed Mum. 'What has that man done now!'

We could all see a large shape propped up in the back. From a distance it looked like a totem pole. Soon enough we could see what it really was: a wooden statue of a man, as tall as me. Dad was grinning from ear to ear.

'Jimmy, what is that?'

'Meet Molitoni. Isn't he great?'

'You mean you bought him?'

'Yes, I met this woodcarver on the way back from the farm. I thought this statue was just brilliant. I'm naming him after the man who carved him.'

The statue was made from a single tree trunk, about five foot high, of a warrior with a tattooed face, poking out his long tongue.

'And where are we going to put him?'

'I'll think of something.'

Molitoni ended up in the aft cabin and he slept next to Mum in the double bunk. She called him Fred. 'He's my other man,' she joked.

* * *

Calao sailed with us to Samoa and the French island of Wallis and then we parted company. They were heading for Fiji and then Australia.

'We're even thinking of staying there,' Erick explained. 'I can't see myself going back to France to my old job working in an insurance office.'

'Guess we'll see you there then,' said Dad. 'You never know, we might decide to stay as well!'

Poetry in Samoa

MUM WAS READING about the Pacific travels of Robert Louis Stevenson and so when we arrived in Western Samoa she insisted we make the long climb up the hill above the capital Apia to the tomb of Tusitala, the Teller of Tales, as he became known here, where he lived for the final years of his life.

It was a long, hot walk but Ivan liked the climb. I remembered how he had shot up the hills around Machu Picchu, looking for Paddington Bear. Now the hill sapped my strength and left me tired and irritable.

At the top though, looking out at the view, my mood changed. Around us were hills, waterfalls, and lush jungle, while far below Ivan spotted a tiny dot in the harbour that was *Aventura*. Mum read aloud the verses which were inscribed on the white tomb.

Under the wide and starry sky
Dig the grave and let me lie.
Glad did I live and gladly die,
And I laid me down with a will.

This be the verse you grave for me:
'Here he lies where he longed to be;
Home is the sailor, home from the sea,
And the hunter home from the hill.

Those words filled me up and took away the annoyance of the long climb. I whispered them under my breath as we headed downhill.

Best of all, at the foot of the mountain was a pool with a waterfall cascading into it.

'Time for a pit-stop,' said Dad, but before he had finished speaking Ivan and I were already diving into the cool water. Fresh water was lovely after so much salt.

* * *

Perhaps those verses on the tomb had more of an influence on me than I expected. It was evening and we lay off the Samoan island of Upolu, slopping around in a dead calm. The day had been full of squalls massing one after the other black on the horizon.

'People think the tropics are just blue skies and trade winds.' Dad was getting increasingly frustrated. 'But this is just an absolute pain. We aren't going anywhere.'

He rushed up and down the deck, raising all the sails to catch the slightest breath in the calms, and then dropping them quickly and taking reefs in the mainsail when the squalls came. When a squall was about to hit we braced ourselves as the wild weather swept over us in a fury. The boat heeled over, masts and ropes protesting under the strain, and the wind beat the warm rain against our faces. Just as suddenly the squall swept on by, leaving the sails limp and the boat wallowing in the calm again.

As the sun dropped below the horizon and darkness flew over the sea, I felt my eyes taking it all in, just like I had observed the little crabs on the mud flats in Tonga. Everything I saw turned into words and I wrote a little poem, which was one of the first I ever wrote.

An evening at sea

Sunset
Gloomy sky
Black clouds
Sunset:
Drop sun
Drop wind
Drop sails
Calm
Sails flapping
Darker
Wary
No wind
Drop sail
Fly sheet
Wind gone
Lightning flashes
Across darkness
Across blue
Ocean, thunder

Darker
Blocks squeak
Drop sails
Drop wind
Drop sun
Thunder
Sea, sea
Sea
Gloomy
Clouds
Lightning flashing
Thunder at sea
Sea is still
Calm
Wind gone
Gone Ocean

Drop sun

Drop wind

Drop sails.

The Gilberts Turn into Kiribati

'EMPIRES JUST PLONK places together,' said Mum, 'without any regard for the people they're colonising.'

She was giving us a lesson on the Gilbert and Ellice islands as we travelled north.

'Tuvalu used to be joined with the Gilberts as one colony under British rule. But Tuvalu is part of Polynesia, while the Gilbertese are Micronesians, a quite different people altogether.'

'I'm guessing Micronesia means small islands?' I ventured. 'Just as Polynesia means many islands?'

She nodded.

'But what are the Gilberts going to be called when they become independent?'

'Kiribati. Pronounced *Kiribass*. Like *Gilberts* sounds in their own language.'

Having enjoyed the Tuvaluan celebrations so much the previous year, we all looked forward to witnessing the birth of a new nation.

However, it was not the same as before. Tarawa, the main atoll, was densely populated and there was not the family feel to the ceremonies as we had felt in Tuvalu. A different princess came, who discharged her duties as representative of the Queen efficiently, and was never ill or absent, and there was the excitement, the dancing and the feasts, but we did not feel quite such a part of it.

The canoe racing in the lagoon was pretty good though – the canoes went really fast. They had narrow wooden hulls that could hold two or three people, and each had a slim wooden outrigger for balance, on one side, fastened not by nails but lashings of sennit, rope made from coconut fibre. One crew member had to crawl right out onto the outrigger to balance it against the gusts of wind. Ivan and I climbed the main mast to watch and Mum said afterwards that she was sure the princess had

given us 'a good look over' while she was watching the canoe racing, 'probably because you kids were up the mast.'

Tarawa's beaches were littered with rubbish, some of it recent, but also the rusting remains of the Second World War, abandoned vehicles and amphibian craft from forty years before. Fighting had been fierce in this part of the world. Relics lay underwater too, and I went with Dad to snorkel over a sunken plane, overgrown with barnacles and weed. The propeller could still be seen, where now delicate anemones waved their tentacles, and little fish darted among the corroded blades.

Kiribati had at least given Dad plenty of journalistic work. And I celebrated my twelfth birthday there.

'This is for you,' Dad said, handing me a small package after a visit to the Tarawa post office. 'Filed under D for Doina, and some for me under J for Jimmy. That place is so disorganised!'

Granny had sent me a lettering pen and proper handwriting nibs. I wanted to show her what nice writing I had so I copied out my Samoa poem to send her.

'You've mastered that pen well,' said Mum.

I finished off the letter and was quite proud of it. But I didn't feel any different being twelve.

* * *

Time to turn and head south again, back over the equator. Leaving behind the busy, hot, overcrowded land, we sailed out into the clear and clean ocean. The nights were the best. Tiny creatures created luminescence in the waves that only appeared when the boat's hull disturbed the water. Then it was like sailing over a glittering Milky Way of stars, bright and tumbling through the dark salt sea. And above – well, those skies were magnificent. We switched off our navigation lights, so far were we from any shipping lanes, and so there was no light pollution anywhere to interfere with the glories of the stars above. I could have sailed on forever through nights like these, the only sounds the swish of the bow wave and the creak of a rope, the boat leaving a silver living trail upon the ocean that flared up for an instant and was then gone.

* * *

Mum and Dad had befriended the crew of two Australian yachts that had been moored alongside us back in Whangarei, all of three thousand miles away, and had inspired them to go to Tarawa too. *Tarrawarra* was a green boat with two young men crewing it, Tony and Kim, and then there was *Hagar the Horrible.* Gunter had built *Hagar* himself out of steel, and was single-handing. Ivan and I loved the fact that not only was *Hagar* painted bright orange (the only orange yacht we had ever seen), it was also named after a funny cartoon Viking.

A rendezvous was arranged with them a hundred miles south of Tarawa, on the Kiribati island of Abemama. Thanks to Dad's work, the island's assistant district officer, a young man named Kuria, offered to show us around.

'Can we see where Robert Louis Stevenson lived?' Mum asked. 'I've been reading about how he stayed here as a guest.'

'Aren't you going to say as a guest of whom?' said Dad. 'The local tyrant.'

'Tem Binoka,' said Kuria. 'We can see his grave, if you like.'

We walked along the white coral-sand road that cut across the middle of the island and looked at Tem Binoka's grave. He might have been a terrible tyrant but he'd seemed to get on alright with 'RLS' (as we'd started calling him). Kuria showed us a few stones that were apparently all that was left of RLS's house. I was beginning to get a bit bored of this, plus it was very hot.

'There's a dead whale on the other side of the island.'

That definitely sounded more interesting.

Kuria led us from the island's lagoon side to the windward, less protected coast. A flat shelf of dead coral and rock stretched towards the barrier reef, and ahead could be seen the round mass of the carcass. The wind was blowing away

from us and there was no smell. But within a hundred feet of the whale the ground began to be alive with fat white maggots.

'How did they get here?' Ivan and I wanted to know.

'The flies came, laid their eggs,' said Gunter. 'Maggots are the fly larvae.'

Now the smell began. I gasped and quickly put my hand over my mouth. It was the foulest thing I had ever smelt.

The whale was well rotted. The body shape had collapsed and most of the flesh had turned to a rotten yellow goo wriggling with maggots. The black skin was shrunken and split and the bones stuck up out of the mess.

'What sort of whale?' I wondered, trying to speak but keeping my hand over my mouth. I thought I might be sick if I breathed the smell in too much.

Gunter pointed at the head.

'See that square shape, and the long jaw,' he said. 'Sperm whale. Young one, I'd say. I wonder if there are any teeth. I wouldn't mind one.'

But the whale's jaws *gaped* empty. According to Kuria, one of the descendants of the tyrant who still lived on the island had the teeth.

This was not the first time I had seen dead things; lots of fishes had died in our cockpit, but this was different. This was a mammal. So much closer to us, so much bigger, so much rot. However, I was curious rather than disgusted. I stared – I wanted to take it all in and remember it.

I am twelve now, I thought, and here is death.

I imagined the whale's life, swimming deep and free. Surely it would be better to die at sea and sink down, not be stranded high and dry on the land. Better to have the fishes than the flies pick at your bones.

* * *

The following day the three yachts headed across the lagoon to a deserted islet on the reef.

'This is my sort of place,' said Mum as we walked along the white beach. 'An island all to ourselves.'

Kuria had said there were some wild piglets roaming about so Gunter set off hopefully with his knife. We could hear squealing and crashing about, but he came back empty-handed.

'I tell you what I did see though. There's a palm tree fallen over. I reckon we could cut out its heart for a salad. I'm going back to *Hagar* to get an axe.'

Gunter was a trained chef and knew a lot about food.

'Heart of palm,' said Mum longingly. 'I've heard of it but never tasted it. They call it millionaire's cabbage.'

'Why?' I asked.

'Because you have to cut down a whole tree to get one.'

I was glad the palm tree had already fallen down. I didn't like the idea of cutting down a whole tree for one salad.

While Gunter set about cutting out the heart of the palm tree, Dad, Kim and Tony took one of the dinghies over the reef to spear some fish.

Ivan and I collected driftwood on the beach for the fire. When we'd got the fire burning well I saw the divers coming back in the dinghy so I thought I'd swim to them. I left the clear blue water over the white sand and swam above a dark patch of coral. I didn't have my mask and the water was so dark I couldn't tell what might be moving underneath me. Suddenly fear seized up my arms and legs.

'Help!' I choked. I knew there was nothing there, but I was afraid.

'What is it?' Dad called, revving the engine faster. 'Is it a shark?' The dinghy reached me and they hauled me in.

'Nothing,' I gasped. 'Nothing.'

I felt stupid. How could I be afraid, when I'd been swimming in the sea for years? I didn't say anything to the adults but I knew it was that dumb shark film I'd seen with Lisa. With a mask I was okay, because then I could see underwater. But without it, swimming on the surface, I was scared. It was ridiculous.

There was plenty of fish in the bottom of the dinghy.

'We had a bit of an adventure,' began Dad.

'We'd caught lots of fish,' Kim interrupted, grinning. 'But Jimmy decided he wanted just one more.'

'There were a few white-tipped sharks about,' added Tony, 'but they weren't very interested in us.'

'I speared a lovely grouper,' said Dad. 'But it swam under a rock with the spear in it. I was going to dive down but the sharks went into a frenzy.'

'He got out of the water bloody quick, I can tell you!' laughed Kim.

'The blood from the fish made the sharks completely mad,' Dad went on. 'I've never seen anything like it. I did get my spear back in the end. Picked completely clean.'

'Scary,' I said.

'You've swum with white tips loads of times. You don't even remember. Once in Bora Bora lagoon, you'd a barracuda on one side and a white tip on the other. They took a good look at us then swam away.'

'Ooh.' I certainly couldn't remember that.

'Dad,' Ivan said, as the fish were gutted and prepared for cooking over the fire. 'Remember how you used to keep the fish on a ring on your belt, when we were in the Mediterranean?'

'Yes. I wouldn't do that now, I can tell you! The fish go straight into the dinghy.'

A metal grille was placed on the hot ashes, and grilled fish, accompanied by millionaire's cabbage salad, was washed down with the juice of green coconuts cut open by Gunter's useful knife.

'This needs a bit of rum,' said Kim.

'A-ha!' Gunter produced a bottle and added a shot of rum to each of the adult's coconuts.

'A toast,' he proposed. 'To the cruising life!'

'Perfect,' Mum said. 'Absolutely perfect.'

A Nukulaelae Welcome

MUM AND DAD were keen to spend some time in Tuvalu on our way back down to Fiji. In Funafuti Dad ferried his projector ashore and showed the films he'd shot the year before, to great acclaim.

'Finally, Jimmy, you got to use that projector we've been lugging round everywhere,' said Mum.

Then we said goodbye to *Tarrawarra* and *Hagar* and set off south to the island of Nukulaelae.

'Remember when we met them last year?' said Dad. 'They were cutting up turtles, and we gave them the photographs of the dancers. The island President, Tinirau, invited us to visit.'

Dad went to the radio hut in Funafuti and sent a Morse code message to the island.

'What are those for?' Mum asked when he returned with a box of tools.

'We have to take these with us. They've just got a secondhand generator, but it's not working. Anyway, I told them to expect us tomorrow. It's only 60 miles away.'

That afternoon *Aventura* made slow progress out of Funafuti lagoon against the tide. Once in the open sea it wasn't much better as both wind and current were against us. We sailed now on the port tack, now on the starboard, our course a zigzag as the wind wouldn't let us plot a course straight to the island.

'Hell,' said Dad as we went about yet again.

'What?'

'Do you know what today is?'

'What? Friday? So?' Mum said.

'Oh!' I had just realised what he was getting at.

'Exactly.' Dad finished tightening the rope at the winch and sat down. 'Haven't I always said, never leave on a Friday? And also, don't ever say what time you're going to arrive. There's no way we're going to get there tomorrow, if the wind stays like this.'

A second night passed at sea and in the morning we saw Nukulaelae. The island lay invitingly on the other side, beaches, palm trees, lagoon. But there was no anchorage and no pass through the barrier reef.

Four outrigger canoes paddled by strong young men came around the island from the sheltered lagoon side and shot out across the reef, dodging the breakers.

'Anchor here.' One young man waved his arm.

'Isn't it just a steep drop off?' Dad queried, but the depth sounder showed a small patch of about thirty feet depth. He let the anchor go.

'Welcome,' said the young man. 'I'm Tinirau's son. We've been waiting for you.'

Dad put on his mask and dove to check the anchor.

'It's stuck fast in the coral,' he said. 'But I think we'd better put down a second anchor to be sure anyway.'

Soon we were heading to the shore, each of us in a different canoe. The canoes shot fast over the reef, the young men judging the right moment and then paddling hard to avoid the worst of the breaking waves.

'We've only had one other yacht visit and that was about ten years ago,' Tinirau said, welcoming us to his house.

There were lots of women there – part of his family – and also two children a similar age to us, watching and smiling. Tinirau motioned to them to come over.

'This is Fuolo, my son. He is nine.'

'So is Ivan,' said Mum, and the two boys eyed each other up.

'And this is Lieli, my granddaughter.' Lieli smiled broadly. I liked her. 'Lieli means sunshine.'

Lieli was a bit younger than me and didn't know much English but it didn't matter. She took me down to the beach on the lagoon side of the island. Fuolo was showing Ivan one of the sailing outriggers, small enough for one child to sail.

Mum came to find me.

'We have to get ready to go to church.'

'I am ready.'

'No, we need to change. That's what everyone does.'

Some of Lieli's female relatives found clean outfits for us. Mum wore a dress that reached right down to her feet. Dad had to wear a pink wrap around *lavulavu*. At the church men sat on one side and women the other, while we children all gathered at the front. The singing was really beautiful.

Afterwards Dad was taken out to *Aventura* by canoe to get the projector and the tools so the generator could be set up in the *maneapa*.

That evening the *maneapa* was packed and a large sheet had been hung from the rafters as an improvised screen. The Super 8 films did not have any sound to go with the singing and dancing but that did not seem to matter. Many of the people watching had not been able to go to Funafuti for the independence celebrations and they burst out with shouts of laughter when they recognised themselves or people they knew.

Dad then showed some black and white silent films, Charlie Chaplin and Laurel and Hardy. The island children looked in wonder at the moving picture of a train, puffing and steaming across the screen.

Mum, Ivan and I stayed on shore that night.

'I'll go back,' said Dad. 'I can't leave *Aventura* on her own.'

Tinirau's house was traditionally built, like all the houses on the island, thatched with palm leaves and without any outside walls. There was almost no furniture except a few chests in which clothes were kept. People sat and slept on the floor on pandanus mats.

I lay on a mat and felt the warm air cover me. The land seemed so still, compared to the boat, though in fact there were the small noises of people sleeping, the whine of a dog, the whisper of wind through the palm trees.

'We're going to have dancing today,' announced Tinirau in the morning. 'To celebrate you being here.'

'I'm off with Fuolo,' said Ivan. 'Bye Mum.'

'Wait!' said Tinirau to the two boys. They stopped and looked at him solemnly.

'You are friends now and so you should swap names. You,' he put his hand on Ivan's shoulder, 'will be Fuolo now. And you will be Ivan.'

The boys broke out into laughter.

'Come on,' said Ivan-that-used-to-be-Fuolo, 'I'll teach you to sail an outrigger.'

'Okay,' said my brother. He was still my brother, whatever his name.

I rather wanted to learn to sail an outrigger too, but instead I stayed with Lieli.

The women had gathered piles of pandanus and fragrant frangipani flowers and were going to make garlands and decorations for the dancers. They sat comfortably on the ground beside the hut, one leg stretched out in front, and hooked strands of dry panda-nus leaf over their big toes, then began to twist it together, tucking in yellow-white frangi-pani, until the strip was long enough to go round the head. Leili's aunt made one for me as I sat and watched them work-ing. The sweet smell of the flowers filled my head.

A young man dressed only in a *lavulavu* passed by and said something that made them giggle. He looked at me in a knowing sort of way which made me feel quite awkward. I wondered what he had said.

'He thinks you would make a good –' Lieli's aunt paused and tried to think of the word. 'Wife.'

They all laughed and I tried to laugh too but I felt terribly self conscious. I was glad the young man had walked on and wasn't looking at me any longer.

I wished I was smaller, that I could disappear; my body felt too big for me, ungainly, there was too much of it, too much of me. I wished I could be off playing like Ivan, skinny and not noticed.

The dancing, however, made me forget this. I loved it. Afterwards, Lieli and I gathered up some garlands and skirts of pandanus strips and she tried to teach me. We spent ages turning our hands in the air and I tried to copy the facial expressions that the dancers used as well as their bodies to convey the meaning of the dance.

'You have expressive eyebrows,' Lieli's aunt told me, laughing.

'I've never heard of anyone being complimented on their eyebrows before,' smiled Mum.

'Well, you inherited them from me,' added Dad, 'so I should be proud. They are the best dancers in Tuvalu, after all, so they know what they're talking about.'

Lieli and I just kept on dancing.

We spent a second night ashore, Dad on the boat. Lying there in the quiet, I felt at home and wished that we could stay.

But that was not to be. Out beyond the reef, poor *Aventura* was rolling in the big swell, completely unprotected from whatever the sea might throw at her.

'We have no insurance – if anything happens...' Mum left the sentence unfinished. All we owned was on the boat, was the boat.

'I know,' Dad sighed. 'And the wind is getting up...'

I could see they wanted to stay as much as me. But we had to leave.

With flower garlands on our heads, we headed out to sea on the outriggers. We had presents of dancing skirts, pandanus fans, and even a model outrigger for Ivan from Fuolo.

A few of the young men came on board to have a quick look at the boat, which was as interesting to them as their island lives were to us. I hadn't been aboard for two days – I went below to tidy our cabin for sea. One of the men followed me. He was familiar – I had seen him on shore several times. He'd made the joke about me to Lieli's aunt.

'My name is...'

I heard some Polynesian word but didn't catch it. He was tall and he seemed to fill the little cabin. I stared not at his face but at his bare chest. It was brown and smooth and I would have liked to have touched it with my finger.

'...it means Waves.'

I couldn't look at his face. I looked down, at the scattered toys and books, and saw his strong hand gripping the side of the bunk. I smelt a fresh salty odour that was somehow pleasing.

He said something else. In my confusion I was sure it sounded like 'I love you.' That was too much for me.

'We must go,' I said and managed to get past – he stepped aside for me. I went into the cockpit and busied myself doing something and would not look at him as he came out of the cabin. He and the others climbed back into their canoes. Dad was already hoisting the anchor and the boat was heading out to sea, her movement now fitting into the waves instead of fighting them when she was tethered by an anchor chain to the land. Mum took off her garland and threw it with a great sweep of her arm into the sea. Ivan and I did the same. The garlands bobbed in the wake of the boat, foam curling around the sweet-smelling flowers.

'They say you can make a wish and hope you will return,' she whispered, taking her place at the wheel.

I watched the garlands, and the canoeists, rapidly getting smaller as the wind blew us away. I kept thinking about the smooth chest of the young man. Why had he said that to me? I felt unsettled and confused. New feelings, but also, a new realisation: this was my life. Things happened in the blink of an eye and then were gone, bobbing away on the white wake behind us.

All that was left was the sea.

Thank You Granny

24.8.79
Suva Yacht Club
Fiji

Dear Granny,

Thank you very much for the books. Books are about three times more expensive here than in England. Once I have read this one, I will have read all the books about the *Swallows and Amazons*. I have just finished reading the *Lord of the Rings* for the second time. It is one of my favourite stories.

For my birthday, among other things, Mum and Dad gave me a notebook. In this I write poems. When I turn out a good one, I'll send it to you.

It is great being back on familiar ground – actually, water! I am sure Suva is one of my favourite places so far.

I think that the Gilbert's Independence wasn't half so nice as Tuvalu's. For a start the place was two big. No – <u>too</u> big! Sorry about all the mistakes. If Dad is going to sack his typewriter, I'll sack my pen – or, myself?!

Ever since the wastelands of Tuvalu and Kiribati, it has been wonderful. Raw carrots – mmmn! – they're really nice, crisp and crunchy. And delicious ice cream! We never stopped talking about what we'll eat in Fiji. Fresh salad, meat.... it is really nice after papaya and breadfruit.

And mountains galore! We're all sick of 'paradise' – coconut trees, sandy beaches, etc. etc. It's quite nice having a bit of drizzle and cold. When we drove to somebody's house, I really appreciated the vegetation – so different. Before I thought it just for silly grownups to admire vegetation. (I am becoming a rebellious teenager!).

Next week, 'Hurricane' will be on. It will be funny seeing Dad in it! And the set – we'll recognise all the tricks – plastic palms, and the false waves – created in a pool. We're sure to recognise other people too.

Love kisses and hugs, Doina

P.S. At first I felt no difference being twelve, but I slowly am.

Friday 24th August

Dear Granny,

Thank you very much for the book. I chose *Swallows and Amazons* and Doina took *Pigeon Post*. I'm not sure about the jack with the white border. But the St George's flag is to show that it is English not Scottish or Welsh.

After New Zealand we went to Tonga, Samoa, Wallis, Tuvalu, Gilberts and Fiji. I was so glad to get back to Fiji and have an ice cream.

Our last stop before Fiji was Nukulaelae. In the Tuvalu group last year my father met the president of Nukulaelae who said that somewhen maybe you might come to my island Nukulaelae. Anyway we had a fantastic time there and I went for a sail in an outrigger canoe. The sailing canoes are very interesting. To go about they lift up the mast and put it in the other end of the boat. Then they start sailing the other way. When the wind gets too strong somebody goes out to the float.

Yours
Ivan Cornell

Fiji is the Same but I am Not

JUST LIKE THE year before I'd enjoyed being in the Fijian capital Suva because there were so many children to play with in the gardens of the Royal Suva Yacht Club, kids from boats, kids from ex-patriate families that worked in Fiji. Now I was one of the oldest, but I still liked to run barefoot on the grass, and swing as high as I could on the swings.

But it wasn't quite the same as before. When I walked down the street Fijian  men often whistled at me; and people we hadn't seen during our months up north said 'Haven't you grown!' as if it were a compliment. But it only made me feel awkward and self-conscious.

I noticed new things. In town, how the young Indian men wore the latest fashion, high-waisted trousers tight about their bottoms and narrow hips, and widely flared below the knee. On *Aventura*, when sailors came for drinks, the men always sat with their legs wide apart, and sometimes from the sides of their shorts you could see their hairy balls squeezing out, which was rather disgusting, but also interesting, from a detached, scientific point of view.

And on the yacht club lawn, two dogs stuck together, mating, for what seemed a very long time, until someone chased them away.

The world was definitely not as straightforward as it used to be. I didn't think of it as good or bad, I just thought – oh, that is the world. Interesting. Like those photos of naked women in the American magazines, in that Maine tree house, the poor boy having a fit in New Zealand, the dead Abemama whale. Details of life and death that you couldn't learn from books.

* * *

There was a pool table in the club house, but the children weren't supposed to use it. Sometimes we tried to sneak in and have a go at potting some of the balls, but generally one of the bartenders would come and tell us off. There was one, a rather fat Indian man, to whom we took an especial dislike.

'I don't like that guy at all,' someone said. The man had just kicked us out and a few of us were hanging around outside the swings.

'I know which is his car,' said an older boy.

We crept towards the car park. We didn't have anything much in mind. On the way, however, the older boy, whose name was Robert, picked up a dead insect from the ground. It was some sort of grasshopper, very black and as long as my hand. The window of the man's car was slightly wound down, and Robert quickly threw the insect onto the driver's seat. Ivan and the younger children ran off to the swings, giggling about what we'd done. I wandered back more slowly with Robert.

'I wonder what that man will say when he looks in his car?'

'I dunno.' Robert shrugged. 'It was funny though.' He hesitated and looked at me. 'D'you want to go for a walk?'

'Where?'

'Just over there, towards the dinghy dock.'

'Okay.' I hadn't anything else to do. I picked up my flipflops and swung them in my hands.

'Don't you like to wear shoes?'

'Not really. I don't wear them on the boat.'

I pointed out where *Aventura* was, swinging on her anchor in the crowded anchorage.

'I live in Suva,' he said. 'I'm English, but my parents are working here. They're club members though. How old are you?'

'Twelve.'

'Oh. I'm fourteen.'

We walked slowly along the pontoon and looked at the assortment of dinghies tied up there.

'That's my parents' boat.' He pointed to a little motorboat that was anchored near the shore in water too shallow for the yachts to go. 'I'm allowed to use it. We could motor over to the next anchorage if you like. Maybe tomorrow?'

'Yeah,' I said. 'I'll ask my parents.'

I could tell that Robert liked me. But I couldn't help thinking, that his white skin was too pale and flabby. Not brown and beautiful like Waves. Though at least he was not as intimidating as Waves had been.

Ivan was friendly with Robert's younger brother, so the two of them came along too, and in the little boat we chugged across the bay. When the time came to return I stood beside Robert at the steering wheel. He tried to put his arm around me and I moved away. I was embarrassed that people might see us.

After that it was awkward between us on the return journey. When we got back to Suva, and the younger brothers jumped off and ran to the swings, Robert lay on the cockpit seat moping and wouldn't talk to me. I looked at him. I didn't know what to make of him or what I ought to do. So I didn't do anything.

'Bye then,' I said.

'Bye,' he mumbled.

Only later, when I was back on *Aventura*, I wished that I could have thought of something to say.

Robert was better the next day.

'Do you want to go to the cinema?' he asked me.

'Well,' I said. 'We're actually supposed to be going to see *Hurricane*. My Dad had a part in it when we were in Bora Bora. But okay.'

We went with my parents and the two younger brothers, so it didn't seem quite like a proper date. In the cinema Robert sat next to me and his knee touched mine. He reached out and took hold of my hand. His hand was warm and slightly sweaty. My heart beat faster; I rather liked the sensation.

In the film a huge hurricane battered a Pacific island, backdrop to a love affair between an islander and a white woman. The Fijian audience fell about laughing because the special effects of what were supposed to be raging winds and breaking giant waves were so unlike any real hurricane they had ever seen; and they had seen many.

'Where are you?' we whispered to Dad.

Finally for a few brief seconds he appeared on screen as a grinning American sailor dancing with the local girls.

'That was the beginning and end of my Hollywood career,' he said afterwards.

That evening the yacht club put on one of its regular barbecues and the adults sat outside in the garden chatting and drinking beer. The children ran about, playing hide and seek.

'Come on,' said Robert, pulling me by the hand. Together we wandered off to a dark part of the club yard. We lay down on the grass. He wanted to kiss me then and I let him.

I felt a new desire wash through me like the sea. I didn't understand it at all, but I accepted it.

* * *

Suva was always busy for my parents. Mum packed up a pile of our souvenirs like the Molitoni statue from Tonga and had them shipped back to the UK to make the boat a bit lighter. She bought lots of cheap material for making clothes as well.

'Can I sew something?' I asked.

I made myself a pair of baggy trousers out of cheesecloth. Mum said my first dressmaking effort was very good.

'We've finished our Suva jobs,' Dad said at last, 'let's go and find a quiet place

where I can write my programmes. I've got a ton of catching up to do, all that happened to us in Kiribati and Tuvalu.'

'I agree. Too many sailors just get stuck here in Suva when there's a whole archipelago out there to explore. And I need to finish writing my own article about RLS.'

I knew that time was coming again. I had to say goodbye to Robert. Always the same, I thought.

'This is for you,' he put something small into my hand. It was a tiny turtle, carved of Fijian rainwood.

'That is lovely, really lovely.' I thanked him and kissed him.

'I'll miss you,' he said.

'Sorry, Robert.' I didn't know what else to say.

He took hold of my hand for a moment. 'You'd better go then.'

'Bye,' I said.

Afterwards I thought, maybe I said bye too happily. I walked down to where my parents were getting into the dinghy and looked back at him. He stood there rather sadly and raised a hand. I waved back. I couldn't pretend to myself that I was upset. I wasn't. I wondered what it would be like, for once, to be the person on the shore, staying put and waving goodbye.

The turtle went into my wooden treasure box from New Zealand alongside the photo of me and Sione on the stone arch. It was beginning to be like a box of farewells.

Exploring the Fijian Archipelago

EAST OF SUVA, the island of Taveuni is the only place in the world where the International Dateline crosses the land. We had already sailed across the line several times, going west and going east, losing or gaining a whole day. Now we stood in front of a sign that pointed one way for 'today' and one way for 'yesterday'. We had a foot in both.

'We're at 180° longitude,' said Dad. 'That means we are 180 degrees away from the zero meridian which runs through Greenwich in London. A stone's throw from the Royal Albert Docks, where we set off. It feels like a turning point. Until now, going west took us further away, but now we'll be getting nearer again.'

'Four years since we left,' added Mum. 'And we've only gone halfway around the world.'

'Will it take us another four years to get back?' I asked.

My parents looked at each other.

'Who knows? Will we go back? Maybe we'll never stop...'

I thought about all that happened to me in the last four years. I was standing on my own personal dateline now, I was here and there, I was today and tomorrow. And it was very confusing.

* * *

The channels between the Fijian islands were full of fish and four times we caught a big fish on our trailing lure only to lose it again. Each time Dad held the line taut, and Mum was supposed to hook it with the gaff hook behind the gills so he could hoist the fish on board. She approached each big thrashing fish so gently with the gaff she never managed to get the hook in. Four times the fish got away.

Dad was getting fed up. Then we caught a shark. It was big, maybe a six-footer. He put on his gloves and heaved it to the side of the boat.

'I can't land this thing,' he said through gritted teeth, holding the line with all his strength. 'But I want my lure back.'

The shark thrashed against the hull with the strength of a monster; it had a shovel-like head and grey sandpaper skin, mean tiny eyes and a powerful hooked tail like a scythe.

'Get my knife!' yelled Dad.

Mum grabbed the boat knife, which was always kept ready for emergencies in a cubby hole near the cockpit. She knelt on the deck, reaching down hesitantly to those terrible jaws. Suddenly the shark snapped its mouth, and was gone, lure and all. She stood up, white in the face.

Dad was very angry because of the lure being lost.

'That was my best lure! Manu gave to me, in Mangareva.'

'It's not Mum's fault,' I said. I would answer him back, even if Mum wouldn't.

'Don't interfere,' he said sharply.

I said nothing more, but in a flash I saw my parents so clearly; they were individuals with faults like anyone else. Dad was too quick to anger and criticism. And Mum gave in to him too easily. For twelve years, I thought, I've accepted them as they are. That they were perfect, and always right. Now I was not so sure.

* * *

Dad's outburst passed as quickly as a tropical squall and soon the usual harmony reigned again between my parents. Off the island of Vanua Mbalavu we discovered

what we'd been looking for, a place hidden away from yachts and other people, a collection of islands and little rocky islets. *Aventura* was moored between three islets with a rope tied to each one, snuggled right in and as protected as could be. The only sound was the water slapping under the rocks as the tide came in, and for this reason the place was called the Bay of Chuckling Waters. We all agreed it was one of the most perfect anchorages we'd been in so far.

Mum had given Ivan and me the task of drawing a map of the islets and shallows and we spent all our time in the dinghy sailing around the protected waters, exploring the little islands. We found lots of caves where the sea had eroded the rock. One cave we could only get into at low tide, by lying flat in the dinghy. On one of the islets nearest to *Aventura* we discovered a shallow cave above water. We scrambled up the rocks and and sat inside, looking down at the boat.

'Remember when we camped in New Zealand?'

'Let's do it again.'

'We won't get our feet wet this time!'

'For sure. And it's warm. We don't even need a tent.'

We tied our few possessions to a rope and hoisted them up from the dinghy. Neither of us wanted to go to sleep and kept whispering 'Good night', each wanting to be the last to say goodnight. I spoke in an ever quieter whisper hoping Ivan would not hear me, but then he answered back and so I had to reply. The competition went on a long time and it was a game we often repeated when lying in our bunks in our tiny cabin, waiting for sleep to come.

Deeper into Melanesia

FIJI WAS LEFT BEHIND, as we headed west for Vanuatu and from there to the Solomon Islands and Papua New Guinea: a long curve up through the southwest Pacific and the islands of Melanesia. It was six months since we had left New Zealand, and the hurricane season was coming again. We had to move north, and get ourselves out of the zone. A few yachts didn't bother to do this.

'Oh, it's fine,' the captain of one said to Dad.

Months later, we heard his yacht had been smashed to bits in the first hurricane of the season.

* * *

In Port Vila, Vanuatu, the usual lot of kids played about on the waterfront. A little Australian girl on another boat had just had her fifth birthday so there'd been a party with food and games for all the children.

'Let's have a dinghy race!' someone suggested. That kept Ivan busy.

I stayed on the quay. A man came and sat nearby. He was much older than Dad, a white man, and I thought he was from one of the other boats, though I wasn't sure.

'You've got lovely eyes,' he told me, smoking a cigarette and smiling. His teeth were very yellow.

'Thank you,' I said politely. He smelt of stale smoke. I didn't like him at all.

The other children, who were all younger than me, were talking about eating pizza.

'Do you like pizza?' the man asked. 'Maybe we could go for one sometime.'

I deliberately misunderstood this invitation to mean all the children. Though I knew what he meant.

'No, just you,' he insisted. I laughed lightly, as if I still didn't understand, and ran off with the others. It wasn't like what happened with Waves or Sione or Robert; this was just unpleasant.

I was reminded of the shopkeeper, long ago in Greece, when I was about eight. Nothing happened to me but a girl I'd got friendly with told me that he'd tried to put his hand in her pants in the back of the shop. She and I didn't go near the shop again. But we never told anyone either. There were creepy men like that in the world, I knew. You just had to try and avoid them.

It All Blows Up in Honiara

I MET MARIA laughing at the 'whiteys' who got off the cruise ship and walked down the main street of Honiara, capital of the Solomon Islands. The women wore very short shorts that showed their fat white thighs right up to where their buttocks began, and the men's legs were skinny and hairy and pale. I could hardly believe that people could be that white.

'They shouldn't dress like that,' I said to Maria primly. My parents had said it was against the Pacific custom. For a woman to show her thighs and bottom was far worse than going bare-breasted. I'd seen women bare-chested in some remote islands where missionaries hadn't yet persuaded them to cover themselves up; for them, breasts were just functional, for feeding babies.

Those white tourists made me indignant. I don't know if Maria felt the same. But she did laugh with me.

She was Australian and she lived on a yacht that was anchored off the Honiara Yacht Club like we were. She was sailing with her father and stepmother and her half-brother.

'I like your shorts,' she said.

'Thanks. I made them of an old nightie. I quite like sewing.'

I pointed at the colourful bracelets on her wrist, made out of twisted pieces of string and wool.

'I like those too. Did you make them?'

Maria nodded and smiled. She looked quite different from me. Her hair was a mousy brown colour and she had a flat chest and a thick waist. Her skin was much whiter than mine, so I don't know why she laughed at the white tourists. Maybe because those people lived on land. As far as she and I were concerned, they seemed to belong to a very different, far away world.

We spent the afternoon plaiting friendship bands which we tied round our wrists and ankles, and talking about the places we had been to. We went for a swim off the Yacht Club beach. A young man swam out to join us.

'Hallo,' he said, rather shyly. Maria and I looked at each other, giggled, and then dived back into the sea, and swam out to the boats.

Later I saw the young man working behind the club bar. The following day, when we swam off the beach, he came over to us again.

'Hi, I'm Joseph,' he said in a quiet voice. 'It's my afternoon off.'

Joseph said he was eighteen but he didn't seem that old; he was not much taller than us girls. He had a round, innocent-looking face, and he wore his hair slightly long, haloing round his head, like most Melanesians did in those days. His skin was very black, and when it was wet from the water it almost glistened grey in the sunlight.

He swam and chatted with us until it was time for him to go to work. After that we met him most days and swam together off the beach. One day when Maria had to go shopping with her mother, Joseph and I swam together under the quay, out of sight. I let him hold me but he wanted to kiss me with his tongue.

'It is the custom of our people,' he said. But I would not open my mouth.

We met again the next day. This time he held me closer; his hand crept over my body. I pushed his fingers away from slipping under my bikini. I did want to be with him but I wasn't ready for that.

Later on Maria and I talked about it.

'How can people do it? How could two adults bear to look at each other afterwards?'

'I don't know,' said Maria. 'It's just too embarrassing.'

'What about our parents –' I stopped. I couldn't go on. Maria put her hand over her mouth.

'No,' she said, 'I can't even think about that! Yuck!'

I didn't see Joseph for a few days. Dad was on his usual tireless hunt for stories and we trekked across the island to find a war hero. Honiara was on the island of Guadalcanal, where the fighting during the Second World War between the Americans and the Japanese had been especially bloody. The sea bed was so thick with the wrecks of ships one stretch of water was called Iron Bottom Sound. In the end Dad got the interview he wanted, with Sir Jacob Vouza, who helped provide intelligence during the war, hiding out in the jungle, and had been captured, tortured and left for dead, though he managed to escape, and reveal the enemy's position to the Americans. When Dad spoke to him, he had just been knighted by the Queen.

That was my parents' world. Some of it did rub off on me. There were always stories told round the dinner table on *Aventura* about politics and history and the wider world.

But I also had my own little story that was going on at the same time. Though I kept Joseph to myself. I didn't talk about these things with my parents.

Joseph had asked me several times if I would go with him to get our photographs taken.

'So I can remember you, when you go,' he said.

I agreed in the end.

'Only if Maria comes,' was my one condition.

The three of us walked some way into town, to the photographer's studio. We posed for a colour photograph on bright green plastic grass besides plastic flowers in flower-pots. Joseph stared straight ahead, smiling, his arms stiff by his sides. Maria looked to one side and didn't smile.

'I hate having my photo taken,' she whispered to me.

A few people were waiting their turn and watched us, which made me feel uncomfortable. The second picture was taken in black and white. I sat on a chair and I looked down at the ground. Joseph stood behind me, with one hand on the back of the chair. It felt as if we were posing for an old-fashioned oil painting.

The photographs took most of the afternoon. Back at the yacht club Maria went back to her boat and I thought maybe it was time I got back as well, but Joseph persuaded me to stay. He pulled me to the side of the clubhouse and into a toilet cubicle.

'I dreamed about you,' he said, 'and –' but he didn't finish the sentence. It began to be awkward. I wasn't ready to do anything more than a kiss or two.

'Don't go,' he said.

'I have to,' I told him and rowed back to the boat.

My parents were furious. I'd disappeared with the dinghy all afternoon.

'Where have you been?' shouted Dad. 'You never said where you were going!'

Mum's face was twisted with disapproval. 'It seems like every place we go to now, you get involved with boys. What are we to do with you!'

I couldn't reply. Suddenly the whole weight of what I had done fell down on me like a rock. It was exactly the same as when I'd got caught shoplifting in Annapolis.

'*Why* did you do it? *Why*?' Dad was shouting like he had before. Mum's twisted and disapproving expression was exactly the same as before. But just the same as before, I didn't know why. There weren't any *reasons*. I didn't think about it before it happened. I just did it. Couldn't they understand that?

'I don't know why,' was all I could say. 'I don't know.'

The row went on and on.

'It's not just the boys,' said Mum. 'It's getting harder for me to teach you now. You're nearly thirteen, you should be at secondary school. Maybe it's time to send you back to England, to go to school and make friends.'

'We've been thinking about this,' Dad added. 'You could go back to England. Would you like that?'

'I don't know.' I'd never thought about it before.

'We know it's hard for you,' Mum went on, 'not having proper friends, stuck with us all the time.'

'And we're all suffering because of it. It can't go on like this.'

'Yes. It's up to you. What do you want to do?'

I really didn't know what to think. Thoughts whirled around my head. On and on we talked. The row about Joseph was left far behind.

'You're old enough now, Doina, to make up your own mind. You could go back if you want, to school. You could stay with Granny in Cornwall. And we'll sail the boat back.'

'What do you think? It's your decision.'

Ivan was given the choice as well. He had been restless too, and he missed having the company of boys his age.

My head started spinning with possibilities. Going to a real school, having friends for more than a few days, and having my own room. That was all so tempting. But one thought rose above all the rest.

'But if I did that,' I began slowly. 'I wouldn't finish the circumnavigation, would I?'

'No, you wouldn't.'

There was silence, for the first time in hours. I realised in a flash what I wanted.

'I want to stay. I want to finish sailing around the world.'

'What about you, Ivan?' He had sat there quietly, listening. 'What do you want?'

'I want to keep sailing.'

So the family struck a bargain. If Ivan and I stayed, and were good, our parents would get us back to England as soon as possible. And Mum would try to find a correspondence course, to give me a bit more challenge with my schoolwork.

'I'll try to stay out of trouble,' I promised. I agreed that what I had done with Joseph had been stupid. 'I'll try to be more sensible.'

Until then Mum and Dad had never thought of the end. The date for going back to England had never been set. If it wasn't for us, maybe they would have sailed on for much longer.

The row, in the end, was good. It cleared the air and we all knew where we stood. We were good at arguments. Good at having them and good at getting over them too.

For the very first time, returning to England became a real, living idea for me.

Funnily enough, Maria's parents hadn't been very bothered by her absence. They were leaving anyway; *Aventura* as well. We'd only stayed about ten days in Honiara but the anchorage was not well protected and we were between seasons so the wind came from every direction and Mum and Dad wanted to move on.

Before we left, Joseph came to say goodbye, and he gave me prints of the two photographs as well as a silver chain for me to wear. I thanked him and put it round my neck. When I got back to my cabin I took it off and put it into my wooden box, along with my other treasures.

Playing with Custard

'CUSTARD,' SAID IVAN. 'That's what I dream about.'

We were lying in our bunks talking, as we often did, before we fell asleep. What would life be like back in England? We remembered Granny's steamed puddings, and the old TV advert for golden syrup pudding I still remembered from our London days. Custard, though, was what Ivan loved best, and in Honiara Mum managed to get hold of some custard powder as a treat for him.

But custard resulted in one of the worst accidents of our voyage so far. We had left Honiara and were motoring across a wide lagoon.

'Can we make some custard?' we asked, and Mum agreed, as the sea was calm, and it was hours to the next anchorage. We warmed some milk on the gimballed cooker until it was nearly boiling, then added it to the custard powder mixture and boiled it some more.

'I'll pour the custard,' I said.

'No I will,' insisted Ivan.

There may have been a bit of a struggle. Afterwards, I couldn't remember. Suddenly the boat made a little movement, Ivan's hand slipped and the hot custard poured onto his bare chest. He screamed and Mum leapt down the companionway. It was hard to get the sticky custard off his skin quickly and he was badly burnt. Mum wrapped bandages across his chest, criss-crossing his body like a wounded soldier. And I got told off by Dad.

'Good thing you keep the medicine locker well-stocked,' he said to Mum.

'I know. Thankfully until now we haven't needed it much.'

As a trained pharmacologist Mum knew a lot about medicine, though our medicine locker was mostly only used for knocks and scrapes. Those were bad enough. We'd been in the tropics so long, we'd lost our immunity to infections, and the tiniest scratch went septic. Dad had it worst, as he was always bashing his legs on coral reefs when he went snorkelling.

It didn't help that we were in and out of the water all the time. I still suffered from eczema, which had stung so badly all those years ago in the Dead Sea, and the constant warm weather and salt water meant that the soles of my feet and my palms were cracked and sore. Sometimes I took a pillowcase and rubbed and rubbed my fingers until they were raw. The pain felt better than the itching.

Once I had a large spot on my arm that grew red and inflamed.

'Squeeze all the pus out,' Mum told me.

I squeezed and an enormous amount of thick yellow pus oozed out. Squeezing was very satisfying. I kept on until the yellow turned into red blood. Only when I had cleaned it with antiseptic did I see that there was a neat hole in my arm, a perfectly round circle that I stared at with equal horror and fascination.

I got the same feelings from peeking into Mum's copy of *The Ship's Doctor*, a book that described all the possible diseases a common sailor might encounter.

There were colour photos too, of serious wounds and swollen body parts, photos so horrid I could only look at them with my eyes squeezed almost shut.

Now we were sailing deeper into Melanesia we had to take a daily dose of chloroquine as prevention against malaria which was a real risk in this part of the world.

'Yuck. This is *so* bitter,' I said, trying to wash the tablet down with my morning cocoa.

Dad handed me a fluoride tablet.

'Oh no,' I screwed my face up. 'I hate those too.'

'Well, you have to take them, for your teeth. We can try dissolving it in the cocoa if you like.'

'Okay,' I said. That was no better: it just formed a gritty mess at the bottom of the mug.

'You're going to have to eat that,' I told Ivan, as Dad handed us a spoon. We both held our noses and swallowed the horrible stuff.

Sailors had their own remedies too. In Port Vila we had met an elderly Englishman who was sailing around the Pacific on a tiny wooden boat that had no engine and was so small you couldn't even stand up inside. My parents invited him over for a drink and I noticed he had a piece of paper stuck to his leg.

'Toilet paper,' he explained, noticing where I was looking. 'Spit on a bit of loo paper. The best thing for those tropical infections.'

* * *

Not long after the custard accident we anchored off a village called Ugeli on Rendova Island. A little islet shaped like a tear created a protected anchorage. When we arrived the sea was crowded with children. They were paddling little dugout canoes, which were only big enough for one or two of them.

'Look! One kid canoes!' I shouted and waved at the children who all waved back.

As soon as we had anchored they came over to say hello. Four girls invited me into their canoe, which was then so low in the water we were nearly sinking. An-

other girl swam up, and we pulled her in, because the game was to make the water go over the canoe's sides and sink it on purpose. Then we all tipped ourselves out. The wooden canoe never sank completely, even when it was full of water.

The girls showed me how to get most of the water out without having to bother returning to the shore. We swam alongside the canoe and pushed it back and forth fast, until most of the water sloshed over the sides, then we slid in and bailed the rest out with our hands. When most of the water was out we started the sinking game all over again.

Ivan could not swim because of his burns and bandages so he assembled his train track on the aft deck, helped by a group of Ugeli boys.

'I don't suppose they've seen a toy train before,' Mum said to Ivan later. 'And I wouldn't be surprised if you're the first white children they've met.'

Another favourite game was to paddle up to the end of the islet, grab a palm tree leaf from the shore, then hold it up as a sail and cruise all the way to the other end of the islet, pushed by the wind. There a huge coconut tree hung over the water, which we climbed and then leapt as far as we could into the sea, yelling with delight.

I really liked Ugeli. The local children included us in all their games, and didn't ever seem to stop playing. Of course, they did go to school, so we went along too. Ivan and I were always glad to make friends with other children. Children on boats were so few and far between, and in the remote places we visited we hardly saw any other boats anyway.

Becoming a Poet

THE LANDSCAPE OF the Solomons was quite different from the Pacific we had grown used to. Instead of low sandy islands and a few palm trees, these islands were high, and covered in dense rain forest. The green trees crept right to the water's edge, and often kept going, as mangroves spread their roots into the water. As we wound northwards through the archipelago, I spent hours on deck watching the lush green of the land pass by.

One day I found myself staring at the tropical landscape as if I was seeing it for the first time. The palm trees on the tops of the hills looked to me like giant feather dusters, and words came into my head that I kept repeating as we motored on. I kept on adding words, until I had a little poem:

Pluck a feather duster palm tree,
Put it in your cloudy hair,
Sweep away
the cobwebs clinging
to the windswept sky.

Wash away the grime of moon-dust,
In an emerald-jewel lagoon,
Sun heat will
soon warm you gently
basking on the Milky Way.

Nibble stars, the choicest fruits there,
Glittering silver, sweet with brightness,
Travel down
the cloud-paved highway
to your palace on the moon.

I wrote it down, and then Dad let me borrow his old typewriter, on which he bashed out the scripts for his articles and radio programmes, so I could type it.

Over the next few days more poems came to me. It was like a switch had been turned on in my head, and words poured out. I don't know why there, in that place and that time, I suddenly started to write and write. Poems about the tropical landscape and my own feelings, that made sense – but why did I write about cities and noise? Where had that come from? I was so far away from anything remotely resembling a city.

Sometimes it felt like the words were coming from another place, one that I didn't have much control over. Othertimes, it seemed to me that it was just an extension of that look, when for example I watched the crabs crawl out of their mudholes in Tonga. I felt I could really see things for what they were.

Writing the poems was important. It gave me a stronger sense of myself. It didn't matter so much if I was alone, if I had no friends, or if I didn't always get on with my family. I could write, I could be with my own self – like a steady rock in the midst of a swirling sea.

<u>Alone – thoughts</u>

I like to be alone sometimes
to think
no one knows my thoughts
they are scraps of paper
whirling
in the hurricane of my mind
disappear away from everyone
a little creature I am
alone with my thoughts
in an unfathomable space the universe

all alone
I can think anything I want
so free

no one can bother me
my head is a whirlwind of thoughts
blown in a wind of fury
rebellion

thoughts are comforts
no one can be
as close to me as
myself
to be all alone
no frightening thing

I like it

Cousin Klaus Comes to Stay

AFTER LOTS OF little hops through the Solomon Islands, we made it to Papua New Guinea. My cousin Klaus was coming to join us in Rabaul, on the island of New Britain.

'He's dropped out of college,' said Mum. 'And been living in a commune. His father and Jimmy thought maybe this trip might do him some good.'

I wasn't at all sure what a commune was, but it seemed his parents, and mine too, were not very happy about it. We hadn't seen Klaus since he travelled to Israel and Egypt with us, and he would be twenty now, so Ivan and I looked forward to his arrival.

When he turned up he looked much the same. Maybe his hair was longer.

'Hey,' he said, giving us each a hug. Ivan and I stood back and eyed him from a distance.

'Are you a hippy?' I asked.

'No!' he laughed. 'There aren't hippies any more.'

'So what's a commune then?' we wanted to know.

'Are you guys going to give me a hard time?' Klaus said, though he was smiling.

'Leave Klaus to sort himself out,' Mum told us. 'Go and play or read or something.'

Later on, when Klaus had managed to pack his things away into a cubby hole, though there really wasn't much space for him, we sat in the cockpit and ate one of Mum's staple dishes, and one of my favourites, beef stroganoff and potatoes.

'I bought you guys presents.'

He gave me a cassette tape of *Peter, Paul and Mary*, and one for Ivan of *The Eagles*.

'Thanks,' Ivan said. 'We've only got one other tape, that's the *Beatles' Greatest Hits*.'

'Well, we have made our own tapes,' I added. 'You can hear them if you like.'

'Oh, that sounds interesting,' said Klaus.

'Not now,' interjected Dad. 'I don't expect Klaus wants to hear Ooga Booga or whatever on earth you've recorded.'

'I was in a band, you know,' Klaus said. 'I played electric guitar. I'll find you a photo. And I'll play you some of the music I've brought with me too.'

After dinner Ivan and I looked at the photo. Klaus played us his favourite music tapes. There was a band called Pink Floyd and a singer called Frank Zappa. Ivan and I looked at each other and shrugged. It sounded pretty weird to us. We went into our cabin and listened to the tapes we'd been given, while the adults chatted in the cockpit. Ivan started messing around to the music and put a pair of shorts on his head.

'Let's dress up,' I said. We climbed out of the hatch above our bunks and crept along the deck towards the cockpit, where we jumped out and started dancing about madly. Everyone laughed.

'It's the silly hour,' said Mum.

The silly hour happened quite a lot. Mum reckoned it was always in the evening, but I thought it was any time of the day when we felt like messing about. Sometimes Klaus joined in. He could do a very good impression of a gorilla; or he tickled us until we thought we would die laughing. We liked him a lot after that.

Christmas was celebrated Romanian style, with our meal and presents on Christmas Eve. We gave Dad a war club from the Solomons. It was made of a black wood that was as hard as stone.

'Is this to keep you lot in order?'

'Of course!'

Granny had sent a tapestry sewing kit for me, and a model kit of the *Bounty* for Ivan. I started on the sewing straight away. The *Bounty* was fiddly but Ivan really liked doing it.

That night it was so hot Mum decided to sleep on deck.

'I couldn't get to sleep until about 2am, I was just lying there in a pool of perspiration!'

'Not sweat?'

'Ladies *perspire*. They don't sweat. Anyway, we can't stay on the boat. It's stifling.'

'Let's spend Christmas Day at the pool,' suggested Dad. 'I think some of the other yachties are having a barbecue.'

Next door to the Yacht Club was a private swimming pool. We paid a deposit for a family key so we could go there whenever we liked. There was grass around the pool where you could sit, and after the barbecue it was nice being able to cool off in the water.

'We'll have a relaxing time here,' Mum said. 'Christmas holidays for you kids.'

On New Year's day we were invited to some friends ashore. Ivan and I tried a sip of champagne and we got to stay up to half past two in the morning. I didn't feel tired at all.

'At least we don't have to carry you home asleep like when you were little,' Mum said as we rowed back to the boat in the dark. 'You're getting to be quite grown up!'

Rabaul Market

SIX SLEEPING VOLCANOES surrounded Rabaul. In fact, *Aventura* was anchored in an active volcano. The volcanoes had names like Mother, South Daughter and North Daughter. There were volcanologists constantly monitoring seismic activity so as to be able to evacuate people if there was the threat of an eruption. Dad interviewed them and they invited us along on the government launch as they were going to test the temperatures of the two active volcanoes. We climbed right down into one of the smoking craters. There was a horrible rotten egg smell of sulphur, just like the hot springs we had seen in New Zealand.

I remembered how I had clutched onto Blulaki, looking down into the pit of Vesuvius, and the white bodies we saw in Pompeii of those who died. The volcanoes stayed quiet while we were there, but the volcanologists said the town was living on borrowed time.

In spite of this, Rabaul thrived and people grew amazing things in the rich volcanic soil. Mum loved the local market. All the vegetables and fruit sold there, in huge colourful piles, were far bigger and brighter than any we had seen so far.

The people were colourful too, the women in bright smocks that were called Mother Hubbards, left over from when the missionaries had told them to cover themselves. They carried their shopping and babies in bilum bags made of colourful string that they hung on their backs, supported by a strap that pressed against their forehead.

'Very clever,' said Mum, 'because when you think about it, the forehead is a strong part of the body and it can take the weight. Also, it leaves your hands free.'

'Why don't you get one then?' I asked.

She smiled. 'I'd probably look a bit ridiculous.'

Just then a woman near us spat a great gob of red onto the ground. Her teeth and lips were stained bright red.

'Some of the local habits,' Mum steered me round the gob, 'are not so appealing.'

'What are they doing, Mum?'

'It's betel nut. They mix it up with lime powder and chew it.'

I noticed many of the market women were chewing. They had little wooden vials of white lime powder which they mixed up with the nut in their mouth.

'Why do they do it?'

'It makes them feel good... spaced out. Like the kava, remember, in Fiji.'

Kava was a drink made from a special root and drunk in complicated traditional ceremonies. My parents had tried it. Mum said it made her mouth and half her face go numb.

The market women who chewed sat there looking lost in their thoughts. If not betel, then they smoked cheap cigarettes of rough tobacco rolled out of sheets cut from the national newspaper. It was said to be the most smoked newspaper in the world.

Papuan Boy

MUM AND DAD wanted to leave Rabaul and go cruising around some of the islands, and Klaus was especially keen to get sailing, but we had to wait for a new starter motor to arrive from Australia. We stayed in Rabaul for over a month.

Ivan and I spent our holidays at the pool. It was too hot to stay on the boat during the day. Mum and Dad worked on the Yacht Club terrace or by the pool. Mum made sandwiches or bought a takeway for our lunch.

There were a few other people our age who swam there regularly. I watched one boy as he did the butterfly stroke for several lengths up and down the pool. He was fast. Eventually he stopped in the shallow end near where I was standing and pushed his goggles on top of his head.

'Hi,' he said, flashing me a white smile.

'Hi.'

I rather liked the look of him. He was a bit taller than Joseph, not so dark, and better looking, I thought. But then I told myself, *Don't be so vain and conceited. You can't expect every boy to look at you. You're still a child.*

'I've got to train,' he said, grinning again. 'See you in a bit.' He set off down to the end of the pool. After a few more lengths he stopped and got out of the pool. We talked then, as he dried himself with a towel.

'I've got to train,' he said, grinning again. 'See you in a bit.' He set off down to the end of the pool.

After a few more lengths he stopped and got out of the pool. We talked then, as he dried himself with a towel.

'My name's John,' he said. 'What's yours?'

I told him, and said I was from one of the yachts anchored in the harbour. He told me he came from Rabaul, that he was sixteen, on holiday from college, and he'd already won a few swimming races.

'I'm training here most days. Maybe see you tomorrow.'

The next day we met again.

'Watch me,' he said, tossing me his swimming goggles. I watched him underwater as he swam a length doing butterfly. His body was lean and muscled and he pushed powerfully through the water.

'Good eh?' he said when he swam back. I nodded, though I did think, *He does have rather a high opinion of himself.*

I liked him though. It was fun to hang out together. The Yacht Club was showing an open air film, *Young Frankenstein*, and I asked John along. We sat on rickety old chairs in the club garden and watched the film together. John pulled his chair quite close to mine but he didn't touch me. My parents were sitting just behind us.

The following day, when we were swimming together, and talking, about nothing in particular, he caught hold of my hand.

'Let's go for a walk,' he said, and we got out of the pool and dressed.

'Where can we go?'

'There's a tunnel over there,' he waved his arm. 'From the war. The Japanese dug them.'

'Can I come?' asked Ivan.

John looked at me.

'Okay.' I shrugged.

We walked into the dark tunnel.

'I wish we had a torch,' said Ivan. He picked his way carefully along, and I started to follow him but John took my hand and stopped me.

'Let him go in front,' he whispered. He put his arms around me and kissed me.

Ivan's skinny silhouette could be seen against the light at the other end.

'We'd better keep up with Ivan,' I said, and we walked on a few steps, then John stopped me and we kissed again. That was how we went through the tunnel.

The next day I met him again after training. We swam up and down the pool and then stood in the shallow end. John held me close and pressed himself against me. He bent to kiss my neck. At least, I thought he was kissing me, maybe it was more of a playful bite.

'You'll have a surprise,' he said, smiling, and then kissed the other side of my neck.

When I was changing, to go back to the boat, I saw in the mirror that I had a red mark on each side of my neck like a bruise.

'Oh *no*,' I thought. Why did I never think before doing anything? I was angry with John too, because I felt as if he had tricked me.

I managed to get onto the boat without anyone noticing, and got some sticking plaster out of the medicine cabinet to cover the marks. I knew that it looked idiotic. As soon as I came into the main cabin Dad asked me what I had done.

'Scratched my neck on some branches,' I said. He didn't look convinced. I didn't see how I could keep up the pretence. Not when I was sharing a little boat with everyone else, and it was far too hot to cover myself up. 'I was playing with the kids, there were these low trees, I bent to go under, and I got scratched.'

My heart sank with every further lie. I went back to my cabin, feeling wretched. I hated the marks and I hated lying. When Mum was alone in the main cabin I went back and hesitantly told her. I could tell her; I couldn't have faced Dad.

'I feel awful,' I said, hanging my head. 'I wish it had never happened.'

She looked disappointed, but not angry.

'He seemed a bit pushy to me,' she said. 'When we met him at the film. So why don't you just give him the cold shoulder?'

'What's that?' I asked.

'Ignore him,' she said.

So I did. I wasn't doing very well. I hadn't kept the promises I made in Honiara. Why did these boys take an interest in me? I looked too old for twelve, that was the problem. And I wasn't very good at saying no. I liked it, as well, part of me did.

The Best Dive of My Life

MID-JANUARY THE engine part still hadn't come and we had to start school. Mum had been busy doing lots of research and had finally chosen a correspondence course for me. She arranged for all the textbooks and other materials to be sent from England to Madang, the next place we were heading that had a reliable postal address. I was impatient to get started on it.

I kept writing poetry in the meantime. Rabaul library was well-stocked and air-conditioned and I went there as often as the pool. I saw John sometimes but I kept my distance and when the new school term started he went back to college. I was fed up getting into trouble anyway.

Ivan didn't enjoy starting schoolwork.

'You are so difficult,' Mum was telling him off yet again. He was having a little tantrum. Trying to get him to write was the worst. 'I don't know why you're so het up about it all.'

'They have had quite enough of us,' I heard Mum saying to Dad later. I realised she was talking about me and Ivan.

* * *

'I think,' said Dad, 'that I'll organise a trip underwater for you lot with air tanks. How does that sound?'

I clapped my hands. 'Great!'

'Are you sure?' said Mum.

'It'll be fine,' he assured her. 'I'll tell them everything they need to know about the safety side of things. I know they'll be sensible.'

Dad sat Klaus, Ivan and I down and gave us a little lecture.

'If you see anything scary, like a shark, perhaps,' he said. 'Don't panic and take a big breath and swim fast for the surface. That would be the worst thing.'

'Why?'

'Because the air you'll be breathing is compressed, and your lungs will be

squeezed because of the pressure of all the water on top of you. If you take a breath and swim upwards, as you come to the surface there is less pressure, and that air will start to expand. It could burst your lungs. So remember, take it slow as possible, and keep breathing out.'

We headed in the dinghy out into Simpson Harbour. We found a spot that looked promising, by a rocky islet in the middle of the bay. Ivan was to go first but when Dad tried to strap on all the gear and the air tank, it was too heavy for Ivan to swim. So he sat on the bottom in about ten feet and breathed from the tank. Klaus went down next. It was his first dive as well.

When it was my turn the tank was strapped to my back. It was so heavy I could hardly sit in the dinghy. Dad was fully kitted up and he rolled beautifully backwards off the side of the boat into the water. I tried to copy, clumsy with all my gear on.

Bubbles burst all around me, whitening the water so that for a moment I could not see anything. Then I felt myself floating, just below the surface. The tank did not feel heavy any more. I breathed in and out, the air noisy in my ears, the bubbles from my out breaths busily rising to the surface. Dad looked at me and made the okay sign, pressing together the tip of his thumb and forefinger.

I made the okay sign back. Okay – one hundred per cent!

He turned and swam away slowly and I followed. Now I could swim underwater for as long as I liked, without that tightness in my chest and the need to get quickly back to the surface to take a breath. I could swim through the sea just like a fish. I felt utterly free.

Little fish glided past us, and ahead was a wall of coral coloured red, blue and green. Gradually we made our way down the coral face, until the red began to disappear from the colours. The skin on my hands began to look green. I glanced over at Dad and gave the okay sign again. We went on down. There was the noise of bubbles in my head, the sound of my breathing. That was all. Nothing happened, no reason to panic and worry about that quick swim back up.

Everything was beginning to look bluey-green. The bright reds and yellows of the coral had gone. Dad gave me the thumbs up which was the sign to ascend, and we went up, slowly, breathing in and out all the way, to give our bodies a chance to adjust to the changes in pressure. We heaved ourselves back into the dinghy.

'Well done,' he said, 'you did really well. We got down to about eighty feet.'

'My skin looked weird,' I said. 'Why was that?'

'Because the red and yellow light can't penetrate that far down. Anyway, did you enjoy it?'

I said nothing but grinned. Back at the boat I was still grinning. Mum raised a questioning eyebrow and Dad gestured towards me.

'You don't actually need to ask Doina how it went, just look at her face! She took to it like a fish. They all did really well.'

'Just me then who's not turning into a fish,' said Mum.

Madang

THE GREAT SEPIK river travelled through the thick jungle of the New Guinea mainland and came out at the sea near the port of Madang. The Sepik people were famous for their carving and they travelled by canoe down the river to sell their wares. My parents wanted to buy a mask. A crowd gathered round, offering their goods. A hand opened, and I saw a tiny face carved out of the hard shell of a betel nut. The hand held it out to me; the man guessed rightly I wouldn't be able to resist.

'Oh look!' I cried, and then I had the little betel nut face in my hand, and my parents bought a big, big mask, and everyone smiled, contented on all sides.

The Sepik mask, with its flared nostrils and straw beard, and slanting hollow eyes, was hung in pride of place on the bulkhead in the main cabin, beside the brass-cased clock and barometer, the gimballed oil lamp and the Mangarevan shark jaws.

That betel nut became one of my most treasured possessions. I kept it with my other mementoes in my New Zealand box.

All the material for my new correspondence course had arrived in Madang. Mum and I had chosen the courses for Ordinary Level exams in English, Maths and Geography. I loved English. I started to read the set texts – *A Midsummer Night's Dream* and *Pride and Prejudice*.

'Hopefully,' Mum said, 'it will stretch you a bit. I'll be able to concentrate on Ivan now. You have been a lot better though, I'm very happy with you.'

I thought about what she said. I did feel a lot better in myself, after the big blow up in Honiara.

My parents had got friendly with a couple on a Canadian yacht called *Kleena Kleene*. They came over for drinks and after Dad had told them about his work for the BBC and the interesting places it had taken us, he asked what they did.

'Frances and I are both teachers,' said Bill. 'I'm an English teacher.'

'Oh, Doina should show you some of her poems. She is always busy writing.'

Bill gave me a friendly smile.

'If you'd like to show me some time,' he said, 'I'd love to read them.'

I did give him some poems to read and he was encouraging.

'I'll give you one piece of advice,' he said, 'and that is try to write three lines a day, about anything at all, for practice.'

It was good advice. Sometimes I did remember to write three lines. But not always. I was rather lazy.

* * *

One afternoon, Ivan was reading and I was struggling with Geography, poring over colour coded maps of land use, curled up on the seats of the main cabin. We'd chosen Geography because we thought I would know a lot about it from my travels. How wrong that was. The work seemed to be mainly about the agricultural system of East Anglia, and however hard I studied the book, I remained mystified at best, at worst bored and confused.

I heard someone row over in a dinghy and start talking to my parents who were on deck. I recognised Bill's Canadian accent. They talked in low voices as if they did not want us to hear. Mum said repeatedly, 'Oh no.'

We stopped reading and looked at each other. What was happening? Dad rowed off with Bill. Mum looked through the companionway. Her face was pale, even under the tan.

'A child has been drowned,' she said bluntly.

The little girl was only a toddler and she had fallen in, next to the dock where she was playing. Bill had found her, face down in the water, and thought at first she was a large doll.

Ivan and I stared at each other. We didn't really know the little girl.

'Doina –'

'Yes?'

'I suppose she couldn't swim.'

'No one was looking after her.'

'No.'

We were quiet.

Later, there was a funeral that Mum and Dad attended along with the other adults from the yachts.

'Her parents were comforted by the words of the priest,' said Dad when they came back. 'That she had gone to heaven. That seemed to make it alright somehow.'

'Well,' said Mum. 'If it made them feel better.'

My parents, I noted, did not seem to find the idea of heaven very much consolation for losing a child.

The Highlands of Papua New Guinea

THE AIR NIUGINI inflight magazine published some of Dad's photographs of Pacific sailing canoes, and in return they gave us plane tickets to the Highlands of Papua New Guinea. We never could have afforded them otherwise.

'It's only a short plane ride,' said Mum. 'Fifteen minutes. If you had to go overland it would take days. The jungle here is almost impenetrable.'

'Yes,' Dad added, 'There are tribes who have lived here for thousands of years without any contact with the outside world. Some have only made contact quite recently.'

In the highland town of Mount Hagen, we saw men wearing the traditional dress of a long loincloth at the front, tucked up into a wide leather waistband, their behinds covered by a big sheaf of green leaves.

'Arse grass, they call it,' Klaus whispered to us and we giggled.

As we drove in our hire car back from a visit to a wildlife park where we had seen the unbelieveably beautiful birds of paradise, the amusing cassowary and the furry *cuscus*, we passed a few people crossing the road and heading off into the bush. Their faces were brightly painted.

'Where are they going?' Dad asked a young man in jeans and an anorak.

'It's a singsing,' the young man said. 'One of the elders has died and people are gathering for feasting and dancing. Many pigs will be killed in his honour.'

We followed the people to a little village nearby where a young woman was being dressed to take part in the singsing. Around her neck there were as many beaded necklaces as could be fitted, black, yellow and orange, and on her wrists were lots of black rubber bands, that used to be seals for 44 gallon drums and were popular as bracelets throughout the Pacific. She had a headdress on, covered in orangy-brown *cuscus* fur. Over her bare

chest was hung a white ornament of shell, and another one was bound to her forehead. Around her waist hung a skirt made of dried pandanus that reached to her feet.

An older woman was painting white stripes in a star across the young woman's face, dotting these with blue and filling in all the gaps with bright red. Another woman then brought out a headdress that was almost as tall as the girl herself, with black, pink and orange feathers and plumes and a whole bird of paradise pinned to the back. This was carefully placed on her head on top of the other headdress. After two hours of preparation she was ready.

We followed the young woman as a crowd of people, some leading pigs on lengths of string, made their way through the trees, leaping over streams, to the meeting place where the dancers had assembled.

The women were all costumed and painted in the same way. All the men had their faces painted black, with white stripes around or under their eyes, which made them look especially fierce. They were small, like all Highlands people, with black beards, broad hard feet, and wiry bodies.

'Why is their skin so shiny?' I asked Mum.

'I think it's pig fat,' she said. 'It's certainly smelly.'

On the men's heads were black headdresses covered in human hair, white bone circles hung from their noses, and in their hands they held long black spears. Today it was peaceful, though we knew that ritual fighting did sometimes happen between tribes.The spectators were dressed in both traditional and modern clothes, sometimes mixing both together in one outfit. They didn't pay much attention to us, even though we were the only white people there. When a crowd had gathered the dancing began. As beautiful as their costumes and decoration

were, the dancing was about as dull as you could imagine. The men banged on long thin drums, swayed back and forth and chanted a slow dirge-like song. The women stood together in a line, sang the dirge, and shuffled their feet to and fro. It went on for a long time and we stayed patiently and watched.

'Not a lot like the Tahitians and the Tuvaluans, is it?' I said to Mum.

'Well,' breathed Klaus. 'It's the most incredible thing I've ever seen. The costumes and colours, I mean.'

'I've definitely got some fantastic shots,' Dad said, taking photographs as if his life depended on it.

The only pity was that when we returned to the hire car, which we had left parked beside the road, someone had smashed the window and stolen our jumpers, an umbrella, and Klaus' leather jacket.

'I guess it was worth it,' he said with a shrug.

The Islands of Papua New Guinea

'WHERE ARE YOU off to next?' asked Bill from *Kleena Kleene*, when we were getting ready to leave Madang.

'The Trobriand Islands,' said Mum.

'Stock up on things to trade.'

'Why?' I asked.

'No one much visits,' said Dad. 'They're not really on the route to anywhere. Plus the charts aren't very accurate.'

Before leaving the mainland, Ivan and I spent a few days at Dregerhafen High School down the coast from Madang. Dregerhafen was a protected bay, with a German name as it was the Germans who were the first Europeans in these parts. Children came from all over the province to learn here.

Ivan came home from his school day completely exhausted. He had spent the afternoon out in the school gardens planting things. Some of the older boys had to carry him back.

I was sorry to leave. I made a few friends and as I left they gave me a colourful *bilum* bag, a miniature version of the ones I had seen women carrying their shopping in at Rabaul market.

From Dregerhafen we sailed a hundred miles across the Solomon Sea, keeping a sharp look out for any uncharted shoals and reefs, and dropped anchor off the Trobriand island of Kuia.

A fleet of outriggers paddled out and surrounded *Aventura*, several canoes deep. Children and teenagers mostly, but the village headman had come too.

'We haven't had another boat visit for over a year,' he said. 'Have you got anything to trade?'

Mum traded rice, flour and fish hooks for green vegetables, eggs and lobsters. She looked very pleased with the lobsters, and the islanders were happy with what they got in return.

'Money is no good,' the headman explained, when she tried to pay with cash. 'The nearest shop is twenty miles away. A long way by canoe.'

The headman was called Kadim and he invited us ashore. The islanders lived in simple thatched huts raised on stilts. The women wore only grass skirts and they cooked over open fires made from coconut shells. Here and there a pig rooted about. A group of friendly children, who wore short grass skirts, or mostly, nothing at all, followed us as we walked through the village.

Kadim offered us drinking nuts at his hut.

'Do the children go to school?' Mum asked.

'No. The school is ten miles away. It is sad that the children don't learn English like me.'

On our way back to the dinghy we stopped to watch an old man making a canoe from a single log by hollowing out the wood with a sharp adze.

Other canoes were drawn up on the beach, their prows carved and decorated with white cowrie shells to ward off evil spirits.

'The Trobrianders are famous for being great sailors,' Mum told us, as we rowed back to *Aventura*. 'They used to go on trading voyages all around the islands with big, sea-going canoes.'

We didn't see any canoes that looked big enough to make a sea passage for trading, but every island we visited had plenty of smaller canoes that were well made and shipshape.

In each place most of the village paddled out to welcome us.

'People are so much more friendly than the mainland,' Mum observed. 'I'm sorry we didn't get out here earlier.'

The Trobrianders were a mixture of Polynesian and Melanesian. Traditions were still strict. On the island of Kaileuna we saw all the teenage girls of one village had their heads shaved and their faces and bodies painted black in mourning. I thought, what if that had been me. I didn't feel here like I wanted to be a part of it, not like before, when we were in Tuvalu.

* * *

We heard on the radio that a hurricane had just struck Fiji, so Dad decided we had to wait a bit longer before heading south.

The Australian port of Cairns, where we wanted to go, was still in the hurricane belt.

'Where to now?' was the question.

'Let the wind decide,' Dad said.

As we headed towards the Amphlett Islands, pushed by a south east wind, Dad spotted two large killer whales swimming towards us. This worried him, because we had heard stories of whales colliding with yachts, sometimes by accident, but also, killer whales had been known to attack.

'I've got an idea,' he said, rummaging in a locker under the cockpit seat and pulling out a can of paraffin. By now we could all see the smooth black skin of the whales pushing up out of the water, drawing ever nearer.

Dad poured some paraffin onto the sea where it spread out in an oily slick, rainbowing at the edges. The whales dived and swam fast away.

'Where did you learn that?' Mum asked.

'Read it in a magazine. It irritates their blowholes, apparently.'

On the second day the sailing was just as good, and we celebrated Klaus' 21st birthday.

On the third day, we were all down below, except for Dad, when we suddenly heard the racket of the fishing reel going out fast.

'A fish! A fish!' Dad yelled and we all ran up to the cockpit.

'Stand back,' he shouted. 'This is a really big one.'

I held my breath as he made a big swing with his arm. And then he slung into the cockpit... an inflatable shark which he had tied to the fishing line.

'April Fool!' he said, and then had to sit down, because he was laughing so much.

It was the first of April.

'I got you,' he said, wiping a tear from his eye.

* * *

In the distance was a sail, very brown against the green of the islands. As we came closer we saw that it was a large sailing canoe, with an outrigger and a pandanus sail. *Aventura* dropped anchor off the village and the canoe came alongside. There was a family onboard, a man and a woman, two small children and a little puppy. They carried a few hot embers on a bed of sand at the front of the canoe.

Dad found batteries for their radio and Mum gave the mother some ointment for the baby who had an infected eye.

The Amphletts were even poorer than the Trobriands. My parents gave away fish hooks and torch bulbs, rice and sugar and soap. The nearest store was thirty miles away over the sea.

'I wish we'd brought more things,' Mum said.

We visited the village of the family that had been sailing on the canoe. The mother was busy making a large clay pot, with her hands only, and no potter's wheel and no kiln. Klaus took the cine camera and filmed the pot making from start to finish. He was fascinated. When she had finished, she pressed a present of a tiny pot into my hand. She wanted to give Mum a large one in exchange for what we'd given her.

'I've nowhere to keep it,' Mum said with regret.

The woman told us that they were leaving the next day to sail twenty miles to get the special clay they needed for the pots.

'I'd like to see them sail,' Dad said, 'and maybe get some photos. We'll leave too.'

That afternoon he recorded his 200th *Aventura* programme. It was due to be broadcast in July on my thirteenth birthday so he decided we all had to say some- thing. Both Ivan and I wrote little poems which he translated into Romanian and told us how to say the words so we could read them aloud.

As we hauled up the anchor the next morning, we saw the canoe being launched and its pandanus sail unfurled. There was only a light breeze but the wind filled the sail and the canoe sped away from us. Poor heavy *Aventura* could barely keep up. Dad jumped into the dinghy and took photos of the modern and the traditional vessels sailing along, side by side.

'Now you can really imagine their ancestors sailing thousands of miles to discover islands,' said Mum. 'Remember how we didn't quite believe it when we started out in the Pacific?

Australia 1980

augur
shell

Back in the Modern World

I WALKED WITH Ivan down a dusty street in the Queensland town of Cairns. Something was wrong and I could not work it out. We passed people walking along, looking into shop windows, chatting to each other. No one paid any attention to us. That was when I realised. No one *was* paying any attention to me. I had got used to the whistles and comments made in all those island places, ever since leaving New Zealand. I hadn't been able to walk down a street without a whistle following me. And now nothing. I was just a twelve year old kid again.

It was a relief.

We passed by a group of Aboriginal people. A man swayed into my path and I smelled the alcohol on his breath. In his face there was a sort of blankness that I'd not seen before in all my travels.

Thoughts raced through my head. Thoughts about empires and former colonies, and the white man making his mark all over the world, in places where other people, brown-skinned and black-skinned, had been living already for thousands, even millions of years – Africans, Incas, Aboriginals, sailing Islanders.

I was nearly thirteen and I was getting radical.

I'd borrowed *The Diary of Anne Frank* from Cairns Library which inspired me to write my own diary more regularly.

I wonder if she would have liked her diary being read by so many people, I wrote. *It must have been terrible for her: besides all the depressions of being in hiding, all her family problems. But she tried to face things cheerfully; I really like her for that.*

Anne sounds so sure of herself. In a way I am like her – in N.Z. I was a flirt and naughty, with lots of friends. Later, on my own, on the boat I grew more serious. I agree with her on most of her opinions – like about happiness: just go out and look at nature, at its beauty, and you'll be happy. I truly love Nature, and we are so close to it on the sea.

* * *

Ivan tried to play with some boys near the Cairns yacht club.

'You're a Pom,' they shouted. 'Go away.'

'What's a Pom?' we wanted to know later.

'A not very nice name for the English,' said Mum.

English? I wondered. Is that what we were?

* * *

Mum and Dad looked up a friend they had made in New Zealand, a lady called Benita. They had asked her if they could use her address for mail, and now we had a fat bundle of letters to read.

I had letters from Emma and Joseph.

'You'll have to write back,' Mum said.

Benita invited us to her house for dinner.

'What are your plans?' she asked.

'We're going to hire a car and drive to Melbourne. We've got friends there, Gunter from *Hagar* is in Sydney. Hopefully we'll meet our friends on *Calao* as well.

'Klaus will look after the boat while we were gone,' Dad added.

'After that I'm going to travel a bit myself,' Klaus said, 'before I go home. And then, well I'm not going back to the commune. I don't really know what I'll do. Maybe I'll study film-making. That film we made of the woman making the pot was really inspiring.'

After dinner we kids watched TV, which was great, because we didn't get to see it very often. There were cartoons and then a film called *Centennial*. A white American with a volunteer militia killed almost a whole village of American Indians, women and children. At the end, an army officer managed to make peace with the survivors. As he embraced the chief, I felt the tears running down my cheeks.

Funny, I thought. I don't cry much any more, not if I hurt myself. But the TV made me cry.

* * *

Off we set to explore the country. Hundreds, thousands of miles. Hours of driving and nothing much to see. At least the car was air-conditioned.

Sugar cane fields after sugar cane fields after sugar cane fields... I wrote in my diary.

In Mooloolaba we looked for *Calao*; we even had presents for them. But someone told us they left a few days before. We hoped we'd see them back in Cairns.

In Brisbane at a beach called Surfer's Paradise we watched dolphins riding the

waves alongside the surfers. On we went to Sydney. Gunter was living there on *Hagar the Horrible,* moored in a big bay north of the city.

We carted all our luggage on board *Hagar* and then took a tour of the bay with some of Gunter's friends. Gunter managed to run *Hagar* aground, so we had to spend hours on a slant until a rising tide got us off. He celebrated by cooking us a meal. Afterwards the adults passed around a tiny butt of a cigarette that they held carefully between tweezers. My parents declined to smoke any. And I pretended I hadn't noticed but I was actually noticing everything. I always did when I came across people doing things I had read about but never seen. There was something in that precious cigarette, I knew, that would make you feel much like those betel-chewing women I'd seen in Rabaul market.

* * *

The temperate climate of Melbourne was a break from the tropical heat we had put up with now for months and months.

Dad was even offered a job at Radio Australia. He was quite keen. 'The Aussies and New Zealanders we've met don't seem to worry about my accent and my non-

Britishness. I didn't like that in England and I think sometimes I had a problem getting on.'

'We'll see,' said Mum sensibly. 'We've had ideas before.'

We stayed with friends my parents knew from that long ago London life, in their rambling house decorated with interesting objects and artworks. Their children had their own room each. Of course I envied them. And there was a TV. Ivan and I watched cartoons all day long.

They took us for a few days out to their holiday home in the bush. At last we got to see some wild kangaroos. We'd been looking for them ever since we'd left Cairns. We'd seen some koalas in Sydney Zoo but they'd been asleep.

* * *

On the way back, somewhere I lost the Anne Frank book. It must have slipped out of the car at one of the many fuel stations we visited on the thousands of miles journey back to Cairns.

Dad was not impressed.

On the boat he and Mum rummaged through our book collection and sorted out a few books that they hoped the library would take in exchange.

Off we went to the library. Dad sweet-talked the librarians into taking our tatty books that had that unmistakable boat smell of salt and diesel that eventually everything started to smell of when it had been on *Aventura* long enough.

I stood there feeling *utterly* embarrassed.

Two months to go to becoming a teenager.

* * *

Aventura was brought from her mooring across the river to the dockside for a couple of days so she could be loaded with stores. Mum bought so much food at the cash and carry the cashier asked if we were opening a shop.

After school work was done Ivan and I escaped to the yacht club and watched TV. There was a BBC series showing of *Pride and Prejudice* which I had just started studying as part of my English course.

'We're looking fairly spick and span,' Mum said at last, having spent ages cleaning and sorting out the boat. 'And you know what, I think we're succeeding in the cockroach war. We're down to the last hardy remnants.'

News came from *Calao* that they were on their way. Ivan and I were looking forward to seeing them again as we didn't have anyone to play with. We were just about to leave when *Calao* turned up with engine problems. Our departure was delayed so Dad could help Erick but we had to get to the start of the Canoe Armada in New Guinea. Dad had commissions to write about it. We arranged to meet them in Port Moresby.

Pacific 1980

Germinated coconut

The South Pacific Festival Of Arts

'WE'RE HEADING BACK to Papua New Guinea,' said Dad. 'The Third South Pacific Festival of Arts is going to take place in the capital Port Moresby and all the countries of the Pacific are sending delegations.'

'It's going to be fantastic,' added Mum.

'First, though,' Dad continued. 'We are heading east of Port Moresby. An armada of traditional sailing canoes is assembling, and we're going to sail with them and finish up at the Festival opening.'

In the end, one canoe, and one yacht, *Aventura*, made the start of the Canoe Armada from Mullins Harbour, on the south coast of New Guinea, but many more joined along the way.

Some canoes were double hulled, with a platform joining the two hulls, and some had a single slim hull balanced only by an outrigger, the crew's possessions kept in plastic bags lashed halfway up the mast out of the reach of the sea spray. Great rectangle-shaped sails, white or brown, canvas or pandanus, filled with wind and pulled them along. Streamers flew from the rigging and colourful flags flapped at the mast tops, while the brightly painted wooden prows were carved into the heads of birds and crocodiles.

By day we travelled, sailing hard to keep up with the canoes, many of which were faster than *Aventura* and well used to long ocean passages. The trade winds blew briskly and the canoes surfed over the waves, the helmsmen holding on firmly to the large paddles they used to steer with.

What we thought in the Amphletts we now knew for sure. The Pacific islanders were great sailors.

Each night we stopped in a different village where feasts were laid on for the tired crews and we were entertained by singing and dancing from men with curved white boar tusks through their noses, children with giant feather headdresses and women with beautiful tattooed faces. More canoes joined daily until at last we arrived in Port Moresby as a real Armada, and the Festival could begin.

Mum was quite right. The Festival was fantastic. Imagine a crowd of people, hundreds of them, men, women and children, dressed in the fanciest of costumes. They have painted their faces all the colours of the rainbow, and sometimes their bodies too. Their bare arms are tight with bracelets, their necks hung with bone and shell ornaments, around their waists are skirts of grass and leaves dyed bright shades, in their ears and noses are beads and tusks, and towering over their heads, huge headdresses made of shells and flowers, fur and exotic feathers. These people sing, too, and dance. The songs and the dances are sometimes hundreds of years old, and sometimes quite new. Their singing is beautiful and harmonious, the music is furious and full of rhythm, and the dancers swing their hips, stamp their feet, and weave stories out of the air with their fingertips.

That was what the Festival was like. Show after show in the open air, and we couldn't get enough of it. Every Pacific country we'd visited had sent a delegation, so we met again lots of the people we had encountered on our way across the ocean. Dad had started off in the Pacific knowing no one, and now as well as the BBC he was working for Radio New Zealand and Radio Australia. His colour photos from the Highlands singsing, and now the Festival, made it onto several front covers of the *Pacific Islands Monthly*.

The shows were scattered all over the town, but journalist friends gave us lifts, and I made friends with Una, a Papuan girl my age whose father worked for the BBC. We had met up with *Calao* again, and there was always a crowd of us going to

the shows. We all wanted to see as much as we could. There were huge crowds everywhere, the majority of them Papua New Guineans, and very few tourists other than the handful of crews from yachts moored in the port.

The show which drew the biggest crowds of all came from the people who were the most plainly dressed of every-one. The Aboriginal dancers from the Torres Strait Islands, off the coast of Australia. The men wore nothing more than a pair of pants, sometimes a tall pointed hat, the women short skirts. Bold, broad stripes of white and ochre were daubed on their arms and legs, a few green leaves bound to their thighs.

But when they danced, the crowd was transfixed. How unlike those people I had seen in Cairns, out of place and shuffling – now their movements were as fluid and light as ballet dancers. They were lean and elegant, straight-limbed, stamping their feet, turning, and raising their long arms as if to fly. They always stopped too soon, and the crowd roared for more. No one ever wanted them to stop.

* * *

I squashed into our cabin with Ivan, Sidonie and Fabien. The Festival had inspired us and now we couldn't stop dancing ourselves.

'Listen,' I said. 'Why don't we put on a show for my birthday? We can use the dancing skirts we got in Tuvalu.'

'Yeah,' said Sidonie in her new Australian accent. She and Fabien had just spent a term at school in Australia and they spoke English fluently.

'Okay,' said Ivan.

Little Fabien wasn't so keen.

'Oh Fay-byen,' Sidonie said, sounding really Australian and not at all French.

'Oh *Fay-byen*,' we teased her and ran away before she could catch us.

Later on we made up some hand movements and practised our songs and dances. Soon enough it was my birthday and I was thirteen.

Dad fiddled with the radio and managed to tune into his programme so we could hear ourselves reading out the poems we had recorded in the Amphletts.

That evening we invited a few people to the boat for a party. Una came, and gave me a lovely necklace inlaid with black and white shells. I put it round my neck with all the other necklaces I had, including the silver chain Joseph had given me, and the green tiki from my grandmothers.

'That looks stupid,' said Ivan.

'I don't care.'

Annoying brother.

The deck of *Calao*, which was moored right alongside *Aventura*, was the stage for our show. Sidonie and I wore the Tuvaluan dancing skirts, and Ivan his wrap around *lavulavu*, like so many boys wore in the Pacific. We sang the song Sidonie had taught us in Tonga, *tu tu e manu ta* and danced the *tamuré* for all we were worth.

That was how it ended, our Pacific time: three years of song, dancing and feasting.

Asia, the Indian Ocean, the Red Sea
1980–81

Pilot fish

Indonesia, Singapore and Thailand

IN SOME WAYS Indonesia seemed just like the Pacific: green volcanic islands, palm trees and beaches, and the channels between thick with sailing boats and fishing canoes.

When we went ashore, though, it was different. A great crowd of boys gathered around us as we stepped out of the dinghy, jostling to touch Ivan and I and pressing so close we could hardly move. They yelled and screamed with excitement and it was so loud I could hardly think. They followed wherever we went, occasionally shooed away by the adults, but then coming back to crowd around us again.

The land was crowded with people and the sea crowded with boats. But there wasn't much in the sea below; for a thousand miles sailing through the Indonesian islands to Bali, we never caught a single fish.

* * *

In Bali people were more used to tourists. In the Balinese port of Benoa we met *Calao* and travelled inland with them to see hills neatly terraced with rice fields, wild monkeys playing among jungle ruins and old women painting wax patterns onto delicate materials to make batik. There were villages of painters, of woodcarvers, and of silversmiths, and we bought lots of souvenirs. I got a small wooden carving of a bird with outstretched wings.

We saw Hindu temple ceremonies where women carried offerings to the gods on their heads, of rice cakes and fruit carefully balanced on silver bowls. We passed a cremation where the body to be burnt was being carried in a decorated tower on the shoulders of about twenty men, and turned round and round to confuse the dead spirit so it would not return home and plague the living.

In another place we saw *Legong* dancing, to mark the end of a cremation. A little girl was dancing, much younger than me, her face painted white, her eyes thickly made up, her body tightly wrapped in gold material. Only children performed Legong.

Indonesia was a big, diverse country, with many different religions, languages and peoples. We spent a week in Java, travelling overland. *Calao* looked after *Aventura* while we were gone, and then we did the same for them.

We learnt some Bahasa Indonesia, the official language of the country. *Selamat pagi*, good morning. *Satu, dua, tiga, empat, lima*. 1, 2, 3, 4, 5. I thought I could speak it well enough so that one evening, as we took a taxi van back to Benoa, and the adults and the people running the taxi disputed over the price, I tried to join in. That just made them laugh.

One thing worried me more than anything. I had read that the left hand was to be used for cleaning your bottom after the toilet. A tap or water bucket was provided, instead of paper. Because of this, the left hand was never used for eating. Food was only to be eaten with the right hand.

'I'm left-handed!' I said. 'What if I forget!'

'So am I,' said Ivan.

And it was true, when I went into a public toilet in Bali there was no paper, only a tap in the wall. I washed my hands thoroughly afterwards.

'If we eat ashore,' I said to Ivan, 'we'll just have to sit on our left hands.'

* * *

Singapore was a country that was not much more than a big city, squashed between Indonesia and the Malaysian mainland. A city full of rules, which began with a very complicated set of formalities that seemed to apply to ships rather than a small yacht like us. We had to be inspected for rats, that was the first thing, and issued with a de-ratting certificate.

Rules that affected children too. I visited the huge public library. It was a real treat, a clean, vast building full of books. So different from the dark cubby hole that stank of diesel, where we stored the books on *Aventura*. Rows of bookshelves, and every desk occupied with someone hard at work studying, reading, writing.

There was nowhere to sit. But I wanted to read. I sat down on the floor, in a corner out of people's way. Within a minute a librarian came over and told me to move. Sitting on the floor was not allowed. The people at the desks looked at me. I couldn't stay in the lovely library.

Mum and Dad meanwhile had a big shopping list. A new dinghy and an outboard engine, two electric fans to keep us cool and a generator so the batteries wouldn't keep getting flat.

'We've spent all the money we've saved from the Pacific,' Mum admitted. 'But things are half the price of England.'

Food was cheap as well in Singapore and the variety amazed us. We visited the street markets where kiosks shared tables, and bought dishes from all the speciality stalls around us. Heaps of noodles and rice, steaming soup, fish and prawns, sticky pork and crisp vegetables.

'This is the best cuisine,' said Mum, 'of anywhere we've been yet!'

We all nodded agreement, our mouths full.

'And that's saying something!'

* * *

A long stopover was made at the Lumut Yacht Club, a protected spot up a river on the west coast of Malaysia. The anchorage was very safe, and the club people were happy to keep an eye on *Aventura*, so the decision was made to travel up to Thailand by land, instead of sailing there. It was a long journey on the train, in third class because no other tickets were available. The other passengers had brought lots of food with them, saucepans of rice and bamboo boxes of all sorts of edible things. It was hot, and by the second day the food began to smell.

The train's conductor refused to accept that I could have a child's half ticket. He marched Dad and I to the end of the train where there was a line marked on the wall.

'She no child, she woman!' he said, pointing to the line.

It was true, my head came above the line. I was almost as tall as him. He would not budge however much Dad argued. After that we couldn't get half price tickets for me anywhere in Thailand.

'Good thing the transport is so ridiculously cheap,' observed Mum.

Snakes, Buddhas and pollution – those three things stuck in my mind when afterwards I thought of Bangkok. The snake farm where Ivan and I got to drape snakes around our necks, and where we watched a man draw out the drops of venom from a cobra's fangs. The busy, smelly city that was so choked with traffic fumes that Mum could barely breathe. And the beautiful temples full of huge Buddhas, sat cross-legged, or reclining lengthways, leaning on one arm, and always, always smiling. Buddhas made of cement, bronze, stone and tin, it felt as if we saw thousands and thousands of  them. There was even a solid gold one that Dad calculated must have been worth at least a billion dollars.

There were beautiful dancers with golden finger tips and delicate buildings with golden spires. Young men with shaved heads and orange robes serving their time as monks. I liked the temples which were cool and quiet after the noisy city outside. The air always had a gentle smell of incense. But we seemed to rush from one place to another, and like once, years before, when we had to visit every single ancient Greek and Roman ruin, every single broken stone relic, Ivan and I began to say: 'Oh no, not *another Buddha!*'

At least Dad had booked us second class sleeper tickets for the train journey back. As night fell, the train ground to a halt in the dark middle of nowhere. For a long time we sat and waited. Then a rumour crept through the carriages that there was fighting on the line ahead.

'We're near the Thai-Malay border,' explained Dad. 'There are insurgents somewhere about, fighting the government.'

The stop dragged into hours. Finally another train pulled up on the track alongside. It was full of young Thai soldiers, conscripts, heading to the frontline. They came on board our train to ask for cigarettes and food. A couple of them grinned at Ivan and I, saw we were playing cards, and sat down to join us for a game. One of their friends came along and perched on the arm of the seat next to them. He looked at my parents and smiled, then pointed at me.

'How old is she?'

'Thirteen.'

I pretended not to listen, and shuffled the pack.

'She get married soon?'

I put my head down and dealt the cards, wishing I could disappear.

'No,' said my parents, as politely as they could. 'She isn't going to get married just yet.'

A Long Stay in Lumut

MUM AND DAD liked Lumut and we stayed there quite a while.

We often talked about what we would do when we got back to England. Mum and Dad still thought we might end up in Australia eventually, but first the London house had to be sold, and all sorts of loose ends tied up. We all agreed we didn't want to live in a big city like London.

'How about you kids staying with Granny at first, and going to school in Cornwall?'

This idea sounded good to me, and Ivan as well. I wrote to Granny to thank her for the Christmas presents she had sent, and I asked her about the schools near where she lived. What were their uniforms like?

I also found a job for myself, baby sitting. Bill and Frances from *Kleena Kleene* had arrived. We had last seen them in Madang, and now they had a six month old baby daughter.

Brandi was a jolly, chubby baby. I fed her baby food and carried her about. I liked babysitting but I definitely didn't want a baby of my own! I was quite happy to hand her back to her parents.

'Still writing?' Bill asked.

'Oh yes,' I said. I showed him some of my poems.

Granny replied to my letter and said that at the school nearest her, the girls' uniforms were red and grey. Definitely not my favourite colours; I preferred blue or green. However, I still dreamed about school. I enjoyed my correspondance courses and Mum and Dad teased me for talking about them all the time.

'I can't help it if I like working!' I answered back. My first assignments that I had sent off to a tutor somewhere had come back in the post with encouraging comments and questions marked in red ink in the margins.

Meanwhile Ivan was driving Mum mad. Or at least, that was what she said.

'You're so good at maths and science.' She was struggling once again to get him to write. 'And navigation as well, now Daddy's teaching you. Maybe you'll end up as a scientist or engineer whose writing no one can read!'

Ivan shrugged. He was never a great one for words. He preferred to be off doing things.

He and I had made friends with the Yacht Club caretaker's children. They taught us lots of card games, how to shuffle quickly and how to count up to ten in Cantonese. Their mother was a great cook and with seven children she didn't mind feeding us too. We loved the food they ate, the piles of flavoured rice and noodles, the spicy sauces and prawns and chicken. The family were part of the Chinese community that lived in Malaysia. The oldest son and daughter were already grown up and lived away from home; the third oldest was a boy of sixteen, Ah-Hua, who used to help behind the club bar.

The clubhouse was quiet during the week, and Ivan and I often took our schoolwork ashore while Mum spread the sails out and stitched and mended. Sundays was the only busy day, when local families came to sail dinghies in the river, and children swam from the beach or played with windsurfers in the sheltered water off the shore. Ivan often got invited to go out in one of the racing dinghies, which he really enjoyed.

One day, I was sitting at the bar and playing patience with a pack of cards. Ah-Hua was cleaning glasses. I heard shouting coming from the beach and a man dove fully-clothed into the water.

'A child has fallen in,' someone shouted in English.

A girl was screaming. Another man who had been relaxing on the club terrace jumped up and ran as fast as he could to the water and jumped in after the other man, while people gathered at the shore's edge.

'What has happened?' I said to Ah-Hua. I did not want to go and look.

He was listening to the shouts. 'A boy has fallen in, off his surfboard, and he has gone under the water. The men are trying to find him.'

My heart pounded very fast and my hands, still holding the playing cards, began to shake. I did not want to move, I stayed there, trying to play patience, my hands shaking, as the search went on and on. They dove desperately into the river, over and over, but could not find the boy, not in the muddy river water.

Soon Mum and Dad came to take me back to the boat, and later, we heard they had found the body. He was laid out near the club house. Ivan went with a couple of other boys to take a look.

'Don't you want to go?'

I shook my head.

'What did he look like?' I asked, when he came back. Ivan shrugged.

'Dunno. A bit green, I suppose.'

At the club house people shook their heads that the boy, who was older than me, could not swim. The family came and took him away. Near the clubhouse they burnt red sticks of incense and special paper notes of money, so he would have some in the afterlife.

* * *

After this I used to talk to Ah-Hua quite often. Once, when I was sitting at the table playing Monopoly with his sisters, he walked behind me, and whether on purpose or not, brushed very lightly against me. I felt a shiver go up and down my spine. I knew then that something would happen. He invited me to go with his older sister and her boyfriend to the cinema. Afterwards, he and I sat on the old swing seat outside his house and held hands. We didn't say a great deal, just sat there, swinging on the seat. And I didn't get into trouble. I was a bit more sensible.

* * *

By now it was time to be thinking of trade winds and oceans again. Christmas had passed along with the risk of tropical cyclones. The north east monsoon was starting, that would blow us across the Indian Ocean with the same good trade winds we had had crossing the Atlantic and the Pacific.

As a farewell, Ah-Hua's mother made us a big meal that she insisted we eat before we left. It was still morning and Dad was itching to get away, but it had to be done. A steamboat was bubbling on the table, and it smelled wonderful. It consisted of a steel pot of stock that was kept boiling away, and all sorts of food like fish, prawns, cuttlefish, vegetables and noodles were cooked in it. Although it was strange to eat for breakfast, it was delicious nevertheless.

'Thank you so much,' said my parents to Ah-Hua's mother. 'We will miss your cooking!' She smiled and nodded. I waved to Ah-Hua as we headed for the dinghy, with his photograph tucked into my pocket.

* * *

Sri Lanka was near enough to India for us that we anticipated trying curry there as much as we had looked forward to those American hamburgers. Especially Mum.

'I love curry,' she said. 'It's ages since I ate a decent one.'

But the Sri Lankan curries defeated us, they were so fierce. They even beat Mum. Ivan and I tried our best to avoid them, so if we went out to eat, we would order omelettes or fried chicken and chips, but even those came well sprinkled with curry powder.

Sri Lanka was green and lush, and we hired a car and driver to take a quick tour and enjoy the spectacular ruins of the ancient civilisation that once flourished here. Buildings built out of solid mountains, carvings of elephants and rock paintings of graceful women holding lotus flowers. A real elephant lugging huge tree trunks and rolling itself thankfully into the cool water. Cute monkeys, snake charmers, and stone Buddhas the size of houses carved directly out of hillsides.

We didn't stay very long. The winds were good and we had a 2,200 mile passage ahead of us.

Across the Ocean Yet Again

AFTER A WEEK at sea Dad was struck down with a fever, and spent several days lying on the bunk in the main cabin, now hot and sweating, now shivering with a cold that wasn't there.

'Can we sail the boat without him?' we wondered.

'I'm strong,' I said, flexing my muscles.

'I can do the navigation,' said Ivan.

But it was frightening, I had never seen him ill before. Fortunately Dad was soon better. Weak, but no longer bed-ridden, and making jokes again. Ivan and I took day watches together, while Mum and Dad slept. It was easy enough, the sails set and the self-steering working hard. The skies were clear and the perfect trade winds blew us westwards.

Kleena Kleene were crossing at the same time as us, and on the fourth and fifteenth day we even spotted them in the distance. Like us they were en route for

the Suez Canal and the Mediterranean after that, and the plan was to sail up the Red Sea together, as it was safer to keep company with another yacht. *Calao* had stayed behind and planned to go up the Red Sea next season.

A lot of merchant ships steamed past us as well. Several changed course to take a look and the crew on the bridge waved. One even sounded its hooter. I guess it was a bit boring for them, crossing an ocean.

One night we hit something, an object big enough to send a great bang through the boat, stopping her dead for a few seconds. It made my heart stop too.

'It was a massive tree trunk,' said Mum, who was on watch. 'I saw it as it went past the boat. I guess it was washed out to sea by a storm or the monsoon floods.'

Aventura, with her sturdy hull that had coped with coral reefs, mud banks and over friendly whales, was undamaged.

'Well, we can congratulate ourselves,' Dad said one day after his sextant sight. He'd been sitting at the navigation table for some time, scribbling lists of figures. 'We've done 50,000 miles since leaving England. You realise that is almost twice the distance round the Equator!'

'*That* is a lot of sailing.'

'And a lot of detours.'

'Not only that. I just worked out how much we travelled overland, in the USA and South America, Australia and so on. And that's the same distance again!'

'My Grandad always used to say his family had gypsy blood.' Mum smiled.

Last time it took so long to cross an ocean it was the Atlantic, and I passed the time playing with Ivan and our collection of toy animals, celebrating birthdays and weddings and re-enacting wars.

Now I preferred to write poetry and think deep thoughts. I guess that was the difference between being nine and being thirteen years old.

It is quiet. I lie peaceful in the quarter berth, thinking of nothing and watching the opposite bulkhead. The lamp there gently swings backwards and forwards; the shadows run to and fro across the hatch-cover; the slanted hollow eyes of the Sepik mask watch me but do not watch. Occasionally a sunbeam falls through the hatch, bringing clouds of sparkling grey-white dust. I watch this mist of tiny stars tumble into the shade, suddenly abandoned and lost: with no sunlight, they disappear forlornly.

I only realise how dim the cabin is when I go out to gaze at the endless sea and whisper to the wind. The light blinds me: I see only a strange blue-white mosaic that hurts my eyes, but goes, and leaves only the wandering, lazy waves, that reluctantly roll beneath us, springing up again to continue their endless journey. The sky is a pure, completely bare expanse of blue. It is the purest thing there ever was, spreading immortal blueness over the world. The sky is the symbol of everything immortal, it reminds you of life, of death, of everything explainable and mysterious. The earth is for mortals; the sea is for the spirits of living things. Immortals – mortals – spirits: everything is complete and nothing matters.

* * *

I stared at myself in Mum's magnifying mirror. Green eyes stared back. Now I looked at my black eyebrows, that met above my nose. Expressive, that was how the Nukulaelae islanders had described them. Too much, I thought. Mum plucked her eyebrows; why shouldn't I? I sneaked her tweezers and holed up in my cabin. Plucking out the hairs was quite satisfying, and I was pleased with the end result.

Not so Dad.

'What have you done!' he shouted angrily.

I retreated to my cabin to sulk. Once this cabin had been Ivan and I's special place. Now it was too small. Ivan was eleven but he seemed far, far younger than me, as if much more than two years separated us.

Ivan is really getting on my nerves, I wrote in my diary. *Always being grotty to me. He's really terrible and one day I'm going to blow up.*

On this voyage he and I had, as usual, moved into the main cabin. He slept on a cushion on the floor and I made my bed in the quarter-berth next to the navigation table. We asked Mum for more covers because we were feeling cold.

'Ivan, you've already got two sleeping bags,' exclaimed Mum, looking at the temperature. 'It's just above 20°. I'm afraid we're used to temperatures in the 30s.'

'What are we going to do when we get back to England then?'

'I don't know. We'll freeze!'

I pulled on another jumper and settled down to write my diary. When I had finished I took a book and went and lay down on the floor. Ivan and Mum were in the cockpit and Dad was sleeping in the aft cabin.

'Get off my bed!' Ivan said, putting his head through the companionway.

'Why? I haven't ever lain here before. You can go in the quarter berth.'

He leapt down the steps and pushed me in the stomach with his hands. Then he punched me. I grabbed his face. He went back into the cockpit.

I tried to start reading again, but I started crying. I went and told Mum.

'He kicked me in the stomach,' I said. Okay, maybe I should have said 'pushed'.

By now Ivan had stomped onto the foredeck so she called him back.

'Don't be so vicious,' she told him. 'You know Doina doesn't cry much. Daddy will be angry with you for behaving like this. We're all fed up with it. Say you're sorry.'

'No!' he yelled. 'Anyway, I'm bored!'

'Why don't you read something?' she suggested.

'Boring!'

'Do some drawing.'

'No! Boring!'

I gave up and went back to my book. Then it went quiet and I saw he'd started playing happily with his Lego.

He is my only brother and I love him, I wrote. *Maybe he's lonely like me, and he wants a true friend to talk to. But perhaps I only think that because that's how I feel. Not lonely in the normal sense; I have so many people around, my family, and all our friends on other boats. A true friend, a girl exactly the same as me. When we get back to England, I hope I find one there.*

The Red Sea

THE YEMENI PORT of Aden was full of bombed-out buildings left over from a war that had happened over ten years ago, rubble that no one had bothered to clean up. Russian naval ships bristling with guns and communications equipment were anchored in the harbour. In 1981, it was the height of the Cold War between the Soviet Union and the United States. Yemen was allied to the Soviet Union, and let its navy have a base in Aden.

'Bill is slightly mad,' Dad commented. 'He keeps trying to take pictures of the Soviet warships out of his portholes. Like he's some sort of spy.'

Ivan and I noticed that the Russian sailors seemed just as interested in us. Whenever we appeared on deck one of them gave us a friendly wave.

'I think they probably can't imagine families doing this sort of thing,' said Mum.

That night, when Ivan and I were in our bunks, though not yet asleep, we heard a panicked call from Frances. Dad rushed over in the dinghy. We waited up until he came back.

'What happened?' asked Mum. 'And why are you laughing?'

'Bill found a rat onboard. He leapt on it and caught it, but he couldn't let go, and he was completely naked! Frances panicked and couldn't do anything.'

'Maybe it was a Russian rat.'

Aden was a useful stopping point before the long haul up the Red Sea.

'I'm not looking forward to this,' said Dad. 'As far as I can tell, the winds are mostly going to come from ahead. And we have to avoid the eastern coast at all costs.'

'Why?' I asked.

'Because it's Saudi Arabia and no foreign yachts are welcome there – if you get too near you're likely to be arrested. We're going to have to keep as near as possible to the west coast. And there are plenty of reefs, not all of them marked on the chart, not to mention the offshore oil rigs and the shipping lanes busy with Canal traffic.'

'Sounds wonderful,' said Mum. 'The sooner this part is over, the better.'

There were not many places to stop and rest. We stayed overnight in the Sudanese port of Suakin, where we anchored behind a sandbank on which lay a rusty old wreck of a ship. Ashore were a few brown tents of some sort of military camp, ruined buildings, and three abandoned minarets. The whole town looked deserted. Beyond the ruins, a sandy expanse stretched off towards distant hills.

'Aren't we going to go ashore?' I asked. I wanted to take a closer look at the African desert.

'We can't – Port Suakin isn't a port of entry. We've only stopped here so we can have a rest. There are no officials here for us to complete entrance formalities into Sudan.'

Not all was ruins and desolation in Suakin. White flamingoes were feeding in the shallows, and solid pelicans floated on the waves nearby, their pouched beaks folded to their chests. I watched the birds until the sun set great and red, behind the far hills of the desert.

After Suakin we cleared into the country at Port Sudan. The whole town was covered in a thin layer of dust and skinny stray camels wandered the streets, scavenging for food in the rubbish skips.

The shipping traffic grew busier and busier as we got closer to the Suez Canal. From Port Suez in the south to Port Said in the north, the Canal cut across the desert, joining the Red Sea to the Mediterranean, and making sailors' lives much easier as they did not have to take the long route round the Cape of Good Hope, on the tip of Africa, in order to travel from Europe to Asia and back again.

For us, the excitement grew. The other side of the Canal, in Port Said, there was an imaginary line in the water, and when *Aventura* sailed over that line, we would officially cross our own tracks and we could say, Yes, we have sailed all the way around the world.

* * *

A Red Sea anchorage. Fried fish for dinner.

'There's so much,' said Mum. 'We'll probably have to eat it for breakfast too.'

'No thanks,' I said, 'not when it's cold and greasy.'

'But I thought you liked fried fish.'

'I never said I didn't like it, just not for breakfast.'

'Don't be such a nag,' Dad said, and he and Mum started discussing the impending end of their supply of wine.

'At least we'll find wine in Greece,' said Mum. 'So running out won't be a tragedy.'

'It wouldn't be a tragedy even if you didn't have it for the rest of your lives,' I remarked irritably. 'I'd rather drink water!'

'Nag, nag,' they repeated.

I shut up.

I wasn't nagging, I was only expressing my dislike of their dependence on wine; they always express their dislikes. Also, they always think I'm answering back grumpily when I'm not, truly, truly! Talk about my voice: don't they listen to theirs? Mum is naggy and screamy, and always swears. They swear too much; what's the point? Sometimes they discuss such boring things and tease me about 'being a poet and so grumpy'. I like writing poetry; they don't write it, what do they care. They talk about what is better for the world, but never do anything. I respect them, but sometimes I hate their perfect manners (though I don't want to be piggy either). I just watch them ever-so-daintily eating, and I hate it! Don't ask me why – I want to have good manners too, and I love my parents, in spite of what I say here.

Mediterranean 1981

We Become Circumnavigators

'IS IT NOW? Is it now?' we kept yelling back to Dad, who was standing on the aft deck. Mum was at the wheel.

Ivan and I were squashed together on the pulpit, at the very bow of the boat. We both wanted to be the first, just like when we came out of the Panama Canal into the Pacific. We were motoring out of the Suez Canal, past the buildings of Port Said, past the huge ships waiting to make the journey south, back to the Red Sea.

Nothing could be seen in the murky water. Where was the line we needed to cross?

'Now,' Dad shouted. 'It must be now!'

We cheered. We had done it, we had crossed our six year old tracks, we were officially circumnavigators!

Thousands of nautical miles under *Aventura's* keel, and more than fifty countries visited. Thousands of miles travelled on land, exploring the interiors of

countries and continents. We had made a slow journey, staying as long as we could in places we liked, with people we liked, and going back again to the best places, twice and even three times. Only the weather could prevent us from doing what we wanted. We hadn't had any interest in being the fastest or going around the world non-stop: why would you want to do that, when the world, and the people who lived on it, were so amazing, so worth getting the time to know.

When we had sailed this way last time, in 1976, there had been war; now there was a new peace between Egypt and Israel. But we were not going to stop here, we were heading out into the Mediterranean.

We arrived on the Greek island of Patmos and that evening we all sat around the wooden table in the main cabin. I remembered how Dad had made it all those years before, in the London docks, and how proud he was of it, and how it could be hooked up to the bulkhead when we were at sea, and kept out of the way.

Now the table was down, and we sat and ate our meal.

'So,' said Dad, looking at Ivan and I. 'This is the plan. If you agree.'

We said nothing, just looked at him.

'We'll go to Romania first,' he said. 'That has to be done. After all these years that I've been sending the programmes back, I haven't heard much about whether people in Romania have actually been listening to them. And then you two will go to Braşov, with Omi. Okay?'

We nodded.

He glanced at Mum before continuing.

'You'll stay with Omi, while we get the boat ready to be sold.'

'No!' Ivan and I gasped.

'Well, we need the money. If we're going to settle back in England.'

'We'll come and collect you,' said Mum. 'So we can travel back to England in time for you to start school in September.'

Once upon a time, years before, we hadn't had a plan. When we sailed away from England. But that was over, and it looked as if everything was planned out and set in stone from now on.

I was looking forward to going back to England but I did not want to think too much about the other part, which was that we would be selling *Aventura* soon. That was a painful price to pay, for a new life on the land.

A Greek Easter

IVAN AND I were desperate to get off the boat.

'Can we go ashore?' we pleaded.

'Yes,' said Mum. 'Take some biscuits and water.'

It was great to stretch our legs, to walk and walk until we were tired. When we had been little, somehow it hadn't mattered so much being cooped up on the boat for days.

'Let's climb those hills,' said Ivan. We walked through the town and up towards the first peak. Many Greeks were making their way to church in their finest clothes. It was the Sunday before their Easter, which was a week later than the English Easter because they were part of the Eastern Orthodox Church and worked out their Easter dates differently. We had been surprised that morning by Dad producing Easter chocolates for us, which were now squashed in our pockets as we climbed.

I remembered how I had loved the ancient myths when we were in Greece before, for our first two sailing summers, and how I had almost believed that those gods and goddesses still walked through the parched summer landscape.

This Greece was far from being parched. A wheat field rippled in the strong wind like a green sea, and there were wild flowers growing everywhere among the rocky outcrops on the hill tops. There were bouncy white lambs, silly kid goats, and grazing donkeys who stared at us forlornly as we passed. The sun was warm in a friendly way – everything was so green after the deserts of the Red Sea – a moist, growing freshness was in the air, quite new to me – this was spring. After so long in the tropics, I had forgotten about the four seasons of the temperate world. I looked down the slopes to the sea, the sparkling Mediterranean, and I believed it would always be as good as this.

* * *

From Patmos we sailed to the island of Tinos, where all those years before Dad had made friends with George, who brought us the lovely Greek pastries. George had invited us to share his family's Easter celebrations. Best of all, he had a daughter, Marika, who was only a little bit younger than me.

Marika had long black hair and a white smile. She always wore clean clothes that looked as if they had been freshly ironed. When I first visited her house, and looked into her room, I felt a real pang of envy when I saw that she had her very own wardrobe, full of clothes, each one hung on its individual hanger. All we had on the boat was a tiny hanging locker, stuffed with heavy weather gear, lifejackets and a few clothes such as Mum's dresses she attempted to keep looking smart. At least five items of clothing were crammed onto every hanger.

Marika and I laughed and chatted together, went to the beach for a picnic, rode a donkey, played cards and swam in the sea. She played me her music and said, 'Have you heard this group? Do you like this song?' I tried to have an opinion, though I did not really know of any groups or songs.

* * *

Easter came, the biggest celebration of the Orthodox Christian year. I had been baptised as a Romanian Orthodox as a baby, when we still lived in Romania, so Easter meant something to me too. I did love all the ritual which went with it, and in my New Zealand box I had a painted wooden egg from a Romanian Easter when I was very little.

Marika's mother made piles of hard-boiled eggs, which she dyed bright red and green. A special bread was made, of plaited lengths of sweet dough, into which a coloured egg was placed, and this was taken to the village baker. The baker's large

ovens were filled with dishes and bread brought by all the local families.

Later on the evening of Easter Saturday we made our way to the church, and waited outside with unlit candles, as there was no more space inside. At midnight the light of resurrection was brought out and we lit candles one to the other, until the yard outside the church was alive with tiny yellow lights. Marika lit her candle and then turned to me.

'*Christos anesti*', she said. *Christ is risen.*

'*Alithos Anesti*,' I responded, *He is risen indeed*, and lit my candle from hers. When everyone had a light, we processed around the church.

Easter Sunday and a whole lamb was stuffed with herbs and placed upon a wooden spit, over an open fire in the garden. The lamb turned and turned on the fire for hours, and at last we could all gather, Marika and her family, and mine, to share the Easter feast, in the spring sunshine.

All too soon though it was time to go. I wrote in my diary:

Will I ever get to say 'Ella, come on, Marika' again? I've quite, quite, quite enjoyed our stay here; I loved it, in fact. We've had great fun and done so many things. Having friends again is lovely.

A Diary Entry

I think I am looking forward a lot to Romania, not only because of family and friends. Since my last visit, when anyway I was so small I noticed little, I have read* and learnt a good amount about communism and communist countries. I am eager to visit such a country now I know more. Not, of course, that I know that much. Staying a month there will be good, especially for Ivy and I's Romanian! I do not think the lack of things will bother us a great deal, for we are used (on long passages) to eating from tins.

* Animal Farm *was my first. Then* Cancer Ward, One Day in the Life of Ivan Denisovich, Dolgun's Story, Darkness at Noon... *I have, I am sure, learnt from these books. But, as Jane Austen says in* Pride and Prejudice, *one is an experiencer and reasoner, and cannot be a reasoner without experience, as Mary Bennet tried to do. I don't have experience for such things as communism and understanding it. Or do I? I certainly have a good quantity of experience because of seeing so many countries, governments, cultures, and peoples. Perhaps I do have that sort of experience, maybe a little... no, I can't possibly have anything of the sort: shut up, Mary Bennet, before you have experience you can't reason. So go to bed and leave reasoning and getting muddled up to more experienced people. It's 10.13 p.m. Good night.*

13.5.81, Büyükderi, Turkey.

Romania 1981

On Our Way to Transylvania

YACHTS RARELY VISITED Romania, so *Aventura* would have drawn a crowd anyway when she moored in the Black Sea port of Constanţa. As it was, we were over-run by visitors. Omi came, of course, and old friends, but also journalists – because Dad was officially the first Romanian to sail around the world – and lots of people we didn't know at all, who had been listening to his radio programme all these years.

'What are they saying?' I asked Mum as the visitors talked and talked.

'That it's bad. Worse than when we were here last time.'

'What sort of bad?'

'Food mostly. The basics are rationed, like sugar, butter and meat. And there are lots of power cuts.'

'Why?'

'Because President Ceauşescu is obsessed with paying off the country's foreign debt and is selling everything overseas. But more than that, the government is repressing the people to keep its power.'

Walking around the town of Constanţa, it looked pretty normal to me. Though I did notice that there were lots of pictures of Ceauşescu. President, Party Leader, Comrade. Pictures in bookshop windows, huge posters on the side of buildings. His face was everywhere.

We packed a few bags and took the train to Bucharest with Omi and Mum. Dad stayed behind to sort the boat out. The second class compartment was dirty and the seat kept coming out, so all through the journey we had to keep standing up to push it in again. Sitting opposite was a woman with a great bushy hairdo. She insisted on having the window closed even though it was hot. That made the compartment terribly stuffy, and she kept sighing and fanning herself.

'Romanians definitely don't like draughts,' whispered Mum. 'They think they are dangerous! When you were a baby if I took you out in your pram without a hat, people would stop me in the street and tell me I was killing you.'

In Bucharest we changed trains for Braşov and went into first class.

'Much nicer,' said Mum.

The lady who sat next to me was a doctor and she gave me some pastilles because I had a sore throat. We talked in French and I told her about our voyage and my schoolwork.

'I'm studying *A Midsummer Night's Dream*,' I told her. 'It's by William Shakespeare. Have you heard of him?'

Everyone laughed.

'I don't know what's so funny,' I said, and folded my arms and looked out the window instead.

Gradually the scenery outside became more mountainous, after the flat plains around Bucharest; there was even a little snow on the peaks. Houses had steep roofs, and everything was green and fresh.

'We're in Transylvania now,' Mum said. 'And those are the Carpathian mountains. We'll be in Braşov soon.'

I thought that the mountains were beautiful, but when we pulled into Braşov train station. all I could see outside was a sprawl of high rises and factories that looked drab and ugly.

Our only relatives in Braşov, besides Omi, were Omi's younger sister Böszi and her family. Böszi's son-in-law Gabor was waiting for us at the station, and drove us to their house. Böszi and her husband, whose name was Constantin, though everyone called him Titi for short, lived there with their daughter Gabi who was a bit younger than Dad. Gabi had a little daughter, Juli. She was only three; she had been born while we were in the middle of the Pacific. She immediately fell in love with Yellow Teddy and carried him off. It was only a small family but it was nice to see them all again.

'You must be hungry,' Gabi and Böszi said. We weren't really that hungry, but we sat down to eat. Böszi had made stuffed cabbage.

'A winter dish,' she said to Mum, 'but I know you like it.'

Böszi, I thought, was like a smaller, more nervous version of Omi, and Gabi was like a younger version of Böszi. Gabi and Böszi fussed, while Gabor and Great Uncle Titi were rather quiet and let them get on with it.

'Have another helping,' Böszi insisted, piling up Mum's plate and adding a dollop of sour cream.

Böszi wanted us to have thirds, but we couldn't, and she looked offended then, though we were full to bursting.

The conversation was a mixture of English, Romanian and Hungarian. Böszi had married a Romanian, just like Omi. So they spoke Hungarian to each other, and Romanian to Titi. Our family was so mixed up.

Eventually Gabor drove us to the old centre where Omi lived. I thought it was

much nicer than around the station. The houses were painted different colours, the roofs were red, and right in the middle towered the massive gothic Black Church. The town was tucked right up against the high mountains, which rose behind, green with thick forests.

When I saw the old house where Omi's apartment was, it all came back to me: I remembered playing in the cobbled yard, and I remembered the apartment too, stuffed full of furniture and knick-knacks in glass cabinets, the yellow walls crowded with pictures. Of course I had visited the apartment the last time we were here, when I was eight, but I hadn't noticed my surroundings so much then.

I remembered the toilet as well. It was outside the apartment, and had to be shared with the people who lived across the landing. And the horrible toilet paper, which was brown and shiny.

'Things must be bad,' I said to Ivan when I came back. 'There's no soft toilet paper.'

Mum had borrowed Titi's car to drive back to the boat the next day.

'I'll be back in a week with Dad,' she said. 'Please do some school work every day. The children here are still at school, it's not the summer holidays yet! And listen to Omi and try to help her as much as you can.'

Mum left early, and then Omi went to the police station with our passports, as she had to register us because we were foreigners. When she returned, she said, 'Now, to the cemetery,' and we walked across town to the little cemetery on the hill, to visit the graves of her husband and daughter; that is, my grandfather and aunt. The old flowers were thrown away and we helped her rinse out the jars and fill them with clean water at the tap before putting in the fresh flowers she had brought with her.

It began to thunder and we rushed back to the apartment, just before the rain started. Omi sat down heavily in an armchair and breathed out, tired after the long walk. She looked at me and wiped a tear away from her eye. Thinking about the past made her sad.

'But we are here now, Omi,' I said, patting her hand awkwardly. I wanted to say something that would help, but didn't know what. Later that night, as I lay in my quiet bed, two thoughts went through my head: that I was now very far from the sea, and that I'd never known my grandfather, Ivan, and I didn't remember my aunt, Doina, at all.

A few days later Mum and Dad returned and as soon as they arrived, a big discussion started. I had no idea what it was about. Dad seemed quite angry though.

'What is it?' I asked Mum eventually.

'Omi said that the *Securitate* phoned Gabi and Gabor. That's the secret police. And they said that, if Gabi and Gabor had dinner with us they had to write a report of all that was discussed. So now they're frightened and don't want to meet Dad. That's why he's angry.'

'Of course I'm angry,' said Dad, reverting to English. 'I mean, they weren't even supposed to tell me. So what if they didn't turn up, and didn't tell me why they wouldn't come, what would I assume, as a 'foreign journalist'? Anyway, I have nothing to hide.'

He picked up the phone.

'I'm going to phone Gabi.'

A long conversation started. To my surprise, Mum began to laugh. Dad eventually put down the phone and he was laughing too.

'What happened?' Ivan and I asked, fed up with not understanding anything.

'I phoned Gabi and I teased her about her name. I asked whether she had a green car (which she does), and whether her father was a greengrocer (which he isn't). She never guessed that it was me!'

'Jimmy,' said Mum. 'You've been winding poor Gabi and her mother up since you were very young.'

'True,' he agreed. 'But then it's so easy with them!'

After that all the family turned up at Omi's apartment. There was a lot of conversation and I heard the word *Securitate* mentioned often but it all seemed alright. We gave Juli her present, a toy koala from Australia. She decided to call it Jimmy. Then she weed on the carpet but the grown ups just laughed and did nothing.

It was a proper family dinner. We got to bed very late.

'We had a bit of a fright,' Mum told us the next morning. 'We wanted to take *Aventura* out of the water. Only when we were craning the boat out a cable snapped and she fell back into the water. It was nasty – the crane's hook was swinging all over the place.'

'Thank heaven it happened over the water,' added Dad. 'If it was over the quay the boat would have been half destroyed. So we've decided not to leave her here. The port isn't safe. We'll head back to Greece and find a yard near Athens. You'll just have to stay a bit longer with Omi.'

'That's okay,' we said. 'We don't mind.'

'Sorry we keep changing the plans. I think we've got up to plan 18D.'

That day the phone never stopped ringing and a stream of people came to visit. Dad headed off to his 25 year school reunion and in the afternoon we went with Mum up to the mountains above Braşov, to the high meadows called Poiana, for a picnic with Dad's old schoolfriends. A few days later, Mum and Dad packed and left for the boat. We wouldn't see them for a month at least. I was sad then.

Staying with Omi

MAY TURNED INTO JUNE. School every morning, helping Omi with shopping and cleaning, visits to the cemetery. There was always enough for us to eat, but Omi did worry about not having enough food. It was true that sometimes you saw queues for things and the shops were generally empty. I'd never seen any bread, for example, in the bakery at the end of the street.

Omi had food hoarded away in various places. Once she took us to a friend's house to get a chicken out of the freezer. She seemed to have meat in all her friends' freezers. There was a big cupboard on the landing outside the apartment that was packed with preserves and jams and pickles, and she kept potatoes and apples in the building's communal cellar.

Omi loved to play gin rummy and most days she had friends round or went to visit them for a few games. It was her turn to be host one afternoon and I didn't want to stay in so I went for a walk on my own. It started to rain but I walked as far as the cemetery. It was very windy and the tree in the churchyard made a rustling great sound like the sea. There was shelter in the arcades where the graves were. I sat there for a while.

I didn't like to think about the fact that Omi was like her old woman friends with their dyed hair and those shapeless house dresses they loved to wear that buttoned up the front. They laughed at what Ivan and I said as if it was cute, as if we were two year olds. I couldn't bear to be there.

It was no better if I thought of *Aventura*. Then I felt my heart tighten in my chest like someone was squeezing it. All I could think about were the stickers we'd collected over the years and put on the fibreglass bulkhead above our bunks. We couldn't peel them off to take with us.

'Stupid, stupid,' I told myself as I realised that I never properly said goodbye to the boat, I left her without a care.

I sat in the cemetery feeling thoroughly fed up. It was so quiet there though, that slowly I started to feel better, and as I wandered back I realised I quite liked walking in the rain with no people around.

The old ladies were still playing rummy. The number tiles click-clacked on the wooden boards, and they bet tiny amounts, a few coins here and there, on who would win. They chattered away in Hungarian. They looked happy enough. Who was I to judge them? There was Margit, with scars on her cheeks where shrapnel had hit her in the war. And Kichy-Tante, Little Aunt we called her, whom Omi got to know when they had young families and struggled to make ends meet because their husbands were both in prison. These old women had had pretty rotten lives, I thought, but they had their friendships. That was good.

On the side table was my favourite, a wafer sandwiched together with caramel and nuts. I grabbed a piece, mumbled a greeting and slunk into the room next door where Ivan was trying to glue a model plane together. I picked up my diary and sat and wrote.

Later that evening I leaned out the window to catch a glimpse of the moon beyond the courtyard. Not even the mountains could make up for this, being cooped up in a building, with no horizons.

Friends

GABI TAUGHT ENGLISH in the high school that both she and Dad had attended, just a stone's throw from Omi's apartment in the shadow of the Black Church. It was founded several hundred years ago to educate the children of the German community, but Romanian children now went there as well.

'Ivan,' Gabi said, on one of her visits to see us during her lunch break, about a week after we arrived. 'I'm going to take you to meet one of my classes. I'll come and get you tomorrow morning.'

So Ivan made some friends, boys from the class. After school finished they took him off to play and we didn't see him again until the evening.

The next day it was my turn to go with Gabi. I had to stand up in front of the whole class and tell them about myself. I felt very shy and gabbled as quickly as I could, 'We left England and went to America and from there to South America and through the Pacific, New Zealand and Australia, and to Asia and then up the Red Sea to the Mediterranean.'

'Which country did you like best?' Gabi asked me.

'Um,' I said. I hated that question. People always asked it, and I didn't know the answer.

'I liked the Pacific best,' I said, hoping that was good enough. The class sang some English songs. Though I did think they were rather American.

'We're going on a class trip to Bran at the end of term,' Gabi said. 'Would you like to come?'

'Yes,' I said. Inside I thought, yipee!

After school finished, I invited three girls back to the apartment. They greeted Omi politely and sat on the overstuffed sofas. I drew a terrible plan of the boat and showed them our trip on a globe. Then they read my poems and I copied out the Sea-poem for them.

'Do you want to go swimming tomorrow?' Corina asked. She had long black hair and a nice smile.

'Sure,' I said.

'That's great,' said Marion. She was tall and blonde. Her family were Saxon, as they called those German-speaking families that had lived in Transylvania for hundreds of years. 'We'll be going to Germany soon,' she told me. 'Many people have already left.'

Brandusa was small and had short curly hair.

'Let's meet at my house,' she suggested.

The next day the four of us went swimming and then walked in the park. We passed by Brandusa's grandparents' house.

'I'll see if I can borrow some money,' she said. She managed to get 20 lei. 'I had to beg!' she laughed. 'But now we can buy strawberries.'

In the nearby market we bought a punnet of wild strawberries and ate them at her grandparents'. Her grandfather gave us a rose each from his garden, and we had fun watching TV and criticising a silly show that was on because it was international children's day.

After that I met my friends and we went swimming every day.

* * *

At the end of term I joined the class for the trip to Bran. The class occupied the whole back of the bus. I sat on top of a pile of rucksacks with Corina. We stayed in a cabin and I shared a room with Corina and a few other girls. There was an endless war of toothpaste, it was smeared everywhere, on the handles of the doors especially. In the evening the boys made a fire and after dinner everyone was supposed to go and dance. I was shy but in the end Corina and I danced. I'm getting better, I thought to myself.

The following morning we visited the museum, a castle on a small hill. The tourist brochures said that it was Dracula's castle but we knew that was just made up. Corina and I decided it wasn't that interesting.

I talked a lot to Corina. I thought some of the other girls were rather childish but like me she liked to sit and think, and walk and talk about more serious subjects.

On the way home that afternoon she sat on my lap because the bus was so crowded and I taught her how to count in Indonesian.

After Bran, the long school holidays began. I met my friends every single day. We went to the cinema often. The tickets were cheap and there were several cinemas in town that showed American films with subtitles.

All my friends spoke English very well, so that was how I talked to them. Though my Romanian was better than when we arrived, and I could understand some conversations now.

I rarely saw Ivan; he was always off playing with his own friends. A friend of Gabi's had brought some of our things from the boat including my skateboard, the one I got for my birthday in New York. I taught Corina and Marion to skateboard on the leafy roads behind Omi's street. Sometimes Ivan turned up with his friends and tried to grab the skateboard off us. Then we would all run as fast as we could up and down the hills, trying to catch each other.

Brandusa came back from her seaside holiday looking tanned. Marion and I tried to teach her to skateboard but she wasn't very good.

'Do you like Corina?' they asked me.

'Yes,' I said.

'She studies too much,' Brandusa said.

I didn't reply. I liked all three of them, but Corina the most.

* * *

My fourteenth birthday was only a few days away and I was planning a party. Corina came to visit me and stayed for lunch. Ivan turned up with a friend, a slim boy with dark hair.

'Hi,' he said rather shyly. 'My name's Serban.'

'Can he stay for lunch too?' Ivan asked Omi. Omi smiled and laid another plate. She didn't seem to mind all our comings and goings.

After lunch Brandusa arrived.

'We should do something, all of us together,' she said.

'Let's have a picnic,' I suggested. 'We could go up to the meadows in Poiana.'

For several days we badgered my friends' parents and eventually we managed to get them all to agree. Marion was the only one who couldn't make it.

The day of the picnic arrived, the first day of July. Corina's father gave us and Serban a lift to the Poiana bus station and Brandusa and her younger sister Maura met us there. The bus was crowded with people and we all had to squash together as it wound its way up into the mountains. We never stopped talking. Serban made us laugh with his ideas.

'Pretend you're spirits,' he said. 'And Ivan and I will be spirit hunters.'

Once we arrived we bought some fizzy pop to drink and walked into the meadows until we found a good spot. We threw all our food into a pile to share and played softball that ended up in a friendly fight. Serban threw everyone over except for me.

'Hey!' someone shouted. 'Brandusa and Maura have got cherries!'

'Attack!' cried Ivan and he tried to grab them.

'Stop it!' I shouted at him.

That put him into a huff and he walked off.

'It's time to go anyway,' I said. We packed and went to find him. He was sitting by the road, so I bought him another drink, and then he was alright. On the bus ride back we racked our brains for a good idea for another trip, we'd enjoyed this one so much. By the time we got back to Braşov bus station it was almost 6pm.

'We'll be in trouble,' said Brandusa. 'We were supposed to be home by 3.30!'

She and Corina went home, but Serban invited us to his house which wasn't far. He had a new game called 'Jockey' where you had to bet on horses and make yours win. We played it with his little sister for a while until I won and then Ivan got upset. I tried not to be annoyed with him.

'I better phone Omi, it's late,' I said, but no one answered the phone, and then I forgot. We all piled in for a big wrestling match and I tickled Ivan until he was crying with laughter. We only got home at 8.30 and Omi was angry at first.

'We had a lovely time,' I said. 'Really lovely.'

She was happy then, to see how much we'd enjoyed ourselves.

I lay in my bed, tired out and thinking about the day. About how happy I felt when I lay in the warm grass in the sun, when we took the bus up through the forests, when we played games and had lunch and told silly jokes. Everything had been just right.

*   *   *

The next day we spent at Serban's. He was only a few months younger than me. I liked him. We had lunch there, played games and messed about. Ivan and I walked home via the cemetery and changed the water in the flower jars.

*   *   *

'Omi,' I said. 'Do you remember the cake you made me in Greece, when I was nine?'

'Yes,' she said. 'And I will make you another, even better this time!'

I tidied up the apartment and at last it was time for my party. All my friends came and they gave me flowers instead of cards. Serban gave me a white rose. The cake of course was wonderful.

Just before 10pm. I had the most wonderful surprise – in walked Mum and Dad. I was so happy, I had to hug Marion and Corina as well as them. We all went outside to look at the car that they'd bought in Greece.

'A Renault 6,' said Ivan.

'Ten o'clock,' said Corina. 'I've got to go.'

'I wish you could stay longer!' I said as all my friends left. 'But it was the best party ever.'

I stayed awake until midnight and saw the date change and sang 'Happy Birthday to me.'

Leaving Again

ON MY BIRTHDAY Mum and Dad and Ivan left for Bucharest, leaving me behind because I wanted to see my friends. But the trip to Poiana we had planned had to be cancelled because in the morning it poured with rain. I spent ages on the phone to everyone and in the end we decided to go to the cinema again.

I phoned Serban to find out what time he wanted to meet us. The phone call went on quite a long time and it leaked out in the way he spoke to me that he really liked me. I liked him too and we sat next to each other in the cinema. He held my hand and his hand was smooth and cool. The film was *A Little Romance* and at the end the girl and the boy went to Venice together. Of course my friends piled back to the apartment afterwards. I found some photos of *Aventura* and gave them a copy each and wrote little messages on the back. In the end only Serban was left. We went walking together up by the swimming pool behind Omi's house.

'We can't go to Venice though,' he said. 'Like in the film.'

'Maybe when I come back and I'm older,' I said, and I held his hand tight.

* * *

Mum, Dad and Ivan returned and the little apartment was crowded.

'Is it really seven weeks?' Omi said.

'It doesn't feel like that, Omi.' I started reluctantly to pack up my things.

It was so hard to say goodbye to my friends. We'd spent every day together and done so many things. After the girls had left I stayed talking alone with Serban by the big gate that led out of the courtyard and into the street. He held me and we kissed, just a little, and he pressed his cheek against mine.

'Goodbye,' he said.

'Bye,' I said.

And that was it.

Afterwards we had to go to Bözsi's for dinner. I talked on the phone with Corina.

'I'm sad,' she said. 'You've been such a good friend.'

Then I spoke to Serban for about half an hour.

* * *

Our last day. It never stopped raining. The car was packed. I phoned Serban but now I didn't know what to say. I was sad to leave him and my other friends, but I knew I was glad to be going to England.

Ivan and I squeezed onto the back seat. The car was full to the brim.

'Bye! Bye!' we called to Omi, standing there in the rain.

'Ghastly weather,' commented Mum as we drove slowly on the wet roads.

Ivan and I looked out at the rain and felt bored. We spent the night in Oradea near the frontier with Hungary.

'Pretty forsaken isn't it?' said Dad. 'But here is where I met Mum.'

'I was a tourist,' Mum explained. 'On holiday with my friends. We were in the street looking at a sort of lottery thing and trying to work out what it was. We asked this young man if he could tell us. He spoke good English.'

'Was that Dad?'

'Yes.'

* * *

Two days on the road.

'I used to drive this route regularly,' Mum said, 'when Jimmy was still stuck in Romania. Doina, you've done it several times yourself as a baby. In fact, I remember doing this journey when I was eight months pregnant with you. I just made it back to England in time for you to be born there!'

'Remember that guy we met in Florida?' said Dad.

'Oh, the one with the electric car windows?'

'The Cadillac,' Ivan reminded me.

Dad made an impatient gesture. 'There was more to him than the car windows! Anyway, now you know why Gwenda loved that car seat he sent her so much. You were stuck in it for thousands of miles.'

I stared out the window. We were driving fast on straight level roads to Budapest past bright yellow fields of sunflowers. It felt like I'd never stopped moving, not since I was in the womb.

After we crossed into Austria and joined the motorway, the old, laden-down Renault did its best, but everything overtook us, even VW Beatles and ancient Citroëns. Near to Munich Dad phoned Klaus for directions to their house.

Marianne was there – she was tall now and I really liked her clothes.

'I'm studying photography,' she said.

'You've had a hair cut!' we laughed when we saw Klaus Junior. He looked quite respectable. He'd worked in Australia to earn his flight home.

'I'm working as a cameraman now,' he said.

It was great to see them again, and it didn't feel as if we'd been away for years.

And then on we went. Long miles across the continent. 'Going to England, going home,' I told myself. But really, home for six years had been the boat, and I'd left her without much thought. And yet, it would become home, just as soon as I got there. Of that I was sure.

England 1981–83

*The colour of your skin depends on
who you're standing next to.*

London Again

THE LONDON HOUSE in Venner Road, Sydenham, where we lived before we went sailing, was still ours. I liked that house. It was Victorian, and it had lots of rooms. My bedroom was right at the top on the third floor, next to a room that had been converted into a second kitchen for the tenants who lived there while we were away.

'Are we going to live here now?' I asked Mum. She and I were standing in the little kitchen. It looked like it had never been cleaned. Years of grease stuck to the walls in brown sticky layers.

She sighed. 'Honestly, I don't know. We have to clean this place, whatever we do.' She left me to the kitchen. It was my job was to clean that. I scrubbed and scrubbed. It was disgusting work, scraping off the grease.

A decision had to be made. It was July and Ivan and I had to start school in September.

'I'm going to check out some of the local comprehensives,' said Dad. The summer term had not finished yet, unlike in Romania where the holidays began in June. He sat outside one school when the kids came out at the end of the day.

'No,' he said on his return. 'I can't believe what I saw. Kids fighting outside the gates... I don't think it'll be any good for you. Too rough.'

'So what then?' asked Mum.

They talked about the offer from Radio Australia. But the BBC had already said he could have his old job back. And we all rather wanted to stay in England.

'What about Cornwall?' suggested Mum. 'We talked about it before. Granny is down there, we can stay with her while we look for a house. We'll be near the sea, and the children might fit in better in a smaller school. At least we can try it for a while, until we know what we want to do.'

So the Venner Road house was to be sold. *Aventura* was to be sold.

I revisited the places I remembered from when I was six and seven. Mayow Park where I played with my friend Emma on the swings, Crystal Palace where life-sized models of dinosaurs peered out from the trees. Those memories did not help me feel like I belonged here. Too much had happened in the meantime.

'What an amazing time you must have had,' people said politely, but they didn't pay much attention to our answers.

'Were you in any big storms? Were you afraid out there in the ocean?' they always asked me, and looked vaguely disappointed when I shook my head. I had been scared a few times, but never in the middle of the sea.

One Saturday I took the train with Dad into central London, while he went to work at Bush House, and wandered on my own around the city. It wasn't long since Covent Garden had opened as a new shopping centre, now that the old fruit and vegetable market had moved out, and I liked to go and browse the shops and watch the street performers.

On my way back along the Strand, I sat on the top deck of a red London bus and looked out to see a young man running fast down the road, stopping only to kick a litter bin across the pavement. He was lean and wiry, his clothes ripped and his head partly shaved. Was that what I should be like? There was a new world out there, young, self-enclosed, exclusive of parents, full of music and defiance for its own sake. Perhaps I should try to be part of it.

But I didn't know how you did that.

* * *

One person I was looking forward to meeting again, and that was my friend Emma. We had written a few letters to each other over the years. Her family had moved down to Surrey, so we went to visit. With her I felt as if I could pick up where we had left off all those years ago, and it was easy to talk and laugh. We stayed for the weekend, and together watched the Royal Wedding on the television, watched along with the rest of the nation.

Yet even then. Emma had a firm group of friends, made through years of school and shared experiences. She looked so much as if she belonged. I liked being with her, and yet, I felt as if I always said the wrong thing, didn't get the joke. Where did I fit in?

Cornwall Again

IT RAINED ALL the way to Cornwall and although it was August, it was cold. The cold was unfamiliar to me and I disliked it. But here was the village where Granny lived, which I remembered well, with its grey stone houses, and the muddy lane behind her house where I had learnt to ride a bike.

The secondary school where we were to go was not far, in the nearest town.

'There's a school bus you can take from the village,' Mum said. She had got all the information about the school and I looked at the list of subjects I had to choose from, that I would study for the next two years, before taking my O Level exams. I ticked the subjects I wanted to do, with a thrill of anticipation going through me.

'We'll have to hurry up and get all this,' Mum was looking at the uniform list.

'I'll knit you a jumper,' said Granny.

Finding school shoes was trickier, because our feet were so broad after our years going barefoot. I ended up with a comfortable pair of brown moccasins.

Mum and Dad soon had to drive back to London.

'I'll be back for your first day,' said Mum. 'Aren't you excited?'

I nodded. Though nodding was an understatement as to how I felt.

'Sorry I'll miss it,' said Dad. 'I have to work. But I'll be down at the weekend. You can tell me all about it then.'

'Let's go for a walk,' Granny suggested after they had gone. The sun had come out and it was warm. We climbed the hill out of the village, and in the distance saw the sea glinting in the sunshine.

'Tide's out,' said Ivan, peering out to the horizon. Beyond the beach, with its miles of ribbed sand, the sea was a far-off silver band.

We took the coastal path that wound along the cliffs to a little sandy bay caught between two headlands.

'I often brought you here when you were small,' Granny said. 'You swam and played among the rock pools.'

Further along the coast was the headland, where a red and white painted landmark looked out to sea, the mark which had watched *Aventura* sail out of the Fowey River all those years before. And across the fields, on the other side of the headland from where we were, was the new school. I couldn't see it but it felt as if it was watching and waiting for me. Waiting – the promise of my exciting new life.

On the way back through the narrow lanes we picked wild blackberries, which Granny cooked into a delicious blackberry and apple pie. There was homemade cake for afternoon tea, and proper Sunday lunch with roast meat and potatoes, and then golden syrup pudding, with custard. Ivan and I tucked into the pudding and grinned at each other. We didn't need to say anything. All those talks on the boat, how we'd longed for that pudding all these years, and now here it was, tasting even better than we remembered.

The day before the term began, Mum returned as she said she would. Ivan and I put on our new uniforms and posed in the sun for a photograph outside the house. I thought we looked pretty smart.

First Day at School

MY FIRST DAY at school started with the register, and no one smiling back at me, and the blonde girl calling me Paki.

Between my expectations and reality there was a car crash.

My form teacher taught English and that was my first lesson so I stayed put. The blonde girl stayed too. I heard her friends calling her Tina and they sat together in a clump at the back of the class.

'Can you please write a list of which books you have read in the past year,' the teacher said. I started writing furiously.

'Look at Paki,' Tina said. 'What's she got to write about?'

She turned up in my French class too. We had to introduce ourselves. The other pupils struggled to answer the questions, but I was eager to speak.

'Where were you born?' the teacher asked in French.

I put up my hand.

'Cornwall,' I said, and there was an audible gasp from Tina and her gang from the back of the class. They had not expected *that*, I thought. It felt like a tiny victory. Though it didn't stop them calling me Paki.

I ate my packed lunch on my own in the hall and wondered how Ivan was getting on. When afternoon register was over I set off for Physics. Only I couldn't find the lab, nor anyone to ask, so I was late. When I found the door and looked in, I saw that the rest of the class were all boys. They looked back with mocking smiles. My heart sank.

'Please come in, young lady,' the teacher said gallantly. He was an older man with bushy grey eyebrows and a stained white coat. 'There's a free seat there.'

I forced myself through the door, wondering if girls ever chose physics as an option and sat on my own at a desk. When we had to divide into pairs for an experiment, of course no one wanted to work with me. The teacher insisted, so I was lumbered with a reluctant boy who barely acknowledged my existence and kept talking to his mates all the time.

At the end of the lesson the bell went and the boys rushed headlong for the door.

'Stop!' bellowed the teacher. 'Ladies first.'

I scooped up my books and headed for the door, past the resentful eyes of the boys. I wished I could disappear through the floor. I knew the teacher was trying in a clumsy sort of way to be nice, but that was worse because it just drew attention to me.

Next was PE. I copied the other girls changing into my shorts and followed them out to the netball court. I'd never even heard of the game before and I hadn't a clue about the rules. No one offered to explain them and I was too afraid to ask. I concentrated on trying to guess, and not let on that I didn't know. The teacher was impatient and the other girls annoyed with my mistakes.

Afterwards in the changing rooms a girl pointed at my bare feet and laughed. 'Look, square feet!'

Until then I had rather liked my feet. At least they weren't bent and cramped like people who'd worn tight shoes since they were little. Now my feet were just a trouble, because I couldn't find shoes to fit, and all the other girls had narrow feet so they could wear any fashionable shoes they liked.

* * *

'Good day at school?' Mum asked when I came home.

'Fine,' I said. I made her laugh when I told her about the physics lesson. I didn't mention how embarrassed I'd felt. I didn't mention being called a Paki.

'What about you?' she asked Ivan.

'Okay.' He shrugged. 'They asked me what football team I supported.'

'What did you say?'

'Well, nothing. I don't know any.'

When Dad arrived that weekend, Ivan had to repeat this story. They thought it amusing. I knew he had found it humiliating. And neither of us said a word to tell them the truth.

That first night as I lay in bed, a great dread settled on me for the next day. I didn't cry. This is just how it is, I told myself, I can't do anything about it.

Days and Days at School

I WOKE UP the next morning and every morning after that with dread clutching at my stomach. At the bus stop people joked and chatted to each other but no one spoke to me.

The double-decker wobbled through the high hedges of the narrow Cornish lanes, past the stench of the pig farm that always made people shout and hold their noses, up onto the main road that led to the school.

Tina had her allies on the bus.

'Oh, doesn't Paki fancy...' and they shouted out the name of some boy I'd never heard of.

The bus was full and the seat next to me couldn't stay empty. A girl with a pinched face and threadbare clothes sat beside me. She was very thin, and her bare legs were pink and blotchy from the cold. Her name was Jenny and from the comments thrown her way from the back of the bus I gathered she and her brother came from a poor estate at the other end of the village.

'I'm a Jehovah's Witness,' she said to me.

I said nothing and stared out the window at the hedges speeding by. The back of the bus had momentarily given up on me and had started on a Welsh boy instead.

'Hey, Jones,' they cried, 'there's a sheep! Don't you fancy it?'

We drove past a lot of sheep every day. And they said the same things about Jones every day, even though he was their friend.

'Do you believe in evolution?' Jenny suddenly asked me.

'Well, yes,' I said slowly, turning to look at her and wondering if I wanted to have this conversation. A vague memory of a book given to me once on the life of Darwin surfaced in my mind.

Jenny screwed up her face in disgust. 'But how could *we* be descended from monkeys?' she said scornfully.

I didn't reply.

But at least she talked to me.

Our bus was the first to arrive at the playground because the driver had to do a second run to another village. I wished we could have arrived at the last minute, and not have that interminable wait. I stood there on my own, excluded from all the little chatting groups, and felt like a cold island, surrounded by an unwelcoming sea.

Once the school day began it was better. Classes filled the time. I liked having a proper chemistry lab, the wealth of painting materials in the art class, and all the new English texts we got to study. I did notice though that the others liked to pretend that they knew nothing, that they didn't care about school. I couldn't help but throw myself into school work. That of course made things worse.

Slowly I made a few contacts with people. I went around with a couple of girls that I sat next to for registration. I didn't really feel like I had much in common with them, but at least I had someone to talk to and eat my sandwiches with at lunchtime. At least they kept me company and didn't whisper insults behind my back.

In Maths there were two boys who sat behind me. I'd seen them at break-times talking to Tina. During lessons they whispered, loud enough for me to hear, about my thick eyebrows and my hairy legs. At home I looked at myself in the mirror. I'd never really noticed I was hairy before. Mum waxed her legs on the boat but I'd never thought that was something that applied to me. That Saturday I found a disposable razor and shaved my legs, managing to cut myself in the process. The cut was obvious and Dad noticed.

'What have you done?' he asked.

'Shaved my legs,' I said. Before I even said it, I knew he wouldn't approve.

He frowned. 'Why did you have to do that?'

What could I answer? I wasn't going to tell him about the boys in Maths and the endless teasing. I shrugged and said nothing.

I rarely saw Ivan at school. He was in a different playground at break and lunchtimes. I did know he got into fights sometimes. But we didn't really get on now, and we didn't say much to each other at all.

I never told anyone about what was happening at school. Never told my parents, never told a teacher, not even one of those I quite liked. I don't know why. I guess I thought I just had to put up with it.

Winter Blues

AUTUMN AT FIRST had been pleasant, because it was a new season to me, following on from my Greek spring and Romanian summer. I liked the fallen golden leaves and blackberries to pick in the lanes and many warm days. I didn't notice that the days were getting shorter, as I was so busy with school. Then suddenly I realised I was always getting up in the dark and coming home in the dark. I hated having to wear so many clothes, and shoes all day long. I was always cold and my feet hurt.

At school, we had to go on long cross-country runs. I was very far from that run on the beautiful Polynesian island of Bora Bora. Now I felt just heavy, and not free at all.

I remembered my success in the New Zealand swimming competitions, so I joined a club at the local pool, but the training lengths up and down the pool were just boring, and the coach always said, not good enough, do it again. I had no sense of competition, and I had lost the edge I had as a twelve year old large for my age. At fourteen all the other girls were bigger and stronger than me.

I didn't want to run and swim when they said I had to. There was no freedom or joy in it, not that I could see anyway.

One weekend I wandered down to the beach. I wanted to see a glimpse of the sea. I crossed the sand dunes with their scanty, prickly grass. The sand was grey like the sky, and the tide was right out, so the sea was grey and distant. Clumps of black seaweed were tangled up with rubbish: plastic bottles, rotting fish, old shoes, brought by the storms. I walked on the sand and wrote my name with a piece of driftwood.

The scene was desolate, and I felt utterly alone.

I never cried. I felt like I had turned into a rock, dry and hard and far from water. I lived right by the sea but it wasn't my sea any more. I never sailed on it or swam in it.

* * *

Winter came. Days on days of getting up in the dark and trying to swallow down a few mouthfuls of cereal though my stomach was tense with worry. Waiting at the bus stop as the icy wind whipped round my legs. Sitting on the bus as it wound along the narrow lanes, ignoring the insults. Waiting again in the playground, cold outside and cold inside.

My parents took a long trip to Greece to get *Aventura* ready to be sold. Then *Aventura* was sold, and the London house. A house was bought in the same village as Granny. Our life was fixed on the land.

We moved in and painted all the rooms white. Mum began to cultivate the garden and write a book about our travels in the Pacific. The Sepik mask, the Tuvaluan dancing skirts, and all our shells, decorated the living room. The wooden statue from Tonga, Molitoni, which had been shipped back to England in a crate, stood in my parents' bedroom. And at last, I had my own room. Properly, not like in London, or at Granny's, when it was temporary. I could close the door, and be on my own. At least one of my wishes had come true.

I pinned up the big colour postcard of Bora Bora that I'd been given for my eleventh birthday, and laid on my desk my little treasures: the betel nut mask from Madang, the rainwood turtle from Fiji, and the box from New Zealand. I'd lost the green *tiki* my grandmothers gave me. And I still had the photos of me sat on the stone arch with Sione, and in the studio, sitting stiffly on a chair next to Joseph, and the dance show I put on in Port Moresby with Ivan and Sidonie. I was glad to see these familiar things again.

A wave of sickness overcame me – missing the boat so much it hurt. I couldn't bear to think of *Aventura* being sold, and strangers living in her. I remembered little details – the wooden toe-rails going round the edge of the decks, warm beneath my feet when I sat up at the bow, watching the cut of waves below while the foresail billowed out huge and taut above me. The crust of dried salt on the smooth white fibreglass of the cockpit, where the water was forever gurgling in the scuppers. The wind whistling through a hole in the boom like your breath whistles when you blow over a bottle. I remembered how in port Ivan and I curled the ropes into round flat spirals that lay neat and tidy on the aft deck, how we laced on the stiff blue sail covers to protect the sails, and climbed the mainmast to sit on the spreaders and talk and joke, legs dangling high above the deck.

Remembered how I lay at night in my bunk, before sleep came, at anchor, with the chain rumbling as it caught some obstacle on the sea bed, crackles coming through the hull of shellfish walking down below; and at sea, best of all, listening to the rush of water just outside, that comforting noise, which meant the push on to the horizon, towards new places, which meant the sea was just there, my lullaby...

I remembered all this and my boat-sickness passed. I put it all away; it was my old life now, to be packed away with the photographs, and the toy animals, very tatty now, with missing eyes and limbs and bald patches, that had been mine and Ivan's loyal companions all around the world.

* * *

That night thunder and lightening cracked and crashed outside. I looked out – what a storm! The trees were almost bent double in the wind and the rain was driven horizontal, beating against the windows. It was wild and in a second my misery was gone. The storm broke it.

I came to love the frequent winter gales that blew up from the Atlantic and battered the Cornish coast. Sometimes I even went out in them and danced around the garden until I was drenched through. I felt a wildness inside me, stirred up by the wind and the salt memories of the sea that came with it, and I wanted to run outside and yell. I wanted... well, I did not really know what I wanted.

* * *

I decided I would turn myself into a proper teenager. I listened to the radio and taped songs from the pop charts, which made Ivan laugh but I didn't care. I had my ears pierced, dressed in old dresses from jumble sales, painted my eyes very dark, and had my hair cut as short as the village hairdresser would dare.

'Will your Mum like this?' giggled the girls as I said, 'Shorter, just a bit.'

Slowly I began to make a few friends, with those, like me, who were at the bottom of the school heap. Sometimes I would make the wrong choice, like trying to be friends with one girl I ended up fighting in the girl's cloakroom, a silly, quick fight that ended with no one the victor.

Spring came, and lighter days. I joined a youth club in the village and made friends for the first time with people who just accepted me as I was and did not label me or call me names.

I wasn't that different though from the girl in Tonga who stayed still and waited for the crabs to come out of their mud holes. I still loved to go and sit in the garden and watch birds, snails and spiders going about their business. In the field opposite were the first lambs of the new year, jumping and running about in gangs; all sort of wild flowers peeped out from the high Cornish hedgerows.

And sometimes, in my room, I put one of my new records on my new record player and danced on my own, remembering all those Pacific dances, as I moved my hands and my feet.

It Gets Better at Last

OUR LIFE WAS not working too well for my parents either. Dad was having to commute to London so we hardly ever saw him. The decision was made to move up to Surrey. We were going to go to the same school as Emma. It was a good school, and it would be easier for Dad to get to work and still spend time at home with us. A house was found, and the Cornish village house was sold, just over a year after we moved there.

Only I had to spend one more term in Cornwall, while Ivan got to move. I was to stay with Granny until the summer, when I had to do my O Level exams.

When the Cornish house was empty, I asked if I could have a party. I had a few friends by then to invite. But those people that hated me, they came uninvited and I was nice and let them in. The next morning I looked at the damage. In fact, I lay on the floor, because I had just started my period and the cramps were crippling me. Someone had thrown up in the sitting room, and someone else had punched a hole in the bathroom door. Mum, her mouth set thin and tight, started to clean up. I was mortified.

In my second year at school I was made a prefect. I knew that Tina and her friends still didn't like me, but I also knew it wasn't the whole school against me. I knew who my enemies were and tried to avoid them.

That wasn't always possible. Some of them had been made prefects too. I walked into the Prefects Room one morning to see 'Paki (puke) fancies....' scrawled in big letters across the wall with the name of a boy who sat behind me in Maths.

Tina and her friends were there, laughing, 'Here she is.' I put my head down, looking at no one and ran quickly past into the second, smaller room where the coats were left, where the 'unfashionable' ones went. The first, larger room, where the popular prefects hung out, terrified me, and I tried to avoid going into it.

The Prefects Room was a privilege, and we were allowed to go there at the start of the day, cutting out that long cold wait in the playground. It was a place to eat lunch, make cups of tea. But it was no haven for me. That graffiti hit me hard, just when I thought I saw an improvement. They always found a new way to hurt me.

I even wrote a funny poem about the Room and pinned it onto the noticeboard. Only to find the next day that 'Paki ugh' had been scribbled on it. The day after that, the paper had been torn down, and lay on the floor, covered in tea stains and footprints.

I didn't let it get to me. I had a couple of boyfriends. I joined the school drama club and had a starring role in a school play. I went camping with my friends from the village youth club. I passed my O Levels with top grades.

I was free to go.

The new house in Surrey was surrounded by a big garden, and when I arrived, it was a lovely summer's day. Blooming scented roses lined the front path.

'Look at all these fruit trees,' said Dad, and Mum showed me the vegetable patch, and the raspberries and blackcurrants ripe and ready to pick. Dad was going to build himself a proper darkroom upstairs, and Mum's book about our Pacific journey was about to be published.

'I've counted how many wild birds come into the garden,' said Mum enthusiastically. 'At least ten different sorts.'

I took a handful of earth from the dug-up soil and squeezed it, feeling its moist warmth; perhaps now, it would be alright.

'Here is my room,' said Ivan, as we went upstairs, 'and that's yours.'

He was much happier in his new school. He was more talkative, and even had a girlfriend. In the past few months he seemed to have lost his skinny boy looks and grown up. He was taller than me now. I hadn't even noticed him changing.

'You can walk to school,' he said, 'across the playing fields. No more school bus.'

I was going to start A Levels in September, and at the end of the summer term I attended an introductory session in the new school. Emma was Head Girl. She showed me where to go for the English A Level class.

'I'm doing all sciences,' she said. 'So we won't be in any classes together. Meet me in the common room later.'

'Okay,' I said. 'Emma –' as she turned to go.

'Yes?'

'Do you remember that silly note we wrote, when we wanted to run away together?'

'Don't tell me you've still got it! I remember we wanted to take the sugar tongs. What was that all about?'

'I do still have it, you know. It's sailed around the world.'

'You'll have to let me see it. Anyway, better go. See you later.'

I walked into the class and sat down in a free seat, next to a girl with lots of brown curly hair. She looked at me and smiled and asked my name.

'That's interesting, I like it,' she said.

I knew then it would get better.

And it did.

Ten Years Later

'I'M BUYING A BOAT,' Ivan announced at a family dinner. 'I'm going to sail around the British Isles this summer. I can't do it all in one go, but I've got lots of friends who'd like to join me for short hops.'

'What about me?' I said. 'I'd love to do it.'

At the end of August I joined him for a week on the leg from Wales to Cornwall. The weather was bad, a big Atlantic low sweeping eastwards, and we spent the first few days holed up in a grey bay on the edge of Anglesey while the wind howled above our heads. Squashed together in the tiny cabin, hanging on the radio shipping forecast for an improvement in the weather, we never argued once.

At last we could leave and we sailed to Ireland and then on towards the coast of Cornwall.

'You really know a lot,' I said admiringly as he navigated through shipping lanes and sandbanks, and fixed the things which broke. 'Why can't I do any of that?'

'I guess you've never been interested,' he said.

'You're right. Anyway, you're the captain,' I laughed. 'And I'll try to be the best crew you've ever had!'

Near to Land's End everything that could go wrong did – the strong wind was against us, and the tide too.  The engine kept coughing and stopping because of dirty fuel. The cockpit was quite open to the waves and the sea hurled itself against the little boat and crashed all over me. I'd been steering by hand for hours and my aching hand could barely hold onto the tiller. Despite my waterproof layers, I thought to myself 'I've never felt this cold before in my whole life. In all the seven years of sailing on *Aventura*, I never felt this uncomfortable, never.'

But – I looked ahead to the wild dark cliffs of Land's End, and I realised – it was beautiful. For the first time, I was happy to see Cornwall again.

* * *

At last we made it to Fowey near where Granny lived. We had not sailed back here since we left with *Aventura* all those years before. How pretty it was as we sailed into the river-mouth from the sea, the white-faced houses gathered in lines upon the steep slopes. A glimpse through the cedars and pines of the blue-topped school on the hill above. Ha! I didn't care at all now.

When we stepped ashore, I felt the hard ground roll under me.

'Remember Barbados?' I said, swaying a little. 'When we wanted the land to roll, because we'd read about it in a book, but nothing happened. We were so annoyed!'

Ivan shook his head. He couldn't remember.

'I was much younger than you,' he said. 'I don't remember much at all from the start.'

That night we slept in beds in Granny's house, after a good meal of meat pie and pudding and even custard for Ivan. After two days and two nights of pounding into the wind, as I lay in the quiet bed, I felt the sea racing on and on through me – opening up again inside, that forgotten, familiar, beloved place.

The boat was left for a rest in a nearby marina, Ivan returned to London to his job, and I stayed with Granny for a gentle week of tea and home-made cake and conversations about the garden.

The day after Ivan left, the Atlantic storm had swept away. The first day of September, blue and warm and calm.

'I think I'll go for a walk,' I said. Since we had moved away from Cornwall I had only come back for brief visits at Christmas, when I barely left the house, dreading meeting anyone I knew from school.

I left the village and walked along the cliff-tops, the way I had gone with Granny in the last days before my first school term. The narrow path wound its way between gorse bushes, which burst with flowers like sharp yellow kisses. The ribbed sand of the beach was no longer the horrid grey I remembered – now it was shining silver and gold in the sun. The sea was blue and on the rocks black cormorants spread their wings, turning themselves towards the sun.

Here was the place, I remembered, and I scrambled down the rocks to a small

beach caught between two tall headlands where Granny used to bring me when I was a tiny thing, just walking. There was no one on the beach and I thought I might paddle in the sea – but the water was warmer than I expected and so I stripped to my pants and bra and dove in. I chattered to myself as I swam, and I was happy. Then I dried myself on my shirt as a man passed, with a dog who ran along the wave line. He glanced at me briefly but I didn't care. I sat on a rock and turned myself towards the sun, breathing the salt air.

Across the wide and shallow bay was the town where I was born. I had sailed all around the world to come back to this place. And at first this place did not want me; nor I it. It took years of work to learn to belong to this land.

I climbed back up to the path, carrying my shoes, to walk barefoot on the warm earth. I remembered how I had run along that road in Bora Bora, so many years ago now. That simple happiness had never left me.

But then I had been a visitor to someone else's country; and this was my earth. For the earth was what I wanted now, I'd had enough of the sea.

Now

AVENTURA IS STILL sailing the oceans. Last I heard, she was in Africa, having just completed another circumnavigation. That was news to warm my heart.

I don't sail very much any more, but I still love the sea. Most people don't think about the sea. They pollute it with plastic and oil, and they kill whales and dolphins and drag up every last fish. This makes me sad. Our seas are beautiful, and we should look after them. Many of the places I visited as a child, those islands in Tuvalu, are under threat now from rising sea levels. Those traditional cultures we witnessed are slowly being lost, as people become modern and leave the old ways behind.

I have travelled so much, I like living in England now. I have my own two children, and sometimes I wish they could have travelled as much as I have and seen all the things I have seen. Then again, they have something I didn't: they are settled in a school, with the same good friends they have had for years, and a neighbourhood where they feel that they belong.

Those children in Cornwall, to try to understand them a little better, never had any contact with people from different countries. And the worst thing that I did was that I never told anyone I was being bullied. These days children know they should talk to someone, and that is good.

Finally, the best thing about sailing around the world as a child is this: you feel related to the whole world. No person is a stranger, because you know we are all humans together, and children, and families, are the same everywhere. And now, when I close my eyes, I can see the whole world turning, and I can feel it inside. I know it is a round, beautiful world: I have sailed all the way from east to west, and never fell off the edge!

About the Author

Doina Cornell has been travelling ever since she was born, and this book is a true account of her childhood spent growing up on a small yacht with her family.

These days she lives in Gloucestershire, a bit further from the sea than she would like, with her husband Julius and their two children Nera and Dan, as well as various pets.

Visit her website www.childofthesea.org for more photographs, films and music of *Aventura*'s voyage.

Other books by the Cornells

Jimmy Cornell

World Cruising Routes
978-0-7136-8777-4 (print)
978-1-4081-9797-4 (ebook)
The seminal guide to 1,000 sailing routes through all the oceans of the world.

World Cruising Destinations
978-1-4081-1401-8 (print)
978-1-4081-9798-1 (ebook)
This substantial handbook profiles every cruising destination in the world.

World Voyage Planner
978-1-4081-4029-1 (print)
978-1-4081-5631-5 (ebook)
This brand new book is an essential guide to planning an extended offshore cruise.

Jimmy and Ivan Cornell

Cornell's Ocean Atlas
978-0-9556-3965-4
An atlas of 129 up-to-date pilot charts aimed at sailors planning offshore voyages.

Gwenda Cornell

Pacific Odyssey
978-1-4081-1738-5 (print)
978-1-4081-7386-2 (ebook)
The Cornells' voyages through the Pacific from the perspective of Doina's mother.

'This childhood sails on a sea of gold. Children of seven to ninety-seven should be as enthralled as I am.'

Susie Morgenstern

'Bursting with life, here is a rare memoir of tenderness and exquisite detail, about a young girl's voyage with her family around the world. Doina learns about politics and race, responsibility and love, all through a kaleidoscope of international friendships, a strong family, and the infinitely fascinating world she discovers from the deck of a boat named *Aventura*. A must-read for parents thinking of taking the cruising leap, and a little worried about how their kids will react. And it's an equally powerful book for their kids, who long for a glimpse into the wonders they have in store.'

Bernadette Bernon

'This poignant story of the author's round-the-world voyage, one-of-a-kind experiences, and coming of age at sea – told from the perspective of a child as she grows into a young woman – is truly unique in this genre. Unlike most seagoing sagas, which are aimed at an adult audience, this one is a must-read for all kids (ages 10 and up), parents, or others who dream either of adventure or exploring the world under sail.'

Lynda Morris Childress

'This is such a fascinating account of a truly different childhood. The images which the book portrays are well laid out, and the prose is very engaging and sharp. With the sea as the backdrop, not only for this book, but for its author's childhood, it makes a real page turner.'

Nikki Owen

'Highly recommended for armchair sailors and travellers of all sorts, or anyone who loves a good story told by an interesting person.'

David Holubetz